186 recipes from 62 top Irish restaurants

In aid of the Irish Hospice Foundation
www.zestcookbook.ie

First published in the Republic of Ireland in 2009 by
The Irish Hospice Foundation
Morrison Chambers, 32 Nassau St, Dublin 2, Ireland

Edited by Vivienne Jupp
Art direction by Stephen Averill - Four5one°Creative
Template design by Tim Allen and Eric Green - Four5one°Creative
Design by Julie O'Boyle

Printed in Ireland by Spectrum Print Co. Ltd

ISBN-13: 978-0-9534880-8-7
www.zestcookbook.ie

The publishers wish to sincerely thank all the photographers whose work has been reproduced in this book. All the pictures included in the book have been supplied to the publishers from relevant sources.

Foreword

The concept of producing this cookbook surfaced in the aftermath of my mother's death. The quality of the hospice care she experienced was, for her and for her family, quite exceptional. The selfless work carried out every day around the country by hospice teams requires substantial funding, often from private donations.

The proceeds of this book will go directly to the Irish Hospice Foundation, the national body concerned with the support and development of hospice services in all care settings nationwide. I hope that this will go some way towards helping ensure that everyone in Ireland has access to the same quality of care as my mother.

This book would not have been possible without the voluntary contributions of the restaurants and chefs and the team of supporters listed in the acknowledgements.

I trust that you will agree with me when I say that 'Zest' is an extraordinary cookbook, which represents a gourmet trail around Ireland. It is a vivid and vibrant showcase for all that is good about Irish restaurants today. It is also designed for those who want to create fine food in their own homes. We hope that you will have as much fun using this book as we did in putting it together.

Vivienne Jupp
Project Director

Introduction

This recipe book has been compiled through the generosity of chefs all around the country who took time out from their busy schedules to write out their recipes. The result is a book that any cook would be happy to have in their kitchen.

Some of Ireland's finest chefs have contributed to this collection, and every chef has given three recipes - a starter, a main course and a dessert. In many cases, the three recipes are intended as a complete meal, designed so that all the elements harmonise. That is not to say that you can't pick and mix; in fact, you might be able to combine recipes in new and interesting ways, depending on what ingredients you have to hand.

I've had the pleasure of reading the recipes as they came in, and I've been impressed with their inventiveness, imagination and thoughtfulness. Some are obviously harder to achieve than others, but there are recipes here that should suit cooks of all abilities.

These days we're all a little fussier than we used to be about ingredients. We want to know more about provenance; we want authenticity; and increasingly, we want food in its season. In a way, that's a return to older values, to a time when convenience foods didn't exist but we had much healthier diets, low in fats and sugars.

This has brought about an increasing awareness of local produce - and using what's local means using what's fresh. You'll find that many of these recipes make wonderful use of Irish ingredients and show what can be done with a little skill without having to import foods from elsewhere. For me, that represents a growing confidence in our own produce and our own culinary skill in preparing it.

I believe that this collection is a showcase for the best of Irish cooking. It proves that good cooking doesn't need to be French or Italian and doesn't need to be complicated - it just needs to be skilful and honest. But 'Zest' is not just an Irish showcase - you'll find recipes here from Italy, France and India. You'll also find cutting edge cuisine, classic dishes, dishes based on organic ingredients, vegetarian dishes and old favourites. Between these pages lies a gastronome's delight.

As someone who finds in good food and the joys of the table the finest expressions of life, I'm delighted to be able to introduce this book that will bring those joys to your kitchen.

Paolo Tullio
Culinary Advisor

Acknowledgements

Project Director
Vivienne Jupp

Project Manager
Anne-Marie Taylor

Culinary Advisor
Paulo Tullio

Restaurant Advisor
Kieran Moore (The Firm)

Art Director
Steve Averill (Four5one°Creative)

Designer
Julie O'Boyle

Recipe Editor
Orla Broderick

Recipes
Chefs and restaurant owners

Photographers
All the amateurs and professionals
who took the food photography

Typing
Ingrid Miller

Project Steering Committee
Caroline Lynch, Mary Millea, Eugene Murray, Tim O'Dea, Eileen Pearson, John Waters,
Carmel Woods

Special thanks
Kevin & Gemma Barry, John Browne, Emer Connolly, Grainne Duggan, Sarah Farrell,
Lory Kehoe, Ger McCarthy, Michael McGinn & Ruth Geraty, Brendan Moran, Gordon
Murray, Frank & Maeve O'Dea, Joanna O'Driscoll, Fiona Power, Sean & Linda Shine,
Philip Toomey, Ciara Walsh, Biddy White Lennon.

Sponsors

⊕ Investec

Contents

Ananda Restaurant

At Ananda, contemporary creativity is at the core of the distinctive design, décor and menu, which offers modern Indian food. Expect the unexpected - innovative spins on classic Indian dishes, which are interestingly spiced, visually stunning and impeccably served.

starter

Hiran ki champ - venison chop served with wild berry chutney and robata grilled figs

main course

Macher jhol – Calcutta fish stew with turbot

dessert

Bibinca

Dundrum Town Centre, Sandyford Road, Dublin 16
Ph: (01) 296 0099
www.anandarestaurant.ie

Hiran ki champ - venison chop served with wild berry chutney and robata grilled figs

ingredients

For the venison

550g/1¼lb rack of venison
4 fresh figs
Vegetable oil, for brushing

For the first marinade

3 tablespoons chilli powder
40g/1½oz freshly grated root ginger
15g/½oz garlic cloves, crushed
85ml/3fl oz malt vinegar
1 teaspoon star anise powder

For the second marinade

100g/4oz Greek yogurt
2 tablespoons vegetable oil
Juice of 1 lime

For the chutney

1 tablespoon vegetable oil
Small cinnamon stick
1 onion, chopped
1 teaspoon chilli powder
50ml/2fl oz white wine vinegar
50g/2oz sugar
200g/7oz mixed berries
Salt

Serves 4

method

- Preheat the oven to 200°C/400°F/gas mark 6 and preheat the grill.

For the venison

- Cut the extra fat off the venison. Make the first marinade by simply mixing all the ingredients together in a non-metallic bowl. Put the venison in the marinade, then cover with clingfilm and put in the fridge for 3-4 hours.
- Meanwhile, make the second marinade, again by mixing all the ingredients together in a non-metallic bowl. Add to the venison and leave to marinate for 30-40 minutes.
- Remove the venison rack from the marinade and thread a skewer through the chops. Cook in the tandoori or in the oven for 10-12 minutes for medium, or approximately 15-17 minutes for well done.

- Cut the figs in half. Brush some oil onto the figs and grill for a few minutes, cut side up, until heated through.

For the chutney

- Heat the oil in a pan and add the cinnamon. Let it sizzle, then add the onion and sauté until it becomes translucent. Add the chilli powder, vinegar and sugar. Cook for 5 minutes, then add the berries. Season with salt. Bring to the boil and remove from the heat. Remove the cinnamon stick before serving.

To serve

- Cut the venison rack into individual chops. Serve on warm plates with the figs and chutney on the side.

Macher jhol – Calcutta fish stew with turbot

ingredients

For the stew

2 tablespoons vegetable oil
1 tablespoon panch phoran
(equal amounts of coriander,
mustard, fennel, fenugreek and
onion seeds)
1 bay leaf
1 dried red chilli
½ tablespoon finely chopped
fresh root ginger
1 onion, sliced
100g/4oz Jersey Royal potatoes,
diced (or Rooster potatoes)
1 tomato, diced
100g/4oz carrots, diced
100g/4oz yellow pumpkin, diced
½ tablespoon ground turmeric
½ tablespoon chilli powder
½ tablespoon ground coriander
½ tablespoon ground cumin
450ml/15fl oz fish stock
½ tablespoon sugar
Sea salt

For the fish

4 x 100g/4oz turbot steaks
½ tablespoon fennel seeds
½ tablespoon coriander seeds
½ tablespoon black sesame seeds
1 tablespoon vegetable oil
1 tablespoon softened butter

A few chervil or coriander sprigs,
to garnish

Serves 4

method

For the stew

· Heat the oil in a large pan over a medium
  heat and add the panch phoran, bay leaf
  and chilli. As they crackle, add the ginger
  and sauté for 1 minute. Add the onion and
  sauté for 2-3 minutes, and then stir in all the
  vegetables and sauté for 3-5 minutes.

· Stir in all the ground spices, sauté for 1-2
  minutes and then add the fish stock, sugar
  and some salt. Cook until the vegetables are
  completely tender. Remove from the heat
  and keep warm.

For the fish

· Prepare the turbot by sprinkling the seeds
  over the turbot steaks. Heat the oil in a
  non-stick pan, add the turbot and fry over a
  medium heat for 1-2 minutes on each side.

· Just before finishing, add the butter to the
  pan, let it melt, and then spoon it over the
  fish.

To serve

· Pour the stew into deep dishes and place
  the fish on top. Garnish with chervil or
  coriander sprigs.

Bibinca

ingredients

For the batter

150g/5oz plain flour
5 egg yolks
15g/½oz palm sugar (or brown sugar)
450ml/15fl oz milk
1 teaspoon salt
40g/1½oz vegetable oil

For the Bibinca

125g/4½oz ghee (clarified butter)
50g/2oz palm sugar (or brown sugar)

Cinnamon ice cream, to serve

Serves 6

method

For the batter

· Whisk all the ingredients together. Strain through a sieve. Keep in the fridge overnight.

For the Bibinca

· Preheat the grill. Heat a tablespoon of ghee in a deep dish about 15cm/6 inches in diameter. When it is hot, pour in a cup of the batter and place under the hot grill and grill until brown, approximately 4-5 minutes.

· Remove from the grill, add another tablespoon of ghee and pour in another cup of batter and grill until brown. Continue in this manner until all the batter is used up. When it is done, turn it upside down and cool.

To serve

· Cut it into thin slices. Before serving, heat in the oven if necessary for 10 minutes and serve with cinnamon ice cream.

Ashford Castle

In the grandest hotel in Ireland, the Connaught Room's menus offer mainly classic French cooking conjured from local artisan food, providing a fine-dining experience that is complemented by a stunning wine list and irreproachable service. The slightly less formal George V dining room features excellent meat, seafood, game in season and a suggested wine for each dish. The Drawing Room serves casual meals.

Cong, Co. Mayo
Ph: (094) 954 6003
www.ashford.ie

starter

Crisp strudel of Connemara lamb with a chutney of sun-dried tomatoes and fresh basil pesto

main course

Atlantic seafood broth of local seafood and fish with vegetables and herbs

dessert

Irish stout pudding with vanilla ice cream

Crisp strudel of Connemara lamb with a chutney of sun-dried tomatoes and fresh basil pesto

ingredients

For the chutney

25g/1oz sun-dried tomatoes
25g/1oz stoned green olives
1 small garlic clove, peeled

For the pesto

1 small bunch fresh basil
50ml/2fl oz extra virgin olive oil
1 garlic clove, peeled
25g/1oz pine nuts

For the strudel

6 x 25cm/10 inch sheets spring roll pastry
12 fresh large basil leaves
6 lamb fillets, fully trimmed (preferably Connemara lamb or similar mountain lamb)
1 egg white
1 teaspoon cornflour
Vegetable oil, for deep frying
Salt and pepper

Mixed salad leaves, to serve

Serves 6

method

For the chutney

· Drain the tomatoes and olives if necessary. Combine them with the garlic and process in a food blender until quite smooth. Adjust the seasoning with salt and pepper. Keep chilled until ready to serve. Can be stored in a plastic container in the fridge for later use.

For the pesto

· Combine the bunch of basil, olive oil, garlic and pine nuts and process in a food blender until very smooth. Adjust the seasoning with salt and pepper. Keep chilled until ready to serve. Can be stored in a plastic container in the fridge for later use.

For the strudel

· Arrange two of the basil leaves on each sheet of spring roll pastry and place a lamb fillet on top. Season the lamb fillet lightly with salt and pepper. Combine the egg white with the cornflour and brush the edges of the spring roll pastry with this mix. Roll up each strudel tightly, folding in the sides as for a spring roll.

· Preheat the vegetable oil in a deep fat fryer or a deep-sided pan to 160°C/325°F. Deep fry each roll for 2-3 minutes (rare) or 5-6 minutes (well done), depending on thickness.

To serve

· Cut the strudels into halves. Place some of the chutney in the middle of each plate and arrange the strudel halves on top. Drizzle with the pesto and serve with some tossed mixed salad leaves.

Atlantic seafood broth of local seafood and fish with vegetables and herbs

ingredients

For the broth

25ml/1fl oz olive oil
1 onion, chopped
50g/2oz mussels and clams
300ml/10fl oz white wine
25g/1oz carrots, diced
25g/1oz leeks, diced
25g/1oz fennel, diced
25g/1oz celeriac, diced
½ teaspoon saffron strands
1 small garlic clove, finely chopped
150ml/5fl oz fish stock (or chicken stock)
25g/1oz fresh herbs, chopped (such as chives, basil, tarragon)
Salt and pepper

For the fish

550g/1¼lb assorted fish fillets, fully trimmed and cut into 40g/1½oz individual portions (such as salmon, monkfish, turbot, cod, halibut)
Olive oil
12 Dublin Bay prawn tails, peeled and de-veined
24 shrimps, peeled
6 scallops, shelled and cleaned

Oven-roasted fennel bulbs, spinach and steamed potatoes or, alternatively, large baguette croûtons and spicy sauce mayonnaise, to serve (optional)

Serves 6

method

For the broth

- Heat a little olive oil in a shallow pot. Add the onion and cook gently until soft but not coloured. Add the mussels and clams and stir over a strong heat for 15 seconds. Add 250ml/9fl oz of the white wine, cover the pot with a tight fitting lid and cook for approximately 3 minutes until all the shells have opened. Remove from the heat and allow to cool. Remove all the clams and mussels from their shells, discarding any unopened ones. Strain the cooking liquid through a fine sieve and reserve. You will need about 150ml/5fl oz. Chill the cooked shellfish until they are to be used.

- Heat a little olive oil in a pan. Add the vegetables and cook gently over a moderate heat until soft. Add the saffron and garlic. Continue to cook gently for another 30 seconds. Add the stock with the reserved liquid and remaining white wine and bring to the boil. Simmer for 5 minutes. Adjust the seasoning with salt and pepper. Add the cooked mussels, clams and fresh herbs. Keep hot until ready to serve, but note that the shellfish can become rubbery very quickly so serve as soon as possible.

For the fish

- Season all the remaining fish and shellfish with salt and pepper. Heat some olive oil in a pan and fry for 2-3 minutes or until almost fully cooked.

To serve

- Place all the cooked fish in a large soup terrine or individual deep dishes and ladle over the broth. Serve with oven-roasted fennel bulbs, spinach and steamed potatoes. Alternatively, serve with large baguette croûtons and spicy sauce mayonnaise.

Irish stout pudding with vanilla ice cream

ingredients

For the pudding

25g/1oz dark brown sugar
25g/1oz butter
25ml/1fl oz Extra Stout Guinness
25g/1oz currants
25g/1oz raisins
25g/1oz sultanas
25g/1oz mixed peel
1 teaspoon mixed spice
1 teaspoon ground nutmeg
1 teaspoon ground ginger
1 teaspoon bread soda
1 egg, beaten
75g/3oz plain flour

For the sauce

50ml/2fl oz Extra Stout Guinness
50ml/2fl oz fresh cream
25g/1oz dark brown sugar
50g/2oz butter

To serve

200ml/7fl oz custard
85ml/3fl oz fresh cream
450g/1lb vanilla ice cream
Fresh mint sprigs, toasted almonds, chocolate shavings and raisins, to serve

Serves 6

method

· Preheat the oven to 180°C/350°F/gas mark 4.

For the pudding

· Beat the sugar and butter together until smooth. Transfer to a pot and add the Guinness, dried fruits and mixed peel. Bring to the boil and then simmer for 5 minutes. Chill until cool. Then add the spices, bread soda, egg and flour. Mix well.
· Pour into 5cm/2 inch deep baking tray, 25cm x 15cm/10 inches x 6 inches. Bake in the oven for 18 minutes. Remove from the oven and leave to cool.
· Using a 7.5cm/3 inch round cutter, cut the chilled pudding into 6 portions.

For the sauce

· Boil the stout in a pan with the cream, brown sugar and butter. Pour over the cut puddings, allowing the liquid to be soaked up.

To serve

· Combine the custard with the cream and divide among deep plates. Place a pudding in the centre of each plate and place 1 scoop of vanilla ice cream on top. Decorate with mint sprigs, toasted almonds, chocolate shavings, and raisins which may be soaked in any remaining sauce.

Avoca Cafés

The well-known Avoca group of lifestyle/craft shops incorporate café-restaurants that are much loved for the imaginative, high-quality food they offer. All-day menus feature top-class cakes, pastries and breads; homemade soups and a selection of simple traditional dishes that make the most of seasonal food cooked with care and served in an informal atmosphere.

Kilmacanogue, Bray, Co. Wicklow
Ph: (01) 286 7466

www.avoca.ie

starter
Pea, pancetta, broad bean and goat's cheese salad

main course
Tuscan slow roast pork with Parmesan and olive oil mash

dessert
Pecan and maple streusel cheesecake

Pea, pancetta, broad bean and goat's cheese salad

ingredients

400g/14oz fresh broad beans, podded (about 1kg/2lb broad beans in their pods. You can also use frozen or tinned broad beans that have been skinned)

8 slices pancetta (Italian streaky bacon)

400g/14oz frozen peas

1 garlic clove, finely chopped

150g/5oz soft goat's cheese

Juice of 1 lemon

2 tablespoon extra virgin olive oil

1 large bunch fresh mint, finely chopped

Salt and pepper

Serves 4

method

· Preheat the oven to 220°C/425°F/gas mark 7.

· Blanch the broad beans in boiling salted water for 1 minute, drain and refresh. Remove the skins and discard.

· Arrange the pancetta on a shallow baking sheet and bake for 2-3 minutes until crisp (watch it, as ovens vary widely).

· Blanch the peas in boiling salted water for 2 minutes, or until just cooked. Drain and refresh.

· Mash the garlic into the goat's cheese and season with salt and pepper and lemon juice. Toss the broad beans and peas in the olive oil. Crumble the goat's cheese over the peas and broad beans and sprinkle over the mint.

To serve

· Spoon the goat's cheese mixture onto plates, top each one with a couple of slices of crispy pancetta and spoon over a little more olive oil. Sprinkle with black pepper and serve.

Tuscan slow roast pork with Parmesan and olive oil mash

ingredients

For the pork

1 leg of pork on the bone, approximately 1.75kg-2.25kg/ 4-5lb (this may have to be ordered from your butcher)
50g/2oz fennel seeds
Juice of 4 lemons
10 garlic cloves, peeled
2 teaspoons salt
4 tablespoons olive oil

For the mash (quantities per person)

2 potatoes
1 teaspoon olive oil
1 tablespoon milk
1 teaspoon freshly grated Parmesan
Salt and pepper

Serves 8-10

method

- Preheat the oven to 220°C/425°F/ gas mark 7.

For the pork

- Ask your butcher to score the skin side of the leg of pork.
- Place all the ingredients except the pork into a food processor and blend into a paste.
- Place the pork on a large board and with a sharp knife make about a dozen small incisions in the meat side of the pork. This will help the paste to infuse into the meat. Then rub the paste all over the meat and gently work it into the scored marks. Ideally allow the meat to sit for an hour to marinate.
- Place the joint in the oven, skin side up, covered with a sheet of loose tin foil to prevent burning, for one hour. Then reduce the oven temperature to just 130°C/250°F/ gas mark ½. Turn the meat over and baste regularly. After a further 2 hours turn the meat over again and continue to thoroughly baste every hour or so. Leave to cook slowly for a further 5 hours with the crackling side up.
- The idea is to melt the fat and end up with sticky meat that will fall apart and can almost be carved with a fork. The crackling should be crisp. (The crackling may be crisped up under a hot grill at the end if you wish but be careful not to burn it too much.) Allow the meat to sit for 10-15 minutes before carving. The remaining juices can be used as light gravy.

For the mash

- Place the potatoes in a saucepan of cold, salted water and bring to the boil. Simmer until they yield to a fork. This will take 25-30 minutes. Drain the water and peel the potatoes while they are still hot. Leave the potatoes to dry in a sieve as the steam evaporates.
- Return to the saucepan over a very low heat and mash thoroughly with a potato masher adding the olive oil. At the same time, heat the milk in a saucepan. Add the grated Parmesan and stir but do not boil. When the potatoes have been mashed and are no longer letting off steam, add the warm milk and cheese mixture and beat with a wooden spoon to get it really smooth.

To serve

- Place slices of the pork on warmed plates and add a good sized portion of the mash. Serve the gravy separately.

Pecan and maple streusel cheesecake

ingredients

For the cheesecake

225g/8oz shortbread biscuits
40g/1½oz unsalted butter
(less if the shortbread biscuits
are homemade), plus extra for
greasing
675g/1½lb cream cheese
225g/8oz light brown sugar
3 eggs
120ml/4fl oz whipping cream
1 teaspoon natural vanilla
extract or 1 vanilla pod, seeds
scraped out

For the streusel topping

25g/1oz butter
50g/2oz pecans, roughly
chopped
75g/3oz shortbread biscuits,
crumbled but still with texture
25g/1oz light brown sugar

For the maple sauce

40g/1½oz butter
50g/2oz caster sugar
85ml/3fl oz maple syrup
120ml/4fl oz cream

Whipped cream, to serve

Serves 6-8

method

· Preheat the oven to 140°C/275°F/
  gas mark 1.

For the cheesecake

· Butter a 23cm/9 inch spring-form cake tin
  and line it with non-stick parchment paper.

· Crush the shortbread biscuits (the quickest
  way is between 2 sheets of greaseproof
  paper using a rolling pin). Melt the butter,
  mix the shortbread with it and sprinkle it
  over the base of the prepared tin.

· Beat the cream cheese and sugar together,
  and then gradually beat in the eggs. Stir
  in the cream and vanilla extract or seeds.
  Pour over the biscuit base and bake for 50
  minutes to one hour. It should still have a
  slight wobble when cooked and it may have
  cracked; don't worry, the streusel topping
  covers a lot.

For the streusel topping

· In a non-stick frying pan, melt the butter
  over a low heat. Add the pecans and
  cook gently for 1-2 minutes. Add the
  crumbled shortbread and sugar, and cook
  for 2-3 minutes, stirring frequently. Leave
  to cool slightly and then sprinkle over
  the cheesecake. Allow to cool to room
  temperature.

For the maple sauce

· Put all the ingredients in a saucepan and
  bring slowly to the boil. Cook for about 5
  minutes until the mixture has become a
  light caramel colour.

To serve

· Cut a thin slice of the cheesecake with a
  warm knife. Pour over the caramel sauce
  and add whipped cream on the side.

Ballymaloe House and Cookery School

Ireland's most famous country house remains true to Myrtle Allen's vision of recapturing lost flavours, preserving those in peril and supporting artisan producers. Ballymaloe offers an authentic country house experience, with seasonally driven menus cooked and presented simply but with flair. One can learn to cook the dishes at Darina Allen's Ballymaloe Cookery School just two miles away.

Shanagarry, Co. Cork
Ph: (021) 465 2531
www.ballymaloe.ie

starter
Spinach and rosemary soup

main course
Pork in mushroom, rosemary and ginger sauce with orzo

dessert
Yogurt and cardamom cream with green gooseberry and elderflower compote

Spinach and rosemary soup

ingredients

50g/2oz butter
100g/4oz onions, chopped
150g/5oz potatoes, chopped
600ml/1 pint homemade
chicken stock, vegetable stock
or use water
450-600ml/15fl oz-1 pint
creamy milk (¼ cream and ¾
milk)
225-350g/8-12oz spinach,
tough stalks removed and
chopped
1 tablespoon chopped fresh
rosemary
Salt and freshly ground pepper

Fresh cream and rosemary
sprigs or rosemary flowers, to
serve (optional)

method

· Melt the butter in a heavy-bottomed saucepan. When it foams,
  add the onions and potatoes and toss them until well coated.
  Sprinkle with salt and freshly ground pepper. Cover and sweat
  on a gentle heat for 10 minutes.

· Add the stock and creamy milk, then bring to the boil and
  simmer until the potatoes and onions are fully cooked. Add the
  spinach and boil with the lid off for about 3-5 minutes, until
  the spinach is tender. Do not overcook or the soup will lose its
  fresh green colour.

· Add the chopped rosemary. Purée the soup in a liquidiser or
  food processor. Taste and correct the seasoning.

To serve

· Spoon the soup into warm bowls and drizzle in some fresh
  cream (optional). Garnish with a sprig of rosemary. If you have
  a pretty rosemary bush in bloom, sprinkle a few flowers over
  the top for extra pzazz.

Serves 6-8

Pork in mushroom, rosemary and ginger sauce with orzo

For the pork

1 large/2 small pork fillets
(preferably free range and
organic if possible)
25g/1oz butter
1 teaspoon chopped fresh
rosemary
2 tablespoons shallot or
chopped spring onions
100g/4oz mushrooms, sliced
150ml/5fl oz homemade
chicken stock
150ml/5fl oz cream
1-2 teaspoons freshly grated
root ginger
1 dessertspoon chopped fresh
parsley

For the orzo

200g/7oz orzo pasta
2.25litres/4 pints water
1½ teaspoons salt
15g/½oz butter
1 tablespoon chopped fresh
parsley (optional)
Salt and freshly ground pepper

Rosemary sprigs, to serve

Serves 4

method

For the pork

- Trim the pork of all fat and membrane. Cut into 1cm/½ inch thick slices.
- Heat half the butter in a sauté pan until foaming, put in the pork slices and turn in the butter (do not brown). Add the chopped rosemary, toss and cover with a round of greaseproof paper and the lid. Cook on a gentle heat for 5-7 minutes or until just barely cooked through.
- Meanwhile, sweat the shallot or spring onions gently in a pan in the rest of the butter. Increase the heat, add the mushrooms and season with salt and freshly ground pepper, then cook for 3-4 minutes. Keep aside.
- When the pork is cooked, transfer to a plate and keep warm. Add the chicken stock, cream and ginger to the pan that you have cooked the pork in. Reduce the liquid by

half over a medium heat; this will thicken the sauce slightly and intensify the flavour. (Otherwise, thicken with a little roux.) When you are happy with the flavour and texture of the sauce, add the pork and the mushroom mixture back in. Simmer for 1–2 minutes, taste and correct the seasoning.

For the orzo

- Bring the water to a fast rolling boil and add the salt. Sprinkle in the orzo, cook for 8–10 minutes or until just cooked. Drain, rinse under hot water, toss with the butter. Season with freshly ground pepper and garnish with parsley.

To serve

- Arrange the pork and the sauce on warmed plates. Spoon the orzo to the side. Garnish with some fresh rosemary sprigs.

Yogurt and cardamom cream with green gooseberry and elderflower compote

ingredients

For the yogurt cream

¼ teaspoon cardamom seeds
250ml/9fl oz milk
200g/7oz caster sugar (can be reduced to 150g/5oz)
200ml/7fl oz cream
3 rounded teaspoons powdered gelatine
4 tablespoons cold water
450ml/15fl oz natural yogurt
Grapeseed oil, for brushing

For the compote

900g/2lb green gooseberries
2–3 elderflower heads, plus extra to decorate
450g/1lb sugar
600ml/1 pint cold water

Fresh elderflowers, to decorate

Serves 8

method

For the yogurt cream

· Crush the cardamom seeds. Put the milk, sugar and cream into a stainless steel saucepan with the ground cardamom. Bring to the boil gently, stirring until the sugar has dissolved and the mixture is warm to the touch. Remove from the heat and leave to infuse while you dissolve the gelatine.

· Put the gelatine in a small bowl with the cold water. Put the bowl into a saucepan of simmering water until the gelatine has melted and is completely clear. Add a little of the infused milk mixture and stir well and then mix this into the rest. Beat the yogurt lightly with a whisk until smooth and creamy. Add into the cardamom mixture. Pour into a well oiled ring mould or 8 individual moulds. Allow to set for several hours, preferably overnight, in the fridge.

For the compote

· First top and tail the gooseberries. Tie the elderflower heads in a little square of muslin and put in a stainless steel or enamelled saucepan. Add the sugar and cover with the cold water. Bring slowly to the boil and continue to boil for 2 minutes. Add the gooseberries and simmer just until the fruit bursts. Allow to get cold.

To serve

· To remove the yogurt cream from the moulds, dip the moulds in hot water first and gently loosen at the sides with a round-bladed knife. Place the yogurt cream in the centre of the plate. Spoon the compote onto the plate as you wish. Decorate with fresh elderflowers.

Bang Café

Bang Café is a chic, bistro-style restaurant, where Eurotoque chef Lorcan Cribbin is dedicated to using locally sourced ingredients as a basis for innovative contemporary menus. Located just a few steps from St Stephen's Green, Bang is spread over three floors and includes a roof terrace and a cellar cocktail bar.

11 Merrion Row, Dublin 2
Ph: (01) 676 0898
www.bangrestaurant.com

starter
Blue cheese and toasted walnut salad with chilli pear and Chardonnay dressing

main course
Chicken casserole

dessert
Apple streusel cake

Blue cheese and toasted walnut salad with chilli pear and Chardonnay dressing

ingredients

For the pears

250ml/9fl oz water
50g/2oz sugar
½ red chilli, seeded and chopped
½ star anise
25g/1oz root ginger, chopped
1 lemon grass stick
4 pears, peeled, quartered and core removed

For the Chardonnay dressing

50ml/2fl oz Chardonnay vinegar (or good quality white wine vinegar)
85ml/3fl oz olive oil
50ml/2fl oz vegetable oil
1 teaspoon Dijon mustard
½ teaspoon salt
150g/5oz walnuts, toasted and seasoned
350g/12oz blue cheese (such as Cashel blue)

Salad leaves, to serve

Serves 4

method

For the pears

· Bring the water and sugar to the boil with the chilli, star anise, ginger and lemon grass. Add the pear quarters. Bring back to the boil, then reduce the heat and simmer for 10 minutes until the pears are tender.

· Remove from the heat and allow to cool in the syrup. Remove the pears with a slotted spoon before using them.

For the Chardonnay dressing

· Put all the ingredients into a bowl and combine well together.

To serve

· Place the salad leaves in the middle of the plates. Arrange the blue cheese, toasted walnuts and pears on top. Spoon over the dressing.

Chicken casserole

ingredients

Olive oil, for frying
1 onion, diced
275g/10oz baby button
mushrooms, sliced
8 rindless streaky rashers,
chopped into large pieces
2 garlic cloves, chopped
450g/1lb ripe tomatoes,
chopped
1 teaspoon tomato purée
600ml/1 pint chicken stock
4 chicken breast fillets, diced
2 thyme sprigs
1 bay leaf
Dash of Worcestershire sauce
Bunch fresh parsley, chopped
Salt and pepper

Mashed potatoes or rice, to
serve

Serves 4

method

· Heat a couple of tablespoons of the oil in a pot. Add the onion
  and sweat until soft. Add the mushrooms and cook for a few
  minutes until tender. Then add the streaky rashers. Cook for a
  few minutes.

· Add the garlic and tomatoes. Then add the purée and stock and
  bring to the boil. Season with salt.

· In a separate hot pan, heat a little oil and sauté the chicken
  breast fillets until brown all over. Add to the casserole with
  the thyme, bay leaf, Worcestershire sauce and simmer for 30
  minutes until the chicken is tender. Add the parsley just before
  serving.

To serve

· As this is a lovely rustic chicken dish, it is best served with
  mashed potatoes or rice.

Apple streusel cake

ingredients

For the crumble topping

100g/4oz butter, at room temperature
40g/1½oz icing sugar
125g/4½oz flour
1 teaspoon ground cinnamon
1 teaspoon vanilla essence

For the apple

40g/1½oz caster sugar
Zest of 1 orange
1 large cooking apple, peeled, cored and diced

For the cake

100g/4oz butter, at room temperature
100g/4oz caster sugar
150g/5oz self-raising flour
1 teaspoon baking powder
2 eggs
2 tablespoons milk

Ice cream and custard, to serve

Serves 8-10

method

- Preheat the oven to 180°C/350°F/ gas mark 4.

For the crumble topping

- Place all the ingredients in a bowl and rub between your fingers until the mixture resembles crumbs.

For the apple

- Mix the sugar and orange together in a bowl. Put the diced apple in the bowl and mix until it is covered with the sugar and zest.

For the cake

- Beat the butter and sugar together until it is smooth and pale in colour. Add the flour and baking powder, then slowly add the eggs and mix again. Add the milk until the mixture has a soft dropping consistency.

- Pour the mix into a greased cake tin, 20cm/8 inches in diameter. Place the flavoured diced apple on top of the cake mix. Sprinkle the crumble topping mixture over the top. Bake in the oven for 40 minutes or until a skewer comes out clean.

To serve

- Serve warm with ice cream and custard.

Beaches Restaurant

Kelly's Hotel is an institution in Ireland, and Beaches is its fine-dining restaurant. Executive chef Jim Aherne offers classic menus that change daily and reflect the value he places on fresh local produce. The hotel's highly regarded wine list, most of it imported directly, is meticulously sourced, always changing and excellent value; the collection also includes organic and biodynamic wines.

Kelly's Resort Hotel, Rosslare, Co. Wexford
Ph: (053) 913 2114

www.kellys.ie

starter
Cream of nettle soup
with Kelly's high-fibre brown bread

main course
Roast goose with potato,
chestnut and chipolata stuffing

dessert
Hot walnut pudding with fudge sauce

Cream of nettle soup
with Kelly's high-fibre brown bread

ingredients

For the bread (makes 4 loaves)

675g/1½lb brown wholemeal flour

50g/2oz wheat germ

100g/4oz bran

2 teaspoons bread soda

1 teaspoon salt

100g/4oz margarine or butter, plus extra for greasing

2 large eggs (3 if small)

About 700ml/1¼ pints buttermilk

Sesame seeds (optional)

For the nettle soup

50g/2oz butter

50g/2oz shallots, diced

50g/2oz plain flour

600ml/1 pint chicken stock (using 1 stock cube is fine)

4 cups of young nettle tops or leaves, chopped coarsely (sorrel or spinach may be used instead)

150ml/5fl oz cream (keep a little to garnish)

Salt and ground pepper

Croûtons, to serve

Serves 4

method

· Preheat the oven to 180°C/350°F/ gas mark 4.

For the bread

· Mix the flour, wheat germ, bran, bread soda and salt together. Rub the margarine or butter into this mixture. Beat the eggs with the buttermilk and add to the dry mix; stir with a fork. Put into 900ml/1½ pint greased loaf tins. Bake in the oven for approximately 1 hour. Cool on a wire tray.

For the nettle soup

· Melt the butter in a pot, then fry the shallots until they are soft. Make a roux by adding the flour, mix well and cook for approximately 2 minutes. Add the chicken stock slowly and stir well. Continue cooking for approximately 10 minutes.

· Add the chopped nettles and season with salt and pepper. Liquidise and return to the heat. Add the cream and heat until warmed through. Do not boil.

To serve

· Pour the soup into warm bowls. Spoon a little cream on top. Serve with croûtons and some of the brown bread.

Roast goose with potato, chestnut and chipolata stuffing

ingredients

For the goose

3.75kg/8lb oven-ready goose

For the stuffing

2 large onions, diced
Olive oil, for frying
900g/2lb cooked mashed
potatoes
450g/1lb fried chipolata
sausages, chopped
900g/2lb chestnuts, peeled,
skinned and quartered (from a
can is fine)
1 teaspoon chopped fresh
thyme (optional)
1 tablespoon chopped fresh flat
leaf parsley (optional)
Salt and freshly ground pepper

Baked red cabbage and roast
potatoes, to serve

Serves 6

method

- Preheat the oven to 160°C/325°F/
gas mark 3.

For the goose

- Prick the skin of the goose all over with a
fork, taking care not to pierce the flesh, as
the meat will dry out during cooking. Season
inside and out with salt and freshly ground
pepper.
- Roast the goose in a roasting tin with a rack
for approximately 3½ hours. Begin roasting
breast down and turn every 30 minutes to
finish with breast side up. Allow to settle for
about 20 minutes before serving, keeping in
a warm place.

For the stuffing

- Fry the onions in olive oil until transparent.
Combine the onions, mashed potato,
chipolata sausage, chestnuts and herbs, if
using. Keep warm until ready to serve.

To serve

- Carve the goose and arrange on warmed
plates and serve with the stuffing on the
side. Baked red cabbage and roast potatoes
are a nice accompaniment which can be
taken to the table in separate bowls so that
guests can help themselves.

Hot walnut pudding with fudge sauce

ingredients

For the walnut pudding

175g/6oz margarine or butter
175g/6oz brown plain flour
3 eggs
175g/6oz plain flour
 Pinch of salt
50g/2oz shelled walnuts
2 tablespoons milk
2 teaspoons baking powder

For the fudge sauce

100g/4oz butter
100g/4oz brown sugar
100g/4oz golden syrup
300ml/10fl oz milk

Vanilla ice cream or whipped cream, to serve

Serves 4

method

· Preheat the oven to 150°C/300°F/gas mark 2.

For the walnut pudding

· Put all the ingredients in a mixing bowl and whisk for about 5 minutes until smooth. Grease 4 200ml/7fl oz ramekin dishes and pour in the pudding mix. Arrange on a baking sheet and cook in the oven for 45 minutes until well risen and lightly golden.

For the fudge sauce

· Put the butter, sugar and golden syrup into a pot and cook until the mixture becomes a dark colour. Add the milk and bring to the boil, stirring well.

To serve

· Remove the puddings from the dishes and invert onto warmed plates. Serve with the fudge sauce surrounding the pudding and whipped cream or ice cream on the side.

Bentley's Oyster Bar & Grill

Richard Corrigan has brought his many talents to bear on Bentley's, which is housed in an elegant 18th century house on St. Stephen's Green. Here, luxury and fine service are matched by food which is a magical mix of innovation and tradition. While the menu has a strong focus on seafood, carnivores have plenty of choice.

starter
Shellfish cocktail

main course
Fish and chips with mushy peas and tartare sauce

dessert
Strawberry mousse with lemon sablé biscuits

22 St. Stephen's Green, Dublin 2
Ph: (01) 638 3939
www.bentleysdublin.com

Shellfish cocktail

ingredients

For the seafood

40g/1½oz cooked white crab meat

4 cooked Dublin Bay prawns

100g/4oz cooked lobster tail meat

100g/4oz cooked brown shrimps, peeled

Extra virgin olive oil

Sea salt

Dash of lemon juice

2 baby gem lettuces, shredded

1 small cucumber, peeled, seeded and diced

For the cocktail sauce

6 tablespoons mayonnaise

2 tablespoons tomato ketchup

Splash of brandy

Dash of Tabasco sauce

Pinch of paprika

Squeeze of lemon juice

Serves 4

method

For the sauce

· Mix together all the ingredients for the sauce.

To serve

· Take four large, old-fashioned cocktail glasses. Season all the seafood with a little extra virgin olive oil, salt and a dash of lemon juice. Put some lettuce and cucumber at the bottom of each glass, which will give a lovely crunch, then layer up the seafood. Put a dollop of sauce on top and let people mix everything up or keep separate, as they choose.

Fish and chips with mushy peas and tartare sauce

ingredients

For the batter

1 heaped dessertspoon fresh yeast
300ml/10fl oz bottle of beer or ale
100g/4oz plain flour
75g/3oz rice flour
25g/1oz cornflour
2 dessertspoons salt

For the chips

900g/2lb potatoes, peeled (starchy variety, suitable for chipping)
Vegetable oil, for deep frying

For the mushy peas

A little butter
1 onion, finely chopped
2 garlic cloves, crushed
1 celery stick, finely chopped
250g/9oz dried marrowfat peas, soaked overnight
1 tablespoon bicarbonate of soda
100ml/3½fl oz malt vinegar
Pinch of salt

For the fish

4 x 175g/6oz haddock fillets, skinned and boned
Vegetable oil, for deep frying

Good quality tartare sauce, to serve

Serves 4

method

For the batter

· Whisk the yeast into the beer or ale, then whisk in the three flours and salt. Allow to stand in a warm place for about 30 minutes, during which time it will puff up and bubble.

For the chips

· Cut the potatoes as you like. Do not put them in water or you will wash away the valuable starch that you need to prevent them cooking too quickly without softening properly. Heat the oil in a deep fat fryer to 140°C/275°F. Put in the cut potatoes and cook for about 5 minutes, until they are soft but not coloured. Remove and drain on kitchen paper.

For the mushy peas

· Heat the butter in a pan, add the onion, garlic and celery and cook gently until soft but not coloured. Drain the peas and add them to the pan, along with bicarbonate of soda. Add enough water to cover by 2.5cm/1 inch. Bring to the boil, then turn down the heat and simmer for 1–1½ hours, topping up with more water if necessary. Do not stir the peas during cooking. That is the key to lovely soft peas. Once you stir them, the outside will start to break down, turning the water thick and sludgy and you will end up with mushy outsides and hard insides. Once the peas are soft (test one between your fingers), take off the heat and leave to cool. Stir in the vinegar and a good pinch of salt.

For the fish

· Increase the temperature of the oil to 160°C/325°F. Dip the haddock fillets into the batter, shaking off any excess, then lower into the oil. Because the fish is quite heavy in its batter, it will want to sink at first, and the oil won't envelop it properly, so support it lightly with a fish slice until the yeast in the batter puffs up and it floats by itself. Fry for about 4 minutes, until golden and crispy, then lift out and drain on kitchen paper.

To finish the chips

· Increase the temperature of the oil to 180°C/350°F, put in the blanched chips, and cook until golden.

To serve

· Place the battered fish on warm plates with the chips, mushy peas and tartare sauce on the side.

Strawberry mousse with lemon sablé biscuits

ingredients

For the strawberry mousse

200g/7oz strawberries, hulled
200g/7oz caster sugar
6 egg whites
4 gelatine leaves
300ml/10fl oz double cream

For the sablé biscuits

250g/9oz butter
675g/1½lb plain flour
250g/9oz icing sugar
Zest of 2 lemons
1 vanilla pod, split in half and
seeds scrapped out
2 large eggs, beaten
50ml/2fl oz cream

Serves 4-6

method

- Preheat the oven to 160°C/325°F/gas mark 3.

For the strawberry mousse

- Place the strawberries in a food processor and blend to a purée.
- In a bowl, whisk the sugar and egg whites together, then add the strawberry purée and mix again. Soak the gelatine in 4 tablespoons cold water for about 10 minutes. Whip the cream until soft peak forms and gently fold into the strawberry mixture.
- Remove the gelatine from the water and squeeze out any excess water. Add the gelatine to the strawberry mixture and ensure it is well mixed through. Pour into a cake tin approximately 675g/1½lb lined with clingfilm and set in the fridge for 2 hours or overnight.

For the sablé biscuits

- Using your hands, rub the butter and flour together to form breadcrumbs. Add icing sugar, lemon zest and the vanilla seeds. Then add the beaten eggs and finally bind together with the cream to form a smooth paste. Wrap in clingfilm and chill in the fridge for 2 hours.
- Roll the paste out on a lightly floured work surface to about 2.5cm/1 inch thick and cut into 7.5cm/3 inch fingers. Place on a greased baking sheet and bake in the oven for 10-12 minutes or until golden brown. Allow to cool on a wire tray.

To serve

- Put tall glasses on plates. Spoon the mousse into the glasses and place a biscuit in each one. Add some additional biscuits to each plate.

Bistro One

Set in the heart of Foxrock village, this popular local restaurant insists on sourcing from small producers who are passionate about food. Prepared and cooked with care, the seasonally driven menu uses the finest Irish ingredients wherever possible to create classic and contemporary European dishes.

Foxrock Village, Dublin 18
Ph: (01) 289 7711
www.bistro-one.ie

starter
Haddock and spinach tart

main course
Roast stuffed 'saddle back' pork fillet with organic turnip mash

dessert
Poached pears, chocolate sauce, vanilla ice cream and toasted hazelnuts

Haddock and spinach tart

ingredients

For the pastry

200g/7oz plain flour, plus extra for dusting

100g/4oz unsalted butter, cut into small cubes and chilled

1 egg yolk (preferably free range)

50ml/2fl oz cold milk

For the filling

275-350g/10-12oz smoked haddock fillets

450ml/15fl oz milk

400g/14oz fresh spinach, washed with tough stalks removed

2 onions, finely chopped

Knob of unsalted butter

500ml/17fl oz cream

2 egg yolks (preferably free range)

2 eggs (preferably free range)

50g/2oz mature Cheddar cheese, grated

Salt and black pepper

Mixed salad leaves, to serve

Serves 8-10

method

- Preheat the oven to 160°C/325°F/ gas mark 3.

For the pastry

- Put the flour, pinch of salt and butter into a food processor and pulse until the mixture has the consistency of breadcrumbs. Add the egg yolk and then, with the food processor running, slowly add the milk, stopping as soon as the dough comes together. Tip out the mixture on to a lightly floured board; knead a couple of times to make a smooth ball of dough and then wrap in clingfilm. Leave in the fridge to chill for 30 minutes.
- Roll the pastry out thinly on a lightly floured surface and use it to line a 25cm/10 inch loose-bottomed tart tin. Then line with a sheet of parchment paper and fill with rice or beans. Cook in the oven for 15 minutes. Remove the paper and beans and cook the pastry for a further 10 minutes until it is dry to touch.

For the filling

- Place the smoked haddock in an ovenproof dish and cover fully with the milk. Place in the oven and poach for 4 minutes.
- Remove the fish from the milk and leave to cool. When it has cooled, remove the skin and bones. Flake the fish into small pieces.
- Blanch the spinach in boiling water for 30 seconds and strain. When it has cooled, squeeze as much water as possible from the spinach.
- Gently sweat the onions in the butter for 10 minutes until they are translucent.

- Whisk the cream, egg yolks and eggs together and season with a little salt and black pepper.
- Place the fish, spinach, onions and cheese in the cooked tart case, then pour the egg and cream mixture on top. Bake in the oven for 40 minutes until lightly set.

To serve

- Serve warm. Cut into slices and serve with mixed salad leaves.

Roast stuffed 'saddle back' pork fillet with organic turnip mash

ingredients

For the stuffing

75g/3oz butter
1 shallot, finely diced
1 apple, peeled, cored and finely diced
½ teaspoon fresh thyme leaves
125g/4½oz fresh white breadcrumbs

For the pork

2 free range pork fillets, about 200g/7oz each
16 slices of pancetta/streaky bacon
Butter, to fry
Olive oil, to fry

For the turnip

I large organic swede (turnip)
Butter
Salt and pepper

Serves 4

method

· Preheat the oven to 180°C/350°F/ gas mark 4.

For the stuffing

· Melt the butter in a pan. Sweat the shallot in the butter for 5 minutes until it is fully cooked, but not brown. Add the apple and the thyme leaves. Only cook the apple for 1 2 minutes so that it does not become too soft. Fold in the breadcrumbs and leave for one minute. Take the stuffing off the heat, season with salt and pepper. Leave to cool.

For the pork

· Cut each fillet in half and flatten out each piece so that you are left with four pieces of thin pork, roughly 10cm/4 inches square. The best way to do this is to place each piece of pork between two sheets of greaseproof paper and flatten with the base of a small heavy saucepan. Place a quarter of the cooled stuffing at the end of each fillet. Roll up the fillet with the stuffing and wrap tightly with the pancetta or streaky bacon to secure.

· Melt some butter and oil in a pan. Seal off the pork fillets on all sides in the hot pan. Put into the oven for 15-18 minutes, after which you can leave to rest for 5-10 minutes.

For the turnip

· Boil the turnip in salted water for about 30 minutes and when it is cooked, drain and mash roughly with butter and salt and lots of black pepper.

To serve

· Slice the pork and serve on warmed plates with the mashed turnip on the side.

Poached pears, chocolate sauce, vanilla ice cream and toasted hazelnuts

ingredients

350g/12oz sugar
600ml/1 pint water
½ vanilla pod
½ star anise
4 pears, peeled and cores removed
75g/3oz shelled and skinned hazelnuts
250g/9oz plain chocolate (minimum 70% cocoa solids)
250ml/9fl oz cream

4 scoops of good quality vanilla ice cream, to serve

Serves 4

method

· Dissolve the sugar in the water and add the vanilla pod and star anise. Simmer for 4 minutes and then add the pears and cook gently for 15-20 minutes until soft but not mushy. Turn off the heat and leave to cool for a couple of minutes.

· Toast the hazelnuts in a hot pan until they are a little golden, then lightly crush.

· Melt the chocolate in a bowl over a pot of boiling water. Allow to cool and then stir in the cream.

To serve

· Cut a little off the bottom of each pear so that it does not slide on the plate. Pour over the chocolate sauce and sprinkle a few toasted hazelnuts onto the plate. Finish with a scoop of vanilla ice cream.

Bon Appétit

Michelin-starred Bon Appétit is one of the country's most exciting restaurants and the ideal place to experience fine dining in stylish comfort. Chef-patron Oliver Dunne's gourmet menus, finely crafted cooking and beautifully presented dishes have acquired a reputation in this laid-back seaside village and beyond.

No. 9 James Terrace, Off Main Street, Malahide, Co. Dublin
Ph: (01) 845 0314
www.bonappetit.ie

starter
Poached Carlingford lobster
with baby carrots, asparagus and lobster bisque

main course
Roast breasts of partridge, confit legs stuffed
with chestnuts, fondant potato and cranberry jus

dessert
Marinated strawberries
with fromage blanc sorbet and sablé biscuits

Poached Carlingford lobster
with baby carrots, asparagus and lobster bisque

ingredients

For the lobster

4 x 675g/1½lb live lobsters
16 asparagus spears, trimmed
16 baby carrots, trimmed
16 green beans, trimmed
2 tablespoons chopped fresh
basil, plus extra to garnish

For the bisque

Lobster shells from the body
(see method)
1 celery stick, sliced
1 onion, sliced
1 carrot, sliced
1 shallot, sliced
2 tablespoons brandy
1 tablespoon tomato purée
50ml/2fl oz white wine
1litre/1¾ pints fish stock
Salt and pepper

Serves 4

method

· Preheat the oven to 180°C/350°F/
  gas mark 4.

For the lobster

· Fill a large pot with water and bring to the
  boil. Poach the lobsters for 10-12 minutes
  and then place in iced water. When cold,
  insert a knife where the tail and body
  meet and cut towards the tail. Remove the
  intestinal tract, the tail meat will now easily
  pull away from the shell. Break off the claws
  and crack the shells with a heavy knife.
  Remove the meat and any excess pieces of
  shell reserving the body shell for the bisque.
  Cut the meat into 1cm/½ inch dice and
  retain until ready to serve.

· In a separate pot, blanch the asparagus,
  baby carrots and the green beans until
  tender. Remove from the pot, refresh in iced
  water and retain until ready to serve.

For the bisque

· Place the lobster shells on a roasting tin
  and bake for 20 minutes. Then add the
  sliced vegetables and bake for a further
  10 minutes. Then deglaze the tin with the
  brandy and scrape all the sediment from the
  bottom. Transfer the shells and vegetables
  into a pot, add the tomato purée and wine
  and boil for 2 minutes. Pour in the fish stock
  and boil for 45 minutes. Strain through a
  sieve. Return to the heat and reduce to
  approximately 600ml/1 pint.

· Place the lobster meat in the bisque and
  slowly heat up but do not boil. Add the
  blanched vegetables and basil.

To serve

· Spoon the lobster bisque into warm bowls.
  If you like, place the lobster shell on top and
  garnish with basil.

Roast breasts of partridge, confit legs stuffed with chestnuts, fondant potato and cranberry jus

ingredients

For the partridge

4 oven-ready partridges
200g/7oz duck fat
10 garlic cloves, unpeeled
50g/2oz chestnuts, chopped
100g/4oz mixed wild mushrooms, chopped
100g/4oz butter
4 large Rooster potatoes (cut into 5cm/2 inch circles using pastry cutters)

For the jus

Partridge carcasses (see method)
2 shallots, chopped
1 carrot, chopped
10 garlic cloves, chopped
2 sprigs thyme
100ml/3½fl oz Madeira
1 litre/1¾ pints chicken stock
75g/3oz cranberries, halved (can use frozen)
Salt and pepper

Serves 4

method

- Preheat the oven to 200°C/400°F/ gas mark 6.

For the partridge

- Remove the legs from the partridges. Carefully carve the breasts from the partridge carcasses. Keep for the jus. Season the partridge legs with salt and pepper. Heat the duck fat with the garlic cloves and submerge the partridge legs in the fat and cook gently for 1½ hours approximately until soft. You will need to start the jus while the partridge legs are gently cooking in the oil. When cooked, remove the thigh bone and stuff with the wild mushrooms and chestnuts. Then roll each leg tightly in clingfilm into a cylinder shape and refrigerate.

- While the legs are cooking, melt the butter in a saucepan and season with salt and pepper. Place the cut potatoes in the butter and cook slowly turning occasionally for 45-50 minutes or until soft in the centre and a golden brown colour.

- Heat a little oil in an ovenproof frying pan. Quickly brown the partridge breasts on both sides until sealed and then transfer to the oven for 10 minutes. After 4-5 minutes, remove the legs from the fridge and place on buttered greaseproof paper and roast for 4-5 minutes.

For the jus

- Put the partridge carcasses on a roasting tin and roast in the oven for approximately 40 minutes or until dark brown. Strain off the fat and add the shallots, carrot, garlic and thyme. Bake for another 10 minutes. Deglaze the tin with the Madeira and reduce ensuring to scrape the sediment from the bottom. Pour in the chicken stock and reduce until sauce consistency. (Alternatively, transfer everything to a pot and reduce on top of the stove.) Strain through a sieve and reduce further. Add the halved cranberries and cook over medium heat until soft. Then allow to infuse in the jus before serving.

To serve

- Place the breasts on warmed plates. Add the fondant potatoes and partridge legs on either side of the breasts. Pour over the jus and serve immediately.

Marinated strawberries with fromage blanc sorbet and sablé biscuits

ingredients

For the strawberries

200g/7oz strawberries
450ml/15fl oz water
150g/5oz caster sugar
1 star anise
1 lemon grass stalk
2 whole cloves
1 Earl Grey tea bag
Juice and zest of 2 oranges
Zest of 1 lemon

For the sablé biscuits

75g/3oz butter
40g/1½oz caster sugar
1 egg yolk
100g/4oz plain flour, plus extra
for dusting
1 tablespoon cornflour

For the sorbet

450ml/15fl oz water
200g/7oz caster sugar
Juice and zest of 2 oranges
Zest of 1 lemon
350g/12oz fromage blanc

Serves 4

method

· Preheat the oven to 180°C/350°F/ gas mark 4.

For the strawberries

· Hull the strawberries. Prepare the marinade by mixing all the ingredients together in a pot and cook over a low heat until the sugar is dissolved. Remove from the heat and put the strawberries in the marinade. Allow to cool, cover with clingfilm and refrigerate until ready to serve.

For the sablé biscuits

· Beat the butter and sugar together until you have a smooth paste. Then add the egg yolk and mix again. Gradually fold in the two types of flour, roll into a ball, wrap in clingfilm and chill for 2 hours. Roll out the mixture on a lightly floured surface and cut into standard sized biscuit shapes. Place on a greased baking sheet and bake in the oven for 8 minutes. Allow to cool slightly and then transfer to a wire rack to cool.

For the sorbet

· Put the water, sugar, juice and zests into a pot and bring to the boil. When the sugar has dissolved, allow to cool. Pour this into the fromage blanc and mix well. Then pour into an ice cream machine and churn until ready. Store in the freezer.

To serve

· Spoon the strawberries onto a plate (reserving four for decoration) with a tablespoon or two of the marinade. Add a scoop of the sorbet in the middle of the plate. Place a biscuit on top of the sorbet. Cut the remaining strawberries in half and place on top of the biscuit on each dessert.

Café Paradiso

People travel from across the country to dine at Café Paradiso, consistently rated the best vegetarian restaurant on this island. The magician behind this enterprise is owner/chef Denis Cotter, whose innovative seasonal menus delight vegetarians and carnivores alike. The stunning food is complemented by the newly refurbished dining room.

16 Lancaster Quay, Cork, Co. Cork
Ph: (021) 427 7939
www.cafeparadiso.ie

starter

Chanterelle mushrooms in brandy cream with nettle and potato gnocchi

main course

Corn-crusted aubergine with green chilli and almond filling, sweet pepper salsa and braised borlotti beans with kale and lemon

dessert

Lavender set custard with honey and berries

Chanterelle mushrooms in brandy cream with nettle and potato gnocchi

ingredients

For the gnocchi

75g/3oz nettle leaves (use kale if nettles are unavailable)

275g/10oz floury potatoes, peeled, steamed and mashed

75g/3oz Cratloe Hills or other hard sheep's cheese, grated

1 egg yolk

50g/2oz plain flour, plus extra for dusting

Olive oil, for frying

For the chanterelle mushrooms

100g/4oz chanterelle mushrooms, cleaned

1 tablespoon softened butter

2 small shallots, thinly sliced

1 garlic clove, finely chopped

1 pinch each of ground nutmeg, cinnamon and cloves

100ml/3½fl oz brandy

150ml/5fl oz cream

Salt and pepper

Serves 4-6

method

For the gnocchi

- Cook the nettles in boiling water for 5 minutes, and then cool in cold water. Squeeze out all of the water and chop the nettles very finely in a food processor. Stir them into the potato mash. Add the cheese and the egg yolk and season well with salt and pepper. Add the flour and quickly work it into the potato.

- Cut the dough into three or four pieces and roll each into a long tubular shape, about the thickness of your finger. Cut into pieces 2.5cm/1 inch long. Roll each one into an oblong shape. As you go, keep the gnocchi on a tray, tossed in a little flour.

- Bring a pot of water to a boil. Cook the gnocchi by dropping batches into the boiling water, but don't overcrowd them. The gnocchi are done when they float to the top. Remove the cooked gnocchi with a slotted spoon and keep them warm in a little olive oil in a frying pan over a low heat.

For the chanterelle mushrooms

- Fry the mushrooms in a tablespoon of butter over a medium heat for 2 minutes. Add the shallots and garlic, lower the heat and stew the mushrooms for another 5-7 minutes until tender. Add the spices and brandy and cook for 30 seconds. Finally, add the cream and simmer for another 30 seconds.

To serve

- Spoon the chanterelle mushrooms onto the centre of warmed plates and surround by the gnocchi. Spoon over the brandy cream and juices.

Corn-crusted aubergine with green chilli & almond filling, sweet pepper salsa & braised borlotti beans

ingredients

For the aubergine

4 medium aubergines
Olive oil, for cooking
4 scallions, thinly sliced
2 garlic cloves, chopped
2-4 fresh green chillies, seeded and thinly sliced
75g/3oz cream cheese
100g/4oz almonds, lightly toasted and finely chopped
2 eggs
150ml/5fl oz milk
50g/2oz plain flour
100g/4oz coarse maize (corn), also called polenta

For the beans and kale

200g/7oz podded borlotti beans (you can use canned or dried)
4 tablespoons olive oil, plus a little extra
1 garlic clove, crushed
Juice and zest of 1 lemon
1 handful black kale, chopped (tough stalks removed)

For the pepper salsa

1 yellow and 1 green pepper, cored, seeded and finely diced
2 garlic cloves, chopped
2 tomatoes, seeded and finely diced
1 red onion, finely diced
50ml/2fl oz olive oil
Salt and pepper

Serves 4

method

- Preheat the oven to 200°C/400°F/ gas mark 6.

For the aubergine

- Slice the aubergine into eight long, thin slices. Brush with olive oil and place on baking sheets lined with parchment paper. Roast in the oven until browned on both sides, about 10-12 minutes, turning once if necessary.

- Heat a little olive oil in a pot. Briefly cook the scallions, garlic and chillies. Then stir into the cream cheese, along with the almonds. Spread a generous layer of this mixture on an aubergine slice, put a matching slice on top. Repeat with the rest of the aubergine slices; you'll need four in total.

- Combine the eggs and milk. Toss the aubergines in the flour, then dunk in the egg-milk mix and finally toss in the coarse maize. Make sure they are well coated, sides and all. Put the finished aubergines in the fridge for 30 minutes to firm up.

- Cook the beans (see below) before finishing the preparation of the aubergines. In a wide pan, heat 1cm/½ inch of olive oil to medium heat. Slide in the aubergines and cook for 5 minutes each side. Drain well on kitchen paper.

For the beans and kale

- Put the beans in a pot of cold water, bring it to a boil and simmer for 15-20 minutes. Drain and transfer to a bowl. Add the olive oil, garlic, lemon juice, zest and some salt and pepper. Leave to stand, off the heat, for at least 30 minutes.

Heat a little olive oil in a pot and wilt the kale over a high heat, stirring regularly. When tender, add the marinated beans and simmer for 5 minutes.

For the salsa

- Place all the salsa ingredients in a small pan and heat gently, without boiling, for 10 minutes. Leave in a warm place and serve at room temperature.

To serve

- Place a mound of bean with kale on each plate with a corn crusted aubergine leaning on it. Spoon some salsa over the aubergine and on the side.

Lavender set custard with honey and berries

ingredients

5 heads lavender flowers
450ml/15fl oz cream
4 egg yolks
75g/3oz caster sugar

Local honey and 18-24 blackberries and raspberries, to serve

Serves 6

method

- Preheat the oven to 150°C/300°F/gas mark 2.
- Put the lavender flowers and cream in a pot and heat gently to just below boiling point. Allow to infuse and then remove the flowers.
- Stir the egg yolks and sugar together. Pour into the hot cream and stir with a spatula. Leave this custard to settle for a minute, then remove the foam that remains on top.
- Place 6 x 150ml/¼ pint ramekins or steel rings lined with cling-film in a baking dish. Fill with the custard. Pour boiling water into the baking dish to come halfway up the ramekins, and place the dish in the oven. Check after 20 minutes and again every 10 minutes until the custards are firm on top but still slightly wobbly when moved gently.
- Remove from the oven and leave in the water dish for 30 minutes, then take the ramekins out of the water and refrigerate for 4 hours. They can also be kept overnight.

To serve

- Carefully remove the custards and place one on each plate. Drizzle with local honey and serve with fresh blackberries and raspberries on top.

Campagne

Campagne was born when Garrett Byrne, formerly head chef at the Michelin-starred Chapter One in Dublin, returned to his native city of Kilkenny to open his own restaurant. It offers modern French-style cuisine for diners who want excellence at affordable prices. Garrett is passionate about supporting artisan food producers and sourcing quality ingredients.

5 The Arches, Gashouse Lane, Kilkenny, Co. Kilkenny
Ph: (056) 777 2858
www.campagne.ie

starter
Organic beetroot, red onion and feta salad with walnuts

main course
Roast corn-fed chicken, gratinated semolina, roast artichokes and herb sauce

dessert
Raspberry crème brulée

Organic beetroot, red onion and feta salad with walnuts

ingredients

200ml/7fl oz red wine vinegar
200g/7oz sugar, plus a little extra
2 organic red onions
4 medium organic beetroots
20 shelled walnuts
100g/4oz feta cheese
Walnut oil
Watercress and/or red chard
Salad leaves
Sea salt

French bread, to serve

Serves 4

method

· Preheat the oven to 180°C/350°F/ gas mark 4.

· Bring the red wine vinegar and sugar to the boil. Slice the onions into very thin rounds. Pour the vinegar and sugar mixture over the red onions. Leave to stand for at least one hour to allow the flavours develop.

· Cover the beetroots with cold water. Add a dash of red wine vinegar and a pinch of salt and cook for 45 minutes -1 hour until tender. Remove from the pan and peel while still warm. Slice the cooked beetroot thinly and add a few tablespoons of the vinegar and sugar mixture. Leave to stand for at least one hour.

· Roast the walnuts in the oven until golden brown for approximately 5-7 minutes. Check regularly. Remove from the oven and place in a cloth and rub together to remove the skins.

To serve

· Drain the beetroot slices and place in a circle on the plates. Season with a few grains of sea salt. Drain the red onion slices and place on top of the beetroot. Next add the feta cheese. Place the salad leaves in a bowl and season with salt and walnut oil, then fold in the roasted walnuts. Arrange loosely on top of the beetroot. This dish is best served at room temperature with some French bread.

Roast corn-fed chicken, gratinated semolina, roast artichokes and herb sauce

ingredients

For the chicken

100g/4oz lardo or pork back fat
(available from a good butcher.)
Alternatively, you can use butter
100g/4oz chopped fresh flat
leaf parsley
15g/½oz chopped basil leaves
4 cornfed chicken breast fillets,
skin on

For the artichokes

2 globe artichokes
Juice of 1 lemon
Olive oil, for frying

For the semolina

200ml/7fl oz milk
50g/2oz butter
50g/2oz semolina
15g/½oz Parmesan, plus a little
extra
A little olive oil
100g/4oz wild mushrooms

For the herb sauce

1 shallot, finely diced
2 gherkins
10 capers
1 handful chopped fresh flat leaf
parsley
20 fresh basil leaves
1 tablespoon balsamic vinegar
200ml/7fl oz extra virgin olive
oil
Salt and pepper

Serves 4

method

- Preheat the oven to 190°C/375°F/gas mark 5.

For the chicken

- Put the lardo, fat or butter in a liquidiser with the herbs and blend until smooth. Put in the fridge for 20 minutes until it sets slightly. Gently lift the skin from the chicken breasts without detaching it and put the lardo mixture onto the flesh, pressing down gently to keep it flat. Place the skin back over the chicken and return to the fridge to set for 20 minutes.
- Season the chicken breasts with salt and pepper. Heat a little olive oil in a pan and fry the chicken breasts skin side down until golden brown. Transfer to the oven and cook for 12-15 minutes. Remove from oven and allow to rest for 5 minutes.

For the artichokes

- With a sharp knife, remove the leaves and the stalks from the artichokes and all the green bits from the flesh. Rub with the lemon juice to keep from discolouring. Bring a small pot of salted water to the boil and cook the artichokes until tender, about 15-20 minutes. Remove from the water and cool. Cut into quarters and fry in a little olive oil until coloured. Season with salt and pepper and keep warm until ready to serve.

For the semolina

- Put the milk and half the butter in a pot and bring to the boil. Whisk in the semolina and cook gently for 10 minutes. Add the Parmesan and season with salt. Turn out onto an oiled tray and allow to cool.

  Cut out 4 circles with a large cookie cutter.
- Sauté the mushrooms in the rest of the butter, drain and place on top of the semolina. Dust with a little Parmesan. When ready to serve, place under a hot grill to glaze for 2-3 minutes.

For the herb sauce

- Put all the ingredients into a liquidiser and blend until smooth. Season lightly with salt and pepper.

To serve

- If necessary, reheat the artichokes and semolina. Place both on large dinner plates. Put the chicken breast to the side and then spoon over the herb sauce.

Raspberry crème brulée

ingredients

4 egg yolks
75g/3oz vanilla sugar (see below for how to make your own)
250ml/9fl oz cream
85ml/3fl oz milk
1 vanilla pod, split in half and seeds scraped out
28 raspberries, plus extra to decorate
100g/4oz caster sugar

Serves 4

method

· Preheat the oven to 110°C/225°F/gas mark ¼.

· You can make your own vanilla sugar by putting a couple of vanilla pods in a jar of caster sugar and leaving for a week.

· Whisk the eggs and sugar together in a bowl until you have a smooth consistency. Bring the cream, milk and vanilla to the boil. Pour onto the egg mixture and pass through a fine chinois or a fine sieve.

· Place a cloth or sheet of newspaper on the bottom of a deep tray and place 4 ramekins on top. Place 7 raspberries in each ramekin and pour the custard mixture on top. Pour enough warm water into the tray to come three quarters of the way up the sides of the ramekins. Place the tray in the oven and cook for 40 minutes until just set but with a slight wobble. Allow to cool in the tray and when cold, place in the fridge for at least 3 hours to set.

To serve

· Dust the brulées with the caster sugar and caramelise with a blowtorch until the sugar is golden brown. Let the sugar harden for 5 minutes before serving. Decorate with some additional raspberries.

Cayenne

Owned by celebrity chef Paul Rankin and his wife Jeanne, Cayenne offers adventurous international food with Asian accents. Fish dishes are a strength; desserts are delicious; and there is an excellent vegetarian menu. The décor is stylish and contemporary; the service friendly and attentive.

7 Ascot House, Shaftsbury Square, Belfast BT2 7DB
Ph: +44 (0)28 9033 1532
www.cayenne-restaurant.co.uk

starter
Spaghettini Molly Malone

main course
Breasts of chicken stuffed with lobster and basil

dessert
Sticky toffee pudding
with Bushmills butterscotch sauce

Spaghettini Molly Malone

ingredients

1 large red chilli, seeded and finely chopped

4 garlic cloves, chopped

8 tablespoons extra virgin olive oil

900g/2lb cockles

900g/2lb mussels

250ml/9fl oz dry white wine

3 tablespoons finely chopped onion

2 fresh parsley stalks

450g/1lb spaghettini (thinner version of spaghetti)

2 tablespoons roughly chopped fresh parsley

Maldon sea salt and freshly ground black pepper

Serves 4

method

· Place the chilli (reserving a little to garnish), garlic and oil in a small bowl, and cook in the microwave on full power for 1 minute. Alternatively, warm over a gentle heat in a small pan for about 5 minutes. Set aside.

· Wash and scrub the cockles and mussels, carefully scraping off the beards from the mussels. Rinse in plenty of clean water, and discard any mussels that are open and do not close when tapped with a knife.

· Bring the wine, onion and parsley stalks to the boil in a large pan over a high heat. Add the cockles and mussels, then cover and boil vigorously for 3-4 minutes, or until all of the cockles and mussels have opened. Discard any that remain closed.

· Drain into a colander with a bowl underneath to catch all that precious cooking liquid.

· Reserve the cooking liquid and as soon as the shellfish are cool enough, remove about two-thirds of the cockles and mussels from their shells.

· Place both the shelled cockles and mussels and the ones in their shells in a pan and pour over the reserved cooking liquid, leaving behind the last few spoonfuls of liquid as it will be full of grit.

· Cook the spaghettini in a large pan of boiling salted water for 8-10 minutes or according to the packet instructions until al dente.

Meanwhile, heat the cockles and mussels in the cooking liquid, adding the chilli and garlic oil to the pan. Add the parsley, reserving some to garnish. Do not allow to boil or continue to cook, otherwise the cockles and mussels will toughen.

· Drain the spaghettini and then toss with the cockles and mussels mixture.

To serve

· Arrange in warmed wide-rimmed bowls and sprinkle over the reserved chilli and parsley.

Breasts of chicken stuffed with lobster and basil

ingredients

For the stuffed chicken breasts

2 live lobsters, each weighing about 450g/1lb

4 large skinless chicken breast fillets, each weighing about 200g/7oz

200ml/7fl oz single cream, chilled

2 tablespoons chopped fresh basil

2 tablespoons snipped fresh chives, plus extra whole ones to garnish

Butter, for greasing

2 tablespoons sunflower oil

For the sauce

Lobster shells from the body (see method)

2 tablespoons olive oil

4 shallots, thinly sliced

4 garlic cloves, crushed

2 tablespoons tomato purée

4 tablespoons port

4 tablespoons brandy

600ml/1 pint double cream

2 tablespoons chopped fresh basil

Salt and freshly ground black pepper

Buttered noodles and steamed mangetout, to serve

Serves 4

method

- Preheat the oven to 200°C/400°F/ gas mark 6.

For the stuffed chicken breasts

- Bring a large pan of water to a vigorous boil. Put in the lobsters, cover and cook for about 12 minutes. Remove the lobsters from the pan, and stop the cooking process by plunging into a sink of cold water.

- Insert a large knife into each lobster where the tail and body join and cut towards the tail, then remove the intestinal tract; the tail meat will now easily pull away from the shell. Break off the claws and any pieces of shell, reserving the body shell for the sauce. Cut the lobster meat into 1cm/½ inch dice.

- Remove all of the small 'fillets' attached to the underside of the chicken breasts, and any sinew from the inside of the fillets. Roughly mash the flesh with a heavy knife or in a food processor. Place in a bowl and add the diced lobster, cream, basil, chives and season to taste. Beat vigorously with a wooden spoon until it comes together.

- Lay each chicken breast flat on a chopping board, and make a long horizontal incision almost completely through it, so that you can open it out like a book. Season each breast with salt and pepper and spoon the lobster stuffing along the middle line. Fold both sides on top of the stuffing, moulding the breast into a good shape with your hands. Butter four sheets of kitchen foil about 25cm/10 inches square and wrap each breast tightly, twisting the ends of the foil to help the breast keep its shape.

- Heat a frying pan over a high heat, add the oil, and seal the foil-wrapped breasts for about 4 minutes, turning every now and then.

Place in the oven for about 15 minutes, take out and rest in a warm place.

For the sauce

- Crush the lobster shells with a heavy cleaver. Fry the shells in a pan with the olive oil over a high heat for 2 minutes. Add the shallots and garlic and fry for 2 more minutes. Stir in the tomato purée, port, brandy and 120ml/4fl oz water and boil until reduced by half, stirring occasionally. Pour in the cream, stirring to combine and continue to boil until the sauce thickens. Strain the sauce through a fine sieve into a clean pan, and add the basil.

To serve

- Carefully unwrap the chicken breasts, allowing any juices to fall into the sauce. Slice each breast and arrange on warmed plates. Spoon around the sauce. Add some buttered noodles and mangetout and garnish with the chives.

Sticky toffee pudding with Bushmills butterscotch sauce

ingredients

For the sticky toffee pudding

225g/8oz fresh dates, stoned and finely chopped

175g/6oz self-raising flour

1 teaspoon bicarbonate of soda

1 teaspoon vanilla extract

1 tablespoon coffee essence

100ml/3½fl oz milk

75g/3oz unsalted butter, plus extra for greasing

150g/5oz golden caster sugar

2 eggs, beaten just to break the yolks

Vegetable oil, for greasing

For the butterscotch sauce

3 tablespoons softened unsalted butter

8 tablespoons light muscovado sugar

200ml/7fl oz whipping cream

200ml/7fl oz Bushmills whiskey

1 tablespoon vanilla extract

Whipped cream, to serve

Serves 6-8

method

· Preheat the oven to 180°C/350°F/gas mark 4.

For the sticky toffee pudding

· Pour 175ml/6fl oz boiling water over the dates and set aside to soak until the mixture has cooled.

· Sift the flour and the bicarbonate of soda into a bowl. Add the vanilla extract and coffee essence to the milk, stirring to combine.

· In a separate bowl, cream the butter and sugar together until light and fluffy. Add the eggs slowly, waiting until each addition has been incorporated, before adding more.

· Fold the flour and flavoured milk into the egg mixture. Lastly, pour in the soaked date mixture. The mix will be rather light and runnier than a cake batter. Ladle into 6-8 greased individual moulds, and place on a baking sheet in the centre of the oven. Bake for about 30 minutes until the puddings are firm and starting to pull away from the sides of the moulds. The time will depend on the size of the moulds you have used. Remove from the oven, then turn out onto a wire rack to cool.

For the butterscotch sauce

· Place the butter in a pan over a medium-high heat. When the butter is bubbling, add the sugar. Stir together for 3 minutes until the sugar has dissolved, and the whole mass is foaming and bubbling. Carefully pour in the cream followed by the Bushmills whiskey and then turn down the heat. Let it all come together, and boil for about

another minute or two, and then remove from heat. Stir in the vanilla extract and allow to cool slightly.

To serve

· Place the puddings on warmed plates, and ladle a generous spoonful of the sauce over each one. The remaining sauce can be served separately in a warmed jug. Dollops of whipped cream will top the puddings off perfectly.

· If wrapped in clingfilm, these puddings keep well for a couple of days, and they can be reheated for just a minute or two in the microwave or covered in some of the sauce in a medium oven.

The Cellar Restaurant

A vaulted dining room and classically appointed tables set the scene at the Cellar, where executive chef Ed Cooney offers menus that change daily. Based on high-quality ingredients that reflect the seasons, the cooking is accomplished with authenticity, skill and flair. Expect excellent service and reasonable prices.

Merrion Hotel, Upper Merrion Street, Dublin 2
Ph: (01) 603 0600
www.merrionhotel.com

starter
Irish Angus beef carpaccio with a wilted watercress, field mushroom and shallot salad and garlic crisps

main course
Steamed fillet of turbot with truffled pea purée, girolles, roasted salsify and a Sauternes sauce

dessert
The Merrion's baked Alaska with strawberry ice cream

Irish Angus beef carpaccio with wilted watercress, field mushroom and shallot salad and garlic crisps

ingredients

75g/3oz beef fillet
6 shallots
2 teaspoons melted butter
About 50ml/2fl oz olive oil
2 field mushrooms
2 garlic cloves, peeled
1 bunch watercress, well picked over, the tough stalks removed
15ml/½fl oz balsamic vinegar (we use Lusk apple balsamic vinegar)
25g/1oz Parmesan shavings
Sea salt and crushed black peppercorns

Serves 2

method

· Preheat the oven to 180°C/350°F/ gas mark 4.
· Trim all the sinew from the beef fillet and slice wafer thin with a very sharp thin-bladed knife.
· Peel the shallots, toss in some melted butter and a little olive oil, then cook in the oven in a small roasting tin for 20 minutes until cooked through and slightly golden, and set aside.
· Quarter and roast the field mushrooms drizzled with a little oil in the oven for 3 minutes each side in a separate roasting tin, season and set aside.
· Thinly slice one garlic clove and fry for 4 minutes in hot oil until golden brown and crisp, set aside to cool. Mix the watercress, shallots and field mushrooms together in a bowl and season with salt and pepper.

To serve
· Cut the remaining garlic clove in half and rub onto each plate. Drizzle a little olive oil onto the plate with some sea salt and black peppercorns. Arrange the beef slices neatly on the plate. Arrange the watercress salad neatly in the middle of the plate. Top with the garlic crisps. Drizzle olive oil around the plate and drop apple balsamic vinegar into this olive oil drizzle. Add 3-4 large shavings of Parmesan on top.

Steamed fillet of turbot with truffled pea purée, girolles, roasted salsify and a Sauternes sauce

ingredients

For the pea purée

50g/2oz unsalted butter
6 spring onions, trimmed and finely chopped
175g/6oz frozen peas (petit pois)
2 teaspoons caster sugar
300ml/10fl oz chicken stock
10 fresh mint leaves
150ml/5fl oz double cream

For the roasted salsify

450g/1lb salsify
900ml/1½ pints water
25g/1oz plain flour
Juice of 1 lemon
300ml/10fl oz white wine vinegar

For the Sauternes sauce

100g/4oz unsalted butter
3 shallots, finely chopped
4 button mushrooms, sliced thinly
200ml/7fl oz Sauternes wine
100ml/3½fl oz chicken stock
100ml/3½fl oz fish stock
150ml/5fl oz double cream

For the turbot

6 x 150g/5oz turbot fillets, skinned
150g/5oz girolle mushrooms
Sea salt and freshly ground white pepper

Serves 6

method

For the pea purée

· Heat a deep non-stick pan. Melt half the butter, add the spring onions and cook until limp. Add the peas, caster sugar, stock and remaining butter. Cover with greaseproof paper and cook for 3-4 minutes ensuring the peas remain vibrant green. Add the mint leaves and cream. Blend in a food processor until smooth. Season and set aside. Keep warm until ready to serve.

For the roasted salsify

· Wash, top, tail and peel the salsify. Cut into 5cm/2 inch lengths. Mix the water, flour, lemon juice, vinegar and a little salt together in a pan. Immediately immerse the salsify in the water. Bring to the boil, then cook gently for 30 minutes until tender. Keep warm until ready to serve.

For the Sauternes sauce

· Put 25g/1oz of the butter in a heavy pan and melt. Sweat the shallots and mushrooms in the butter until soft. Add the Sauternes, bring to the boil and reduce by half. Add the chicken stock, bring to the boil and reduce by half. Add the fish stock, bring to the boil and reduce by half. Add the double cream and simmer for 2 minutes. Pass through a sieve and return to the stove in a clean pan. When ready to serve, finish the Sauternes sauce by dicing the remaining butter and whisking into the sauce. Season to taste with salt and pepper and pass through a sieve.

For the turbot

· Simply steam the turbot over boiling water for three minutes on each side. Heat a little oil in a frying pan and sauté the girolle mushrooms quickly until tender.

To serve

· Place the turbot in the centre of warmed plates, arrange the pea purée in a line, and then arrange the salsify and girolles to the side of the turbot. Drizzle around the Sauternes sauce.

The Merrion's baked Alaska with strawberry ice cream

ingredients

For the sponge

(Alternatively, you can buy a pre-made sponge base)
9 eggs
250g/9oz caster sugar
125g/4½oz plain flour
125g/4½oz cornflour
Butter, for greasing

For the meringue Italienne

6 egg whites
450g/1lb caster sugar
150ml/5fl oz water

For the strawberry ice cream

(Alternatively, you can buy pre-made ice cream)
7 egg yolks
100g/4oz sugar
250ml/9fl oz milk
250ml/9fl oz cream
200g/7oz strawberry purée
35g/1½oz trimoline (inverted sugar) or glucose

Icing sugar, to dust
Fresh mint sprigs, to decorate

Serves 6-8

method

- Preheat the oven to 180ºC/350ºF/ gas mark 4.

For the sponge

- Whisk the eggs and sugar together for approximately 5 minutes. Add the flour and cornflour into the mixture and mix together delicately. Butter and line a 25cm/10 inch baking tin. Spoon in the mixture and bake for 20-30 minutes, until well risen and lightly golden.

For the meringue Italienne

- Whisk the egg whites until frothy and stiff. Boil the sugar and water together in a saucepan. Allow to cool. Gradually add the sugar and water to the egg whites and whisk for a further 10 minutes until stiff peaks begin to form. For best results, use when the mixture is cold.

For the strawberry ice cream

- Whisk the egg yolks and sugar together in a mixing bowl. Put the milk, cream and strawberry purée into a saucepan and boil, stirring all the time.
- Slowly add this mixture to the egg yolks and sugar. Stir with a wooden spoon until the sugar is dissolved and then put back in the saucepan. Continue to stir over a low heat. You will know it is done when you run a finger along the back of the spoon and the line holds. It should have the consistency of custard. Remove from the heat, strain and cool.
- Add the trimoline or glucose and mix well. Pour the mixture into an ice cream machine and churn until frozen. Place in a container

(approximately 1½ litres) and put in the freezer.

For the baked Alaska

- Increase the oven to 190°C/375°F/ gas mark 5.
- Line a baking sheet with parchment or heavy brown paper. Place the sponge bases (1cm/½ inch thick and round shapes) on the baking sheet and set the strawberry ice cream on top of the sponge. Quickly spread the meringue over the sponge and ice cream, creating a spiked effect and to enclose it completely. Bake in the middle of the oven for about 6 minutes or until golden brown.

To serve

- Dust with icing sugar, decorate with mint sprigs and serve immediately.

Chapter One

Michelin-starred Chapter One is among Dublin's finest restaurants. The food here is outstanding: a highly creative approach involving classic French cooking tempered by modern influences, and showcasing specialty Irish products, with a charcuterie trolley and farmhouse cheeses. A meal here is a special treat (reserve well in advance). Lunch and the very popular pre-theatre menu are exceptionally good value. Elegantly appointed, the restaurant has a well-deserved reputation for friendly, well-informed service.

Basement of Writers Museum, 18-19 Parnell Square, Dublin 1
Ph: (01) 873 2266
www.chapteronerestaurant.com

starter
Lime-marinated scallops, avocado purée and crème fraîche

main course
Slow-cooked lamb shoulder, white beans, roast organic carrots

dessert
Baked Ardrahan cheese with strawberry confiture (jam)

Lime-marinated scallops, avocado purée and crème fraîche

For the scallops

Juice of 6 limes
Zest of 1 lime
3 shallots, finely chopped
50g/2oz roughly chopped fresh coriander, plus a little extra to garnish
1 lemon grass stalk, trimmed and crushed
100ml/3½fl oz extra virgin olive oil
1 red chilli, seeded and finely chopped
Pinch of sugar
8 large scallops, cleaned and roes removed

For the avocado purée

2 avocados
250ml/9fl oz crème fraîche
Cayenne pepper
Pinch of sea salt

24 very finely sliced and deep fried potato crisps, to serve

Serves 4

method

For the scallops

· In a non-metallic dish combine the lime juice (saving the juice of half a lime for the avocado) with the zest, shallots, coriander, crushed lemon grass, olive oil, chilli and sugar. Slice each scallop across into 3 individual thin slices and leave in the marinade for 1½ hours.

For the avocado purée

· Peel the avocados and scrape inside the skin for the green pigment (this helps keep the purée green). Purée in a blender with the reserved juice of half a lime and 2 tablespoons of crème fraîche. Then season with a pinch of salt and cayenne pepper.

To serve

· Place 6 dots of crème fraîche on each plate and place a piece of scallop on top. Season with sea salt and place a crisp on each. Garnish with a scoop of the avocado purée, a little of the lime marinade and some coriander.

Slow-cooked lamb shoulder, white beans, roast organic carrots

ingredients

For the lamb shoulder

1 red onion, chopped
10 fresh mint sprigs
1 garlic bulb, cloves peeled
200ml/7fl oz olive oil
1 shoulder of spring lamb, boned
1litre/1¾ pints water
200ml/7fl oz balsamic vinegar

For the white beans

400g/14oz dried haricot beans
2 onions, thinly sliced
2 carrots, finely diced
3 celery sticks, finely diced
100g/4oz butter
2 garlic cloves, finely chopped
300ml/10fl oz cream
1 small swede, finely diced
Dash of sherry vinegar

For the carrots

20 baby carrots
Olive oil, for cooking
Salt and pepper

Serves 6-8

method

· Preheat the oven to at 110°C/225°F/gas mark ¼.

For the lamb shoulder

· Blend the onion, mint leaves, garlic and olive oil in a liquidiser. Spread the mixture evenly over the lamb and marinate overnight. Next day, season well with salt and pepper.
· Heat some oil in a large pan and seal the lamb on all sides until the outside is dark or almost caramelised. Place in a roasting tin just big enough and add water. Cook in the oven for 12 hours. Remove the lamb and allow to cool.
· Strain the stock into a pot, bring to the boil and reduce by half. In a separate pot, reduce the balsamic vinegar by half and add to the stock. Pass through muslin or a fine sieve. Keep warm.

For the white beans

· Soak the beans overnight. Next day drain and cover with fresh water. Add half the onion, carrot and celery and bring to the boil. Cook until soft. Drain, and discard the vegetables.
· Melt the butter, add the remaining onion and the garlic and cook until soft. Add half the cooked beans and all the cream and cook gently for 10 minutes. Liquidise and pass through a chinois or a very fine sieve. Add the purée to the reserved beans and season with salt and pepper.
· Put the remaining celery and carrot with the swede in a pot of salted water and boil for 10-15 minutes or until just tender. Refresh in iced water. Drain and add to the beans with the sherry vinegar.

For the carrots

· Roast the carrots in olive oil in the oven at 180°C/350°F/gas mark 4 until you can pierce them with a sharp knife. This should take about 25-35 minutes. Season lightly and keep warm.

To serve

· Reheat the lamb in the oven at 140°C/275°F/gas mark 1 for about 15-20 minutes. Remove and slice into thick pieces. Place on top of the beans on individual plates. Surround with the roasted carrots and finish with the sauce.

Baked Ardrahan cheese with strawberry confiture (jam)

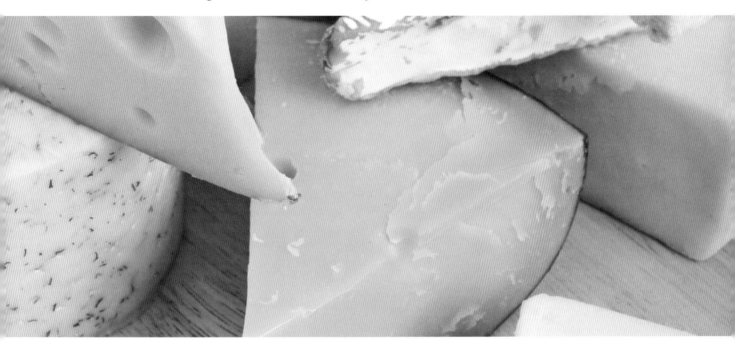

ingredients

For the baked cheese

4 filo pastry sheets, thawed if frozen

50g/2oz unsalted butter, melted

225g/8oz mature Ardrahan cheese (or Cooleeney Camembert, Gubeen or Milleens)

For the confiture

250g/9oz redcurrants

450g/1lb strawberries, hulled

400g/14oz preserving or jam sugar

Knob of unsalted butter

20 green peppercorns, crushed

Serves 4

method

- Preheat the oven to 200°C/400°F/ gas mark 6.

For the baked cheese

- Brush each sheet of filo pastry on both sides with melted butter. Cut the cheese into triangles and place in the centre of each sheet of filo. Wrap carefully to enclose. Put on a baking sheet spaced a little apart. Brush with the remaining butter and bake for 15 minutes or until the pastry is golden.

For the confiture

- Remove the redcurrants from their stalks, place in a pan and cover with about 1cm/½ inch of water. Bring to the boil. Remove from the heat and mash. Then return to the boil and simmer for 15 minutes. Strain the juice through a muslin-lined sieve into a clean pan.

- Add the strawberries to the pan. Slowly bring to the boil, then simmer for 10 minutes or until softened. Add the sugar, stirring until dissolved, then bring to the boil and add the butter. Boil steadily for 5 minutes. Add the crushed peppercorns, leave to cool for about 10 minutes, then spoon into sterilised warm jars. Label and store in a cool dry place until required.

To serve

- Arrange the baked cheese on serving plates with a tablespoonful of confiture to the side. Serve immediately.

The Chart House

Terrific hospitality, top-rate local ingredients and creative, gimmick-free cooking from a talented and enthusiastic team make the Chart House a great place to experience an authentic taste of Kerry at very fair prices. The restaurant also features an extremely interesting wine list.

The Mall, Dingle, Co. Kerry
Ph: (066) 915 2255
www.thecharthousedingle.com

starter
Annascaul black pudding wrapped in filo pastry with apple and date chutney, hollandaise sauce

main course
Roast rack of Blasket Island lamb with cassoulet of beans and vegetables

dessert
Lemon cheesecake

Annascaul black pudding wrapped in filo pastry with apple and date chutney, hollandaise sauce

ingredients

For the pudding

About 100g/4oz butter

12 sheets filo pastry (21cm x 30cm/8 inches x 12 inches), thawed if frozen

275g/10oz black pudding (preferably Annascaul), skinned and cut into 12 pieces

6 tablespoons apple and date chutney (or a good quality relish)

For the hollandaise sauce

300g/10oz clarified butter

2 large egg yolks, beaten

Juice of 1 lemon

Pinch of sugar, salt and cayenne pepper

Salad leaves, to serve

Serves 6

method

· Preheat the oven to 180°C/350°F/ gas mark 4.

For the pudding

· Melt the butter in a pan and leave to cool a little. Cut each sheet of filo pastry in half. Brush 6 sheets of the filo pastry with the butter, place a second sheet on top of each one and brush again with butter. Repeat until you have 4 sheets per portion.

· Put two pieces of pudding and a tablespoon of chutney in the centre of each set of sheets. Pull the corners of the pastry together to form a parcel and brush with butter once more. Bake in the oven for 10 minutes until crisp and golden brown.

For the hollandaise sauce

· In a heatproof bowl over a bain marie or a pot of boiling water, whisk the eggs and continue to whisk while adding the butter gradually until you have achieved a smooth hollandaise. Add the lemon juice and season with the remaining ingredients.

To serve

· Place one filo parcel on each warmed plate and spoon the hollandaise sauce around it. Add some salad leaves on the side.

Roast rack of Blasket Island lamb with cassoulet of beans and vegetables

ingredients

For the lamb

2 racks of spring lamb (6 cutlets
each; a good butcher will
prepare the rack for you)
Sea salt
Sunflower oil

For the cassoulet

Knob of butter
1 red onion, diced
1 carrot, diced
1 celery stick, diced
400g/14oz can butter beans,
drained and rinsed
450ml/15fl oz vegetable stock
6 cherry tomatoes (optional)
Pinch of chopped fresh
rosemary
Salt and pepper

Serves 4

method

· Preheat the oven to 200°C/400°F/gas mark 6.

For the lamb

· Season the meat with sea salt. Heat a heavy-based frying pan, add a
splash of sunflower oil and brown the meat all over in the pan. Place
the racks in a roasting tin and cook in the oven for 10-15 minutes
for rare, or longer depending on how you like it cooked. Remove to
a warm serving dish and allow to rest for at least 10 minutes before
carving.

For the cassoulet

· Heat the butter in a heavy-bottomed pan. Sweat the onion, carrot
and celery in the butter. Add the butter beans and sweat for a further
2-3 minutes. Add the stock and bring to the boil. Add the tomatoes,
if using, and rosemary and bring to the boil again. Then simmer and
allow the vegetables to soften. Season with salt and pepper to taste.

To serve

· Carve the lamb into individual cutlets. Spoon the cassoulet into deep
plates and arrange the lamb on top.

Lemon cheesecake

ingredients

100g/4oz digestive biscuits
50g/2oz butter, melted
400g/14oz mascarpone cheese
Zest and juice of 1 lemon
100g/4oz icing sugar

Fresh seasonal fruit or fruit
sauce, to serve

Serves 4

method

- Crush the biscuits and mix with the butter. Divide between 4
  moulds approximately 4cm/1½ inches deep and 6cm/ 2½
  inches in diameter. Pack the mixture tightly. Allow to set in the
  fridge for 30 minutes.

- Beat the mascarpone with a whisk and fold in the lemon and
  sugar. Spoon into the moulds and level off the top. Allow to set
  for 30 minutes.

To serve

- Remove the cheesecakes from the moulds by running a knife
  around the edges. Place in the centre of large plates and serve
  with fresh fruit or a fruit sauce on the side, depending on what
  is available.

Cherry Tree

The Cherry Tree enjoys a charming location on the lakeside at Killaloe in Co. Clare. Here you will find consistently good creative cooking and impeccable service. The simply worded menu features named, locally sourced artisan ingredients. Beef, mountain lamb and inspired salads take a leading role.

Lakeside, Ballina, Killaloe, Co. Clare
Ph: (061) 375 688
www.cherrytreerestaurant.ie

starter
Girolle mushroom gratin

main course
Seabass with steamed mussels, saffron and vegetable dressing

dessert
Blueberry and apple tartlet

Girolle mushroom gratin

ingredients

10 cherry tomatoes, cut in half
Olive oil, for cooking
100g/4oz girolle mushrooms, unwashed (or any mushrooms of your choice)
50g/2oz hedgehog mushrooms, unwashed (or any mushrooms of your choice)
50g/2oz shallots, cut into small cubes
15g/½oz butter
½ garlic clove, chopped
200ml/7fl oz cream
1 fresh rosemary sprig, chopped
1 fresh thyme sprig, chopped
1 leek, cut into small pieces
Salt and freshly ground black pepper

Balsamic vinegar and fresh watercress sprigs, to serve

Serves 4

method

- Preheat the oven to 150°C/300°F/ gas mark 2.
- Put the tomatoes on an oiled baking sheet. Drizzle with olive oil and season with salt and pepper, then gently bake for 20 minutes. Remove and place in a warm spot in your kitchen overnight.
- Increase the oven to 180°C/350°F/gas 4.
- Clean the mushrooms with a small knife and a pastry brush. Do not wash them. Cut three-quarters of them into small dice. Heat a little oil in a pan and fry three-quarters of the shallots and mushrooms. Keep stirring until the mushrooms have caramelised, then turn down to a low heat. Add the butter and garlic, season and let simmer until nearly all the moisture has evaporated.

- Pour the cream into a small pot. Add rosemary and thyme and let reduce by half, then season to taste.
- Divide the leek and remaining shallot between 4 gratin dishes (or any shallow ovenproof dishes approximately 7.5-10cm/3-4 inches in diameter). Add the mushroom mixture and cover with the reduced herb cream. Slice the remaining mushrooms and put on top, pushing slightly into the cream.
- Bake for approximately 10 minutes until the top is golden brown.

To serve

- Place some of the dried tomatoes on top of the gratin and drizzle with some balsamic vinegar. Garnish with some fresh watercress sprigs.

Seabass with steamed mussels, saffron and vegetable dressing

ingredients

For the vegetable dressing

50ml/2fl oz sunflower oil
1 teaspoon curry powder
(freshly ground)
200ml/7fl oz extra virgin olive
oil
40g/1½oz snipped fresh chives
1-2 shallots, thinly diced
1-2 red onions, thinly diced
1-2 red peppers, cored, seeded,
peeled, thinly diced
1 tomato, peeled, thinly diced
½ red chilli, seeded and thinly
diced

For the fish

4 x 150g/5oz seabass fillets,
boned

For the mussels

Olive oil, for frying
50g/2oz shallots, thinly diced
1 baby leek, washed and cut
into half rings
200ml/7fl oz white wine
20 mussels, cleaned
Pinch of saffron (optional)
2 teaspoons chopped fresh curly
parsley
1 tomato, peeled, seeded and
coarsely diced
2 teaspoons softened butter
Salt and pepper

Fresh chives, to serve

Serves 4

method

For the vegetable dressing

· Heat the sunflower oil and curry powder in a warm pan but do not let it smoke. Remove and let infuse until cool. When the oil is cooled and the curry spice has settled on the bottom, gently pour the oil through a strainer into a bowl. Try not to transfer any of the curry powder. Add the extra virgin olive oil and all the vegetables and herbs. Stir well.

For the fish

· Season the fish fillets with salt and pepper. Heat a pan, pour in some olive oil and fry the fish on the skin side for about 4 minutes. Turn the fish with a fish slice and cook for another 2 minutes approximately until the fish is cooked through.

For the mussels

· Heat some olive oil in a pan. Add the shallots and baby leek and fry for 30 seconds. Pour in the white wine, place the mussels in the pot and cover. When brought to the boil, reduce the heat and let the mussels steam until all the shells are open. Take off the heat and take the mussels out of their shells. Place back on the heat again, and add the saffron (optional), chopped parsley, diced tomatoes and butter. Shake until the butter is melted and remove from the heat.

To serve

· Place a spoonful of the mussels, leek and tomato mixture in the middle of each plate, place the fish on top, and drizzle around the vegetable dressing. Garnish with some fresh chives.

Blueberry and apple tartlet

ingredients

For the pastry

250g/9oz plain flour, plus extra
for dusting
75g/3oz caster sugar
Pinch of sea salt
1 medium egg, beaten
150g/5oz unsalted butter, at
room temperature
1 tablespoon cognac

For the apple mash

1 large Granny Smith apple
25g/1oz caster sugar
Pinch of ground cinnamon
200g/7oz blueberries

For the crème royale

1 large egg
25g/1oz caster sugar
50ml/2fl oz cream

Whipped cream or ice cream,
to serve

Serves 4

method

· Preheat the oven to 180°C/350°F/
gas mark 4.

For the pastry

· Put the flour, sugar and a pinch of salt in a
large bowl. Mix well and form a well in the
middle. Place the egg, butter and cognac in
the well and mix with your hands until it is
smooth but still sticky. Cover with clingfilm
and place in the fridge overnight. The next
day roll out the base on a lightly floured
surface and fill 4 individual baking rings
(7.5cm/3 inch diameter) with the pastry.
Press down and make sure the edges of the
base are completely sealed, otherwise the
crème royale will run out when baking.

For the apple mash

· Peel the apple. Remove the core and cut
into pieces. Place in a pot, cover with a little
cold water and bring to the boil. Remove
from the hob, leave the apple in the water
for another 2 minutes and then strain out.
· Use a fork to mash the apple but not too
much. Add the sugar and cinnamon and mix
well. Allow to cool. Put a 1cm/½ inch layer
of apple mash on the pastry base in each
baking ring. Put a handful of blueberries on
top.

For the crème royale

· Whisk the egg in a bowl. Add the sugar and
cream and beat the mixture until the sugar
is dissolved.

· Pour 2-3 tablespoons of crème royale over
the berries in each baking ring and place in
the oven for 15-20 minutes until just set. Do
not remove the baking rings immediately
when baked but allow to cool down for 5
minutes and then remove the rings.

To serve

· Serve on plates with whipped cream or an
ice cream of your choice.

The Cliff House Hotel

The House restaurant in the Cliff House Hotel is a gourmet retreat for food connoisseurs. Head chef Martijn Kajuiter is passionate about sourcing food locally and has established an organic vegetable garden in Youghal. Martijn has worked with many Michelin starred chefs including Marco Pierre White and Pierre Koffman. The fusion of his experience with fresh Irish produce delivers a wonderfully exciting meal.

Ardmore, Co. Waterford
Ph: (024) 87800
www.thecliffhousehotel.com

starter
Smoked salmon and boxty potato cakes with watercress and horseradish yogurt

main course
Skeaghanore duck with onions four ways and sweet potato tart

dessert
Chocolate mousse

Smoked salmon and boxty potato cakes with watercress and horseradish yogurt

ingredients

600g/1¼ lb smoked Irish salmon

For boxty potato cakes

150g/5oz cooked potatoes, mashed
150g/5oz raw potatoes, grated
1 small egg
50ml/2fl oz buttermilk
Zest of ½ lemon
100g/4oz plain flour
Olive oil, for frying

For horseradish sauce

150ml/5fl oz natural yogurt
40g/1½oz freshly grated horseradish
Zest of ½ lemon
1 tablespoon olive oil
Sea salt and freshly ground white pepper

Watercress or rocket leaves, to serve

Serves 6

method

For the boxty potato cakes

· In a bowl, mix the mashed potato with the grated raw potato. Add the egg, buttermilk and the lemon zest and mix well again. Beat the flour into the mixture and season to taste with salt and pepper. Shape into six equal sized balls and then press them flat.

· Heat a little oil in a non-stick frying pan and fry the potato cakes on a low heat until brown and crisp on both sides.

For the horseradish sauce

· Make the sauce by simply combining all the ingredients in a bowl and mixing well. Season to taste with salt and pepper.

For the salmon

· Slice the smoked salmon 'Cliff-style' (6 slices per person). This means slicing from top to the skin in a straight line (rather like you would slice gravadlax).

To serve

· Put a boxty potato cake on each plate. Top the potato cake with a small mound of watercress or rocket. Place six slices of salmon beside the cake. Pour around some horseradish sauce.

Skeaghanore duck with onions four ways and sweet potato tart

ingredients

For the duck

4 duck breasts, trimmed, with the fat on
Salt and pepper

For the onions

Butter
8 very small round onions
Bay leaf
450ml/15fl oz vegetable stock
2 sweet onions (or normal onions if sweet onions not available)
1 teaspoon caster sugar (optional)
1 fresh thyme sprig
½ garlic clove, finely chopped
2 white onions
Vegetable oil, for deep frying
1 red onion

For the sweet potato

2 sweet potatoes
4 teaspoons organic honey
4 rounds puff pastry (enough to cover the halved sweet potatoes)
Salt and pepper
Extra virgin olive oil, to drizzle

Chive flowers or onion sprouts, to garnish (optional)

Serves 4

method

- Preheat the oven to 180°C/350°F/ gas mark 4.

For the duck

- Heat a non-stick ovenproof frying pan. Salt the fatty side of the duck and put this fat-side down in the pan. Slowly fry until golden brown and crisp, then turn over and place in the oven for 12 minutes. Remove the duck from the oven and let it rest for 2 minutes in a warm place.

For the onions

- Melt a knob of butter in a small pot. Add the 8 small onions, bay leaf and season with salt and pepper. Cover with the vegetable stock. Then slowly cook the onions until soft.
- Slice the sweet onions into small cubes and put in a pot with a knob of butter. If using normal onions instead of sweet onions add the teaspoon of sugar. Add the thyme sprig and the garlic. Cook this very gently until the consistency is like marmalade, smooth with some lumps.
- Slice one white onion and deep fry. Keep the onions in a warm place until ready to serve.
- Slice the red onion and the remaining white onion as thinly as possible and set aside.

For the sweet potato tart

- Peel the sweet potatoes and slice each in two even-sized pieces. With a pastry cutter make them identical. Boil in a pot of salted water for 4-5 minutes. Then strain and arrange on a baking sheet. Season with salt and pepper and cover with a little honey.

- Cover each sweet potato with a round of puff pastry and cook in the oven for 20 minutes or until the pastry is crisp.

To serve

- Place the compote of onion on the plate and build this up with the slow cooked small onions, deep fried onion rings and the raw onion rings. Place the sweet potato on the plate, pastry side down. Carve the duck breasts in half and place on top of or to the side of the onions. Serve with a dash of olive oil. You can use chive flowers or onion sprouts as a garnish.

Chocolate mousse with crushed pistachio

ingredients

300ml/10fl oz cream
250g/9oz plain chocolate
4 egg whites
75g/3oz caster sugar

4 tablespoons roasted, crushed pistachio nuts, Maldon sea salt and extra virgin olive oil, to serve

Serves 4-6

method

· Whisk the cream until it reaches the thickness of yogurt. Avoid over-mixing.
· Melt the chocolate in a mixing bowl over a pot of boiling water. When the chocolate is melted set aside and cool.
· Whisk the egg whites until stiff. Then add the sugar and whisk until a nice shine appears.
· Fold the egg whites into the cooled melted chocolate. When all the egg whites are mixed, fold the cream into this mixture and mix well. Store in a bowl in the fridge covered in clingfilm for at least 4 hours until set.

To serve

· Using a warm spoon, transfer portions of the chocolate mousse onto each plate and sprinkle around the pistachio nuts. Drizzle some olive oil around it and last, but not least, carefully put some sea salt crystals on top of the chocolate.

Danny Minnie's

Located in the village of Annagry in North-West Donegal, the delightful Danny Minnie's features an atmospheric candlelit dining room and a striking collection of antiques. The cooking matches the elegant surroundings, with Donegal mountain lamb, local seafood and delicious desserts taking a starring role on the restaurant's imaginative menus.

Annagry, The Rosses, Co. Donegal
Ph: (074) 954 8201
www.dannyminnies.com

starter
Salad of peach, walnut and Cashel Blue cheese

main course
Fresh Donegal crab
with pineapple and mango mayonnaise

dessert
Cardamom pannacotta
with rhubarb and strawberry compote

Salad of peach, walnut and Cashel Blue cheese

ingredients

For the dressing

2 tablespoons olive oil

2 tablespoons walnut oil

1 tablespoon white wine vinegar

2 teaspoons honey

1 teaspoon mustard

Salt and pepper

For the salad

Mixed salad leaves (include rocket, baby lettuces)

2 ripe peaches

100g/4oz freshly shelled walnuts

225g/8oz Cashel Blue cheese

Edible flowers and/
or fresh herbs, to serve

Serves 4

method

For the dressing

· Combine the ingredients for the dressing in a bowl and whisk well together.

For the salad

· Toss the salad leaves in some of the dressing and arrange them nicely on a large plate or bowl. Decorate the leaves with edible flowers such as viola or calendula and some fresh herbs such as chives, tarragon or basil.

To serve

· Slice or dice the peaches and arrange these on the salad. Dice up the blue cheese and arrange this around the leaves. Finally add some whole walnuts to give some texture.

Fresh Donegal crab
with pineapple and mango mayonnaise

ingredients

450g/1lb fresh white crabmeat
12 fresh crab claws
1 small ripe pineapple, peeled
and cored (ends discarded)
1 ripe mango
100g/4oz mayonnaise

Salad leaves, diced tomato and
fresh herb sprigs, to serve

Serves 4

method

· Cut the pineapple into four even-sized discs. Place a disc on
each plate and top it with the crabmeat. Arrange the crab
claws around the meat.

· Peel the mango and remove the flesh from the stone. Combine
this flesh with the mayonnaise and spoon a dollop of the
mayonnaise on top of the crabmeat.

To serve

· Garnish with some salad leaves, diced tomatoes and herbs.

Cardamom pannacotta
with rhubarb and strawberry compote

ingredients

For the cardamom pannacotta

300ml/10fl oz milk

300ml/10fl oz cream

50g/2oz caster sugar

Zest of 1 lime

Zest of 1 lemon

6 whole cardamom pods

4 gelatine leaves

For the compote

225g/8oz rhubarb, trimmed and cut into chunks

100g/4oz caster sugar

Dash of water

175g/6oz strawberries, roughly chopped

Serves 4

method

For the cardamom pannacotta

· Put the milk, cream, sugar, zest and cardamom into a pot and simmer gently for 15 minutes to infuse the flavours. Allow to cool a little. Remove the cardamom pods.

· Place the gelatine leaves in some cold water for a few minutes until they become spongy. Squeeze out excess water and add these to the cream mix and whisk in. Pour the mix into four individual moulds or ramekin dishes. Allow to set overnight or for at least 4 hours.

For the compote

· Place the rhubarb, sugar and a dash of water in a medium sized pot. Place on a low heat until the rhubarb begins to soften and break up a little. Remove from the heat and add the strawberries. Allow to cool in the fridge.

To serve

· Remove the pannacottas from the ramekins/moulds by dunking in hot water for a few seconds. Turn out onto plates. Spoon around the compote.

Dax

Experience continental and rustic food with quality wines at this popular award-winning bar and restaurant. Olivier Meisonnave, who named the restaurant after a town near his home in France, has assembled an extensive wine selection which can be enjoyed in the restaurant area or at the tapas bar. Head chef Conor Dempsey oversees the kitchen team.

23 Pembroke Street Upper, Dublin 2
Ph: (01) 676 1494
www.dax.ie

starter
Seared king scallops
with sweetcorn purée and raw apple salad

main course
Whole roast pigeon, fondant potatoes,
coco bean purée and cherry jus

dessert
Brioche pain perdu
with fresh apricots and ice cream

Seared king scallops
with sweetcorn purée and raw apple salad

ingredients

For the corn purée

250g/9oz sweetcorn kernels,
fresh or frozen
100ml/3½fl oz cream
150ml/5fl oz milk

For the scallops

Sunflower oil, for cooking
8 large king scallops, cleaned
and roes removed
1 Granny Smith apple, core
removed and finely sliced
Salt and pepper

Wild rocket and lettuce leaves,
to serve

Serves 4

method

For the corn purée

· In a small stainless steel pot, cover the sweetcorn with the
  milk and cream. Bring to the boil and simmer for 10 minutes
  until very soft. Transfer to a food processor and purée until
  smooth, then season to taste. Return to the pot and keep
  warm until ready to serve.

For the scallops

· Heat a little oil in a pan until very hot. If the scallops are very
  large, you can slice them in half. Season with salt and pepper
  and drizzle some olive oil on the scallops and cook for 1
  minute on each side in the hot pan.

To serve

· Spoon the sweetcorn purée onto warmed plates. Make a dent
  in the purée with the back of a spoon. Arrange the scallops
  on top of the purée. Add some finely sliced apple pieces, wild
  rocket and lettuce leaves.

Whole roast pigeon, fondant potatoes, coco bean purée and cherry jus

ingredients

For the pigeons

4 oven-ready pigeons
Olive oil

For the fondant potatoes

4 large Rooster potatoes, peeled
250g/9oz unsalted butter
6 garlic cloves
1 fresh thyme sprig
1 bay leaf

For the coco bean purée

275g/10oz coco beans
(alternatively, white beans or
haricot blanc)
50g/2oz sliced rindless smoked
bacon
½ carrot
1 fresh thyme sprig
1 bay leaf
½ onion
450ml/15fl oz chicken stock
150ml/5fl oz cream

For the cherry jus

Sunflower oil
50ml/2fl oz ruby port
50ml/2fl oz kirsch
50ml/2fl oz cassis
3 shallots, chopped
1 garlic clove, finely chopped
1 fresh thyme sprig
1 bay leaf
12 cherries, pitted
450ml/15fl oz chicken stock
Salt and black pepper
Bay leaves, to serve

Serves 4

method

- Preheat the oven to 180°C/350°F/ gas mark 4.

For the pigeons

- Heat some oil in a frying pan. When hot, add the pigeons and sear on all sides until brown and caramelised. Remove the pigeons from the pan and place, back down, in an ovenproof dish. Place in the oven for 8-10 minutes or until rare in the centre. Cook for 12-15 minutes for medium. Allow to rest for at least 10 minutes.

For the fondant potatoes

- Cut the potatoes into thick cylindrical shapes. Heat a heavy cast iron pan and add the butter. When the butter starts to foam add the garlic, thyme and bay leaf. Cook for a further 2 minutes. Place the potatoes in the foaming butter and brown on both sides. Then place in the oven for 45 minutes until golden brown.

For the coco bean purée

- The night before, soak the beans in water to rehydrate. The next day remove the beans from the water. Wrap the onion in a piece of muslin cloth. Put the beans and the rest of the ingredients except the cream into a large pot. Bring to the boil and simmer slowly for 1 hour or until the beans are soft. Transfer to a food processor and purée for 5 minutes. Add the cream and pass through a fine strainer. Season to taste, then return to the pot and keep warm until ready to serve.

For the cherry jus

- Put a drizzle of oil in a heavy-bottomed pot. When hot, add the shallots and sweat until soft. Add the rest of the ingredients

(except the stock and cherries). Reduce until almost all the liquid has evaporated. Add the stock and reduce by half. Pass through a fine strainer. Return to the pot and add the cherries. Reduce to sauce consistency. Keep warm until ready to serve.

To serve

- Using a boning knife, take the breast and legs off the pigeons. Place in the oven for 5 minutes along with the fondant potatoes. Arrange the coco bean purée on warmed plates. Add the pigeon and potatoes and drizzle some jus over the pigeon. Garnish with some bay leaves.

Brioche pain perdu with fresh apricots and ice cream

ingredients

For the ice cream

6 egg yolks
175g/6oz caster sugar
250ml/9fl oz milk
250ml/9fl oz cream
2 vanilla pods

For the pain perdu

2 eggs
150ml/5fl oz cream
50g/2oz caster sugar
4 thick slices of brioche
Butter, for frying

4 fresh apricots, stones removed and halved, almond slivers, mint sprigs and icing sugar, to serve

Serves 4

method

For the ice cream

· Beat the egg yolks and sugar to a thick creamy consistency. Add the milk, cream and vanilla. Transfer to a pot and heat gently. Then pour into the egg mixture and stir again. Allow to cool, then remove the vanilla pods. When cool, churn in an ice cream maker according to the manufacturer's instructions. Store in the freezer.

For the pain perdu

· Mix the eggs, cream and sugar together with a whisk. Dip the brioche in the batter. Melt some butter in the pan. Fry the brioche on both sides until lightly coloured.

To serve

· Put an almond sliver in each apricot half and arrange on plates. Spoon out some of the ice cream on top. Then set the pain perdu beside the apricots. Dust lightly with icing sugar. Decorate with mint sprigs.

Deanes Restaurant and Bar

The only Michelin-starred establishment in Northern Ireland, Deanes is one of Ireland's great restaurants. Chef Derek Creagh's passion for food, attention to detail and extraordinary skill in blending classic cooking with modern techniques, make a meal here a memorable event.

36-40 Howard Street, Belfast BT1 6PF, Co. Antrim
Ph: +44 (0)28 9033 1134
www.michaeldeane.co.uk

starter
Chicken liver pâté

main course
Roast cod, parsley mash, Chardonnay emulsion and garden peas

dessert
Apple Genoise

Chicken liver pâté

ingredients

For the reduction

100g/4oz shallot, finely sliced
1 fresh thyme sprig
1 fresh rosemary sprig
1 bay leaf
1 garlic clove, sliced
150ml/5fl oz Madeira
150ml/5fl oz port
50ml/2fl oz brandy

For the pâté

400g/14oz chicken livers, trimmed at room temperature
4 whole eggs, at room temperature
400g/14oz butter, melted and kept hot
1 tablespoon pink salt (sel rosé) or sea salt

Brioche toast and fig chutney, to serve

Serves 6-8

method

· Preheat the oven to 110°C/225°F/gas mark ¼ .

For the reduction

· Place all the reduction ingredients in a wide-based saucepan over a high heat. Bring to the boil and reduce to a syrup, then pass through a fine sieve. Discard the herbs, shallot and garlic mixture.

For the pâté

· Place the chicken livers, eggs and syrup reduction in a liquidiser and blend well until smooth. Pour in the hot butter and pink salt and continue to blend. Pass through a fine sieve.
· Pour into a 900g/2lb terrine mould or loaf tin. Wrap tightly in clingfilm, place in a tray of boiling water and bake in the oven for 45 minutes. For a perfectly smooth pâté, ensure that the core temperature does not exceed 64°C.
· Refrigerate for 6-8 hours until thoroughly chilled.

To serve

· Cut a thick slice of pâté and place in the middle of each plate. Serve with a slice of fresh brioche toast and a dollop of fig chutney.

Roast cod, parsley mash, Chardonnay emulsion and garden peas

ingredients

For the cod

Olive oil, for frying
4 pieces cod fillet,
approximately 200g/7oz each
Knob of butter
Juice of 1 lemon

For the parsley mash

550g/1¼lb potatoes, peeled
1 bunch fresh flat leaf parsley
100g/4oz butter, diced
6 tablespoons milk

For the Chardonnay emulsion

4 shallots, finely chopped
1 garlic clove, finely chopped
1 fresh thyme sprig
1 bay leaf
250ml/9fl oz Chardonnay white
wine
100ml/3½fl oz white wine
vinegar
200g/7oz butter, diced
225g/8oz fresh or frozen peas
1 tablespoon snipped fresh
chives
1 tablespoon chopped fresh
mint (the herbs can be varied
according to taste)
Salt and pepper

Mustard cress, to serve

Serves 4

method

· Preheat the oven to 180°C/350°F/
  gas mark 4.

For the parsley mash

· Peel the potatoes and put into a pot of
  salted water. Bring to the boil and then
  simmer for about 25-30 minutes.
· Pick the parsley leaves and discard their
  stalks. Bring a small pan of water to the boil;
  add the parsley leaves for 1 minute. Drain
  well and put the leaves into a food blender
  with some of the cooled blanching water
  (enough to achieve a smooth consistency).
  Blend until smooth. Transfer to the fridge
  and leave there until required.
· Strain the potatoes, return to the pot over a
  low heat and mash roughly. Add the butter
  and mash thoroughly. Heat the milk and
  then, beat into the potatoes until smooth.
  Keep adding the hot milk until desired
  consistency is achieved. Now add the
  parsley purée and beat well.

For the Chardonnay emulsion

· Put the shallots and garlic into a pan with
  the thyme and bay leaf. Cover with the wine
  and vinegar. Bring to the boil and reduce by
  two-thirds. Remove the thyme sprig and the
  bay leaf.
· Whisk the diced butter into the shallot and
  wine reduction over a low heat. Do not boil.
  Keep warm until required. When ready to
  serve, put the emulsion back on the stove,
  adding the peas, chives and mint. Warm,
  but be careful not to boil as it will split.

For the cod

· Heat a large ovenproof frying pan with a
  little oil. Fry the cod over a moderate heat
  with the skin side down until golden. Turn
  onto flesh side and roast in the oven for up
  to 6-8 minutes. Remove from the oven, add
  the knob of butter and some lemon juice
  and then spoon the juices over the fish.

To serve

· Spoon the parsley mash onto warmed
  plates. Spoon the emulsion over the mash
  and place a piece of the cod on top of each
  one. To finish scatter some mustard cress
  over the cod.

Apple Genoise

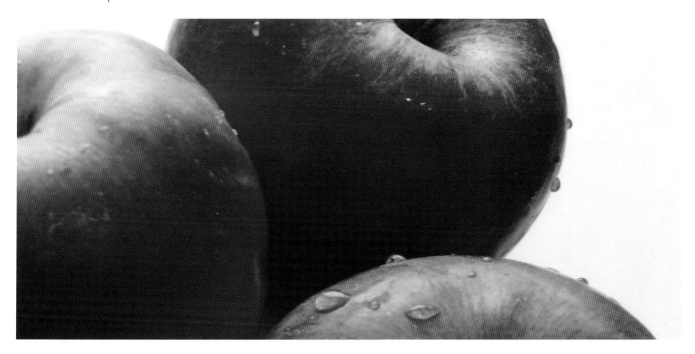

ingredients

6 eggs
200g/7oz sugar
250g/9oz apple purée
150g/5oz plain flour
1 teaspoon baking powder
100g/4oz ground almonds
Butter, to grease
Flour, to dust

Poached autumn fruits, vanilla
ice cream and glasses of
Calvados, to serve

Serves 4

method

· Preheat the oven to 180°C/350°F/gas mark 4.

· Whisk the eggs and sugar together until they are thick and pale
  in colour. Gently fold in the apple purée.

· In a bowl, sift together the remaining dry ingredients and then
  fold into the egg mixture. Take care not to over-mix. Butter 4
  small dariole moulds (approximately 150ml/5fl oz) and lightly
  dust with flour. Pour the mixture into the moulds and arrange
  on a baking sheet. Bake for 10-15 minutes until cooked
  through. Allow to cool before removing from the moulds.

To serve
· Place one apple Genoise on each plate. Place some poached
  autumnal fruits on each plate to decorate. Serve with vanilla
  ice cream and a glass of good Calvados.

Dunbrody Country House Hotel and Harvest Room Restaurant

Kevin Dundon's philosophy of using local produce (he grows his own in extensive kitchen gardens) is a real part of the pleasure of dining at this elegant and extremely comfortable country manor. Dundon's ability to blend classic, contemporary and very individual interpretations of traditional Irish food makes this a place to treasure. An enticing, light, all-day menu is also available.

Arthurstown, Co. Wexford
Ph: (051) 389 600
www.dunbrodyhouse.com

starter
Carpaccio of langoustines with cucumber rolls filled with avocado mousse and citrus-scented oil

main course
Oven-baked poussin
with sage and roasted garlic and Swiss chard

dessert
Dunbrody Kiss

Carpaccio of langoustines with cucumber rolls filled with avocado mousse and citrus-scented oil

ingredients

For the prawns

20 Dublin Bay prawns/
langoustines, peeled and veins
removed
Juice of 1 lemon
1 cucumber
1 ripe avocado
50g/2oz crème fraîche

For the dressing

50g/2oz pine nuts
Juice of 1 lemon
Juice of 1 lime
150ml/5fl oz olive oil
1 dessertspoon freshly chopped
flat leaf parsley, plus extra to
garnish
Salt and freshly ground black
pepper

Serves 4

method

- Peel and thinly slice the prawns and arrange in a circle around the middle of the plate. Sprinkle with a little lemon juice and a twist of black pepper.
- Meanwhile, using a mandolin slice (if you have one) or a sharp knife, cut long strips of cucumber and roll into a tubular shape and arrange in the middle of the prawns on the plate.
- Remove the flesh from the avocado and mash it together with some lemon juice, black pepper and the crème fraîche. Pipe this mousse into the cucumber roll and make it nice and neat in shape. Garnish with some flat leaf parsley.

For the dressing

- Toast the pine nuts in the oven or on a very hot pan. Place the lemon and lime juice in a bowl with the olive oil and mix completely. Add the parsley to the oil and finally mix in the pine nuts. Drizzle the dressing around the side of the plates.

Oven-baked poussin
with sage and roasted garlic and Swiss chard

ingredients

12 spring onions, trimmed
2 tablespoons olive oil
4 oven-ready poussins
75g/3oz butter, at room temperature
8 fresh sage leaves, plus extra to garnish
2 garlic cloves, thinly sliced
225g/8oz Swiss chard, thick stalks removed and roughly chopped
Coarse sea salt and freshly ground black pepper

Serves 4

method

· Preheat the oven to 180°C/350°F/gas mark 4.
· Arrange the spring onions in a roasting tin. Season generously with salt and pepper and toss in half the olive oil until evenly coated.
· Loosen the skin around the neck of each poussin and push under a little of the butter until evenly spread over the breast, then push a sage leaf down each side so that they are clearly visible.
· Arrange the poussins on the bed of spring onions and scatter over the garlic. Drizzle over the remaining olive oil and season with salt and pepper to taste. Roast for 35 minutes until the poussins are completely tender and golden brown. Leave to rest in a warm place for at least 10 minutes.
· Heat the remaining knob of butter in a pan and quickly sauté the chard for a minute or two until wilted. Season to taste.

To serve
· Divide the chard among warmed plates. Add some of the roasted spring onions and sit a poussin on top. Scatter over the sage leaves to garnish.

Dunbrody Kiss

ingredients

For the chocolate mousse

450g/1lb dark chocolate, broken into pieces
5 eggs, separated
600ml/1 pint cream
1 fun size Mars bar, chopped
50g/2oz cornflakes, lightly crushed

For the chocolate shards

50g/2oz dark chocolate, broken into pieces
50g/2oz white chocolate, broken into pieces

For the chocolate ganache

75g/3oz dark chocolate
85ml/3fl oz cream, plus a little extra if necessary

Handful of raspberries, to serve

Serves 6

method

For the chocolate mousse

- Melt the chocolate in a heatproof bowl set over a pan of simmering water. Leave to cool a little. Lightly beat the egg yolks and then whisk into the melted chocolate until well combined. Whip the cream in a bowl until you have achieved soft peaks and then whisk into the chocolate mixture.

- In a separate bowl, beat the egg whites until stiff and then fold into the chocolate mixture. Divide among 6 x 200ml/7fl oz round teacups that have been lined with clingfilm. Chill for at least 2 hours.

- When the chocolate mousse has set, melt the Mars bar in a small pan. Remove from the heat and fold in the cornflakes. Leave to cool a little and then add a layer to each chocolate mousse to form a crunchy base. Place in the freezer for at least 2 hours.

For the chocolate shards

- Melt the dark chocolate in a bowl over a pan of simmering water. Repeat with the white chocolate in a separate bowl. Leave to cool to room temperature. Line a baking sheet with clingfilm. Spoon on blobs of the plain and white chocolate and then cover with another piece of clingfilm. Gently roll until the chocolate blobs meet and form one even layer. Place in the freezer for at least 20 minutes.

For the chocolate ganache

- Place the chocolate and cream in a pan and cook gently for 1-2 minutes until melted, stirring regularly. The consistency should coat the back of a wooden spoon. Leave to cool and use immediately or transfer to a bowl, cover with clingfilm and chill until needed.

- When almost ready to serve, warm the chocolate ganache in a bowl over a pan of simmering water. Remove the teacups of mousse from the freezer, invert on to a wire rack set over a clean tray and then carefully peel away the clingfilm. Ladle a little of the chocolate ganache over each mousse until completely coated, allowing the excess to drip on to the tray below. Using a spatula, scrape the excess chocolate ganache into a small pan and reheat gently. Leave to cool.

To serve

- Using a fish slice, transfer the coated chocolate mousses onto plates and leave to defrost at room temperature for 10 minutes. Then decorate with the raspberries and drizzle around the cooled chocolate ganache. Now working quickly, remove the chocolate shards from the freezer and peel away the clingfilm, then break into shards and stick two into the top of each Dunbrody Kiss.

Earl of Thomond

The Earl of Thomond restaurant in the luxurious Dromoland Castle is the epitome of elegance. It is housed in a magnificent room, with outstanding food and service to match the beautiful views across the lake and golf course. A harpist will accompany your study of the three menus: table d'hôte; à la carte and vegetarian. All menus are based on classic French cuisine using the highest quality Irish ingredients.

Dromoland Castle, Newmarket-on-Fergus, Co. Clare
Ph: (061) 368 144

www.dromoland.ie

starter

Inagh goat's cheese, caramelised salsify and red pepper salsa

main course

Loin of Irish venison, pan-fried courgettes, pomegranate dressing

dessert

Pumpkin and treacle tart

Inagh goat's cheese, caramelised salsify and red pepper salsa

ingredients

For the red pepper salsa

50ml/2fl oz sunflower oil
2 red peppers, peeled, cored, seeded and diced
1 medium red onion, diced
Pinch of sugar
1 garlic clove, crushed
1 fresh thyme sprig
1 tablespoon white wine vinegar
1½ tablespoons port
Pinch of smoked paprika
Drop of lime juice
Pinch of chopped fresh coriander

For the salsify

25ml/1fl oz sunflower oil
4 large sticks salsify, peeled and cut into batons
1 teaspoon sugar
Knob of butter
25ml/1fl oz balsamic vinegar
50ml/2fl oz port

4 thick slices of Inagh goat's cheese
Mixed baby leaves
Olive oil
White wine vinegar
Salt and pepper

Serves 4

method

For the red pepper salsa

· Heat the oil in a pot, add the red pepper, sweat until slightly soft. Next add the onion and sweat until softened too. Add the sugar, a pinch of salt, the garlic, thyme, vinegar and port and cook slowly for 10 minutes. Then add the paprika and cook a little more. Remove from the heat and correct the seasoning and finish with lime juice and coriander. Allow to cool and the flavours to infuse.

For the salsify

· Heat the oil in a pan. Dry the salsify and fry until brown on all sides. Cook for approximately 4-5 minutes, until tender, but still al dente. Add the sugar and a pinch of salt and the butter. Caramelise nicely. Then add the balsamic vinegar and port. Bring to the boil and reduce to a glaze.

To serve

· Warm the plates, season the cheese with salt and pepper and place in the middle of the plates. Place the caramelised salsify on top. Dress the leaves with a drop of oil and vinegar, season and place on top again. Drizzle around the salsa.

Loin of Irish venison, pan-fried courgettes, pomegranate dressing

ingredients

For the venison

2 x 175g/6oz venison loins, skinless and fatless
10 juniper berries, crushed
1 garlic clove, crushed
Pinch of paprika
2 slices thin back bacon
A little oil and butter, to cook

For the courgettes

1 medium courgette, sliced
Olive oil, for frying

For the dressing

Olive oil
1 shallot, diced
Pinch of brown sugar
25ml/1fl oz balsamic vinegar
25ml/1fl oz soy sauce
Dribble pomegranate molasses
25ml/1fl oz vegetable oil
2 tomatoes, peeled, seeded and diced
Salt and pepper

Serves 2

method

For the venison

- Get your butcher to have the venison well trimmed. Mix the juniper, garlic and paprika, and season with salt and pepper. On a piece of clingfilm, place one slice of bacon, rub with a little of the juniper mixture. Place a piece of venison on top and roll up the bacon slice, wrap in clingfilm and tie both ends. Repeat for the second piece.

- Bring a pot of water to the boil and then reduce to a simmer. Add the venison and poach for 6 minutes approximately for medium rare. If you like your venison a little better done, poach for 8-10 minutes. Remove from the water and rest for 5 minutes at least. Remove the clingfilm.

- Heat the oil in a frying pan and add the butter. When melted, add the venison and brown on all sides. Remove and rest again, for 5 minutes.

For the courgettes

- Heat the olive oil in a frying pan, add the courgette slices and season with salt and pepper. Colour on both sides and drain (it only takes a few minutes).

For the dressing

- Heat a little olive oil in a pan. Sweat the shallot until soft. Then add the sugar followed by the vinegar. Bring to the boil and reduce by two-thirds. Next add the soya sauce and molasses and warm through. Add the oil and diced tomato and warm through again. Season with salt and pepper.

To serve

- Place the courgettes in a line on each warmed plate. Slice the venison and place on top of the courgettes and drizzle with the warm dressing.

Pumpkin and treacle tart

ingredients

For the pastry

200g/7oz plain flour, plus extra
for dusting
Pinch of salt
100g/4oz unsalted butter
50ml/2fl oz cold water
Egg wash, for brushing

For the filling

450g/1lb golden syrup
350g/12oz pumpkin flesh, diced
Juice and zest of 1 lemon
Good pinch of ground ginger
100g/4oz fresh white
breadcrumbs
75g/3oz ground hazelnuts

Yogurt, whipped cream, ice
cream or custard, to serve. Mint
sprigs, sugared vanilla pod and
pumpkin seeds, to decorate

Serves 6-8

method

- Preheat the oven to 160°C/325°F/
gas mark 3.

For the pastry

- Sift the flour and salt into a large bowl.
Cube the butter and rub into the flour until
you get a granular texture. Then add the
water and mix until all the ingredients come
together to a smooth pastry. Let the pastry
rest for at least 30 minutes in the fridge.
Roll out on a lightly floured surface and line
a 25cm/10 inch loose-bottomed tart tin or
flan dish; reserve the rest of the pastry for
garnish.

For the filling

- Warm the golden syrup in a saucepan. Add
the pumpkin, lemon zest and juice and
ginger. Bring to the boil and immediately
remove from the heat. Cool slightly and
then add the breadcrumbs and nuts. Mix
well.
- Fill the tart with the mixture. Roll out the
left-over pastry and make a trellis topping
with strips of pastry. Egg-wash the pastry
and bake the tart in the oven for 35 minutes
until the pastry is cooked through and
golden and the filling is just set.

To serve

- Serve with natural yogurt, whipped cream,
ice cream or custard. Decorate with a mint
sprig, sugared vanilla pod and pumpkin
seeds.

Eden

Eden is a busy brasserie where you can dine inside or outside. The buzzy atmosphere is enhanced by excellent food from imaginative menus which have a distinctively Irish flavour and represent good value for money.

starter
Grilled asparagus with mushroom duxelle, hollandaise sauce and Parmesan crackling

main course
Pan-seared scallops with pea and mint risotto

dessert
Irish strawberries with lemon yogurt sorbet

Meeting House Square, Temple Bar, Dublin 2
Ph: (01) 670 5372

www.edenrestaurant.ie

Grilled asparagus with mushroom duxelle, hollandaise sauce and Parmesan crackling

ingredients

20 asparagus spears

For the mushroom duxelle

75g/3oz butter
75g/3oz shallots, finely chopped
400g/14oz button mushrooms, wiped and finely chopped
350g/12oz flat mushrooms, wiped and finely chopped

For the Parmesan crackling

175g/6oz freshly grated Parmesan
75g/3oz Cheddar, grated

For the hollandaise sauce

3 tablespoons white wine vinegar
3 egg yolks
100g/4oz butter, cubed, at room temperature
Salt and ground white pepper

Serves 4

method

- Preheat the oven to 200°C/400°F/gas mark 6.
- Use young green asparagus, otherwise break off the end of the stem if old and woody. Bring a large saucepan of water to the boil. Add a pinch of salt and the asparagus. Bring back to the boil and cook for 2-3 minutes. Remove the asparagus and place in iced water to stop it cooking; you want the asparagus to be green and crunchy.

For the mushroom duxelle

- Heat a heavy-based saucepan and add the butter. Once foaming, add the shallots. Cook until soft, but do not brown. Add the mushrooms and cook on a gentle heat until soft and the liquid has evaporated.

For the Parmesan crackling

- Mix both cheeses together. Spread the cheese evenly in a 10cm/4 inch circle on a non-stick silicone baking mat. Do four at a time. Place in the oven and bake for 5-7 minutes, until golden brown and crisp. Remove with a palette knife and place over a rolling pin while still warm to give a nice curved shape.

For the hollandaise sauce

- Place the vinegar in a saucepan, boil and reduce the amount by half. Bring a saucepan of water to the boil and cover with a tea towel (the tea towel will stop the bowl from slipping). Place the egg yolks in a bowl. Add the vinegar and stand the bowl over the boiling water. Whisk until it holds a figure eight. What you are doing is cooking the eggs without scrambling them.
- Add the softened butter, cube by cube, to the egg mix; make sure each cube is whisked in before you add the next one. Again, do not rush this stage. Check seasoning. Cover with clingfilm and keep warm. The sauce will hold for 90 minutes, but ideally should be used as soon as possible.

To serve

- Reheat the asparagus under the grill. Place spears on each plate. Put 2 spoons of mushroom duxelle at the base of the asparagus spears, drizzle with hollandaise sauce and garnish with Parmesan crackling.

Pan-seared scallops with pea and mint risotto

ingredients

For the pea and mint risotto

2 tablespoons olive oil

2 shallots, finely diced

275g/10oz Arborio rice

100ml/3½fl oz white wine

1¼ litres/2¼ pints vegetable
stock

50g/2oz butter

50g/2oz freshly grated
Parmesan

100g/4oz cooked peas

Juice of 1 lemon

1 tablespoon chopped fresh
mint

8 thin slices of pancetta

For the scallops

20-24 king scallops, cleaned and
roes removed

1 tablespoon olive oil

15g/½oz butter

Salt and freshly ground white
pepper

Lemon wedges, to serve

Serves 4

method

For the pea and mint risotto

· In a heavy-based saucepan, heat the olive
oil. Add the shallots and cook until soft, but
not brown. Add the rice and stir well with a
wooden spoon so that the rice is well coated
with the oil. Add the wine and stir until it
is absorbed. Using a ladle, add the stock,
one ladle at a time to the rice. After each
addition of stock, stir continuously until the
liquid is absorbed before you add another
ladle of stock. Once you have added three-
quarters of the stock, check to see if the rice
is al dente. If still hard continue to add the
stock.

· To finish, turn off the heat. Add the butter
and Parmesan, stir and cover. Allow to stand
for 10 minutes. Before serving add the peas,
lemon juice and mint.

· Heat a little olive oil in a large frying pan.
Cook the pancetta on both sides until crisp.

Remove the pancetta from the pan and
drain on kitchen paper. Keep warm.

For the scallops

· Season the scallops. Reheat the pan that
you have used for the pancetta as the fat
from the pancetta will give a lovely flavour.
Add a little oil and the butter and cook the
scallops. Do them in 2 batches as they will
overcook very quickly. They take only about
40 seconds to cook on each side.

To serve

· Place the risotto in the centre of warmed
plates, arrange the scallops around the
risotto and pour the butter and juices from
the pan over the scallops. Place the pancetta
on top of the risotto and add a lemon
wedge.

Irish strawberries with lemon yogurt sorbet

ingredients

900g/2lb strawberries, hulled and cut into quarters

For the yogurt sorbet

100g/4oz sugar
100ml/3½fl oz water
400g/14oz full fat organic natural yogurt
150ml/5fl oz cream
50g/2oz honey
Juice and zest of 1 lemon

6 fresh mint sprigs, to serve

Serves 6

method

- Place the sugar and water in a saucepan. Dissolve the sugar over a low heat. Bring to the boil and then allow to cool completely. Mix all the remaining sorbet ingredients together and add to the sugar mixture. Mix well.
- Pour into an icecream machine and churn until frozen. Store in the freezer.

To serve

- Place the strawberries in a large martini glass. Top with a scoop of sorbet and decorate with a sprig of mint.

Fallon & Byrne

Located above the irresistible specialty food shop of the same name, this modern bistro-style restaurant offers contemporary European-style cooking in a chic and relaxed atmosphere, with attentive service and good value at both lunch and dinner. The excellent wine bar in the cellar offers a more casual wining and dining alternative.

11-17 Exchequer Street, Dublin 2
Ph: (01) 472 1000
www.fallonandbyrne.com

starter
Seared scallops with cauliflower purée, pancetta and morel dressing

main course
Aged fillet of beef with boxty potato and onion purée

dessert
Mocha mousse with doughnuts and raspberry sauce

Seared scallops with cauliflower purée, pancetta and morel dressing

ingredients

12 large scallops, cleaned and roes removed

For the cauliflower purée

200g/7oz cauliflower florets
200ml/7fl oz cream
Pinch of nutmeg
Juice of ½ lemon

For the morel dressing

3 morel mushrooms (if fresh not available, frozen or dried can be used)
100ml/3½fl oz extra virgin olive oil
50ml/2fl oz Chardonnay vinegar (or any good quality white wine vinegar)
1 tablespoon snipped fresh chives
6 thin slices of pancetta cut into 3cm x 1.5cm (1 inch x ½ inch) pieces
Salt and pepper

Snipped fresh chives or baby leaf salad, to serve

Serves 4

method

· Preheat the oven to 180ºC/350ºF/ gas mark 4.

For the cauliflower purée

· Blanch the cauliflower in salted boiling water until just tender. Bring the cream and nutmeg to the boil, add the cauliflower and bring back to the boil. Take off the heat and add the lemon juice. Blend in a food processor until smooth and then pass through a fine sieve. Season to taste with salt and pepper.

For the morel dressing

· Dice the morel mushrooms and gently sauté in a pan with a small amount of oil. Deglaze the pan with the vinegar and reduce by half. Remove from the heat and slowly whisk in the remaining olive oil. Check for seasoning, and add some chopped chives if you wish.

· Bake the pancetta pieces on a wire rack in the oven until crisp.

· In a hot pan, with a small amount of oil, fry the scallops for 30-40 seconds on each side.

To serve

· Place three dessertspoons of cauliflower purée on each plate and run the back of the spoon through them to create a tear drop effect. Place one scallop beside each line of purée, and a piece of pancetta beside each scallop. Dress each scallop with a small amount of morel dressing and also put a small amount around the plate. Garnish with some snipped fresh chives or baby salad leaves.

Aged fillet of beef with boxty potato and onion purée

ingredients

For the boxty potato

2 large baking potatoes
50g/2oz butter
5 spring onions, finely chopped
50g/2oz chopped fresh flat leaf
parsley
1 egg yolk
Olive oil, for cooking

For the onion purée

1 tablespoon olive oil
1 large Spanish onion, sliced
50g/2oz butter

For the beef

Olive oil
4 x 225g/8oz aged fillet steaks
50ml/2fl oz sherry vinegar
100ml/3½fl oz red wine
225ml/8fl oz chicken stock
Salt and pepper

Serves 4

method

- Preheat the oven to 180°C/350°F/
gas mark 4.

For the boxty potato

- Peel and dice the potatoes, cook until
tender in a pot of salted water. Meanwhile,
heat the butter in a pan and add the spring
onions and parsley. When the potatoes are
cooked, strain off the water and add the
potatoes to the spring onions, parsley and
butter in a mixing bowl. Crush and mix
together then add the egg yolk and season
to taste with salt and pepper.
- Mould the potato mix into 4 rounds. Heat a
large ovenproof frying pan and add a little
oil, then add the potato rounds and seal
both sides until golden. Finish in the oven
for 8-10 minutes until crisp.

For the onion purée

- Heat the olive oil in a pan. Add the onion
and fry until softened but not coloured.
Add the butter and cook for 10-15 minutes
allowing to caramelise a little. Keep stirring
while continuing to cook evenly through.
When completely cooked, blend in a food
processor until smooth. Season to taste.

For the beef

- Rub a small amount of oil on the steaks
and season with salt and pepper. In a hot
pan, cook the fillets for 4-5 minutes on
each side. Depending on how well you
want them cooked, they may need longer.
Remove from the pan and leave to rest in a
warm place for 5 minutes before serving.
- Meanwhile, deglaze the pan with the sherry

vinegar and wine and reduce to a syrup
consistency. Add in the stock and reduce by
half. Strain through a fine sieve into a clean
pot.

To serve

- Place 1 fillet and 1 boxty beside
one another on each plate. Add 2-3
dessertspoons of onion purée beside the
beef and boxty. Run the back of a spoon
through each spoonful of purée to create a
teardrop effect. Spoon over some sauce.

Mocha mousse with doughnuts and raspberry sauce

ingredients

For the mocha mousse

250ml/9fl oz double cream
1 tablespoon freshly ground coffee
25g/1oz caster sugar
1 gelatine leaf
50g/2oz plain chocolate (minimum 70% cocoa solids)
2 small egg whites

For the doughnuts

250g/9oz plain flour
1 tablespoon baking powder
½ teaspoon bicarbonate of soda
1 large egg
75g/3oz caster sugar, plus extra for dusting
150g/5oz natural yogurt
1 teaspoon vanilla extract
25g/1oz butter, melted
700ml/1¼ pints sunflower oil (for shallow frying)

For the raspberry sauce

250g/9oz raspberries
2 tablespoons icing sugar
50ml/2fl oz water

Fresh raspberries, fresh mint sprigs and whipped cream, to serve (optional)

Serves 4-6

method

For the mousse

- Put the cream, coffee and sugar in a saucepan and bring to a simmer. Pour into a clean bowl and leave to infuse and cool for 30 minutes. Soak the gelatine in cold water. Melt the chocolate and stir into the coffee cream. Remove the gelatine from the water, squeeze off any excess liquid and stir into the coffee mixture.
- Whisk the egg whites until they form stiff peaks. Fold the egg whites into the coffee mixture and pour into 4-6 espresso cups/ coffee cups and allow to set in the fridge for 2 hours or overnight is fine.

For the doughnuts

- Mix the flour, baking powder and bicarbonate of soda and set aside. Whisk the egg and sugar together until pale and fluffy. Add in the yogurt, vanilla extract and melted butter and mix well. Gradually mix in the dry ingredients to form a dough. Turn the dough out onto a floured surface and roll out to a 2.5cm/1 inch thickness. Using a pastry cutter, cut the dough into 5cm/2 inch rounds.
- Shallow fry the doughnuts in the sunflower oil, in a medium sized saucepan, turning them with a slotted spoon. They will need around 3 minutes on each side. Place the doughnuts on kitchen paper to drain off any excess oil. You could make the doughnuts beforehand and reheat in an oven for a few minutes when ready to serve.

For the raspberry sauce

- Purée the raspberries, sugar and water in a blender until smooth. Pass the purée through a fine sieve using a spatula to press the sauce through.

To serve

- Toss the doughnuts in a small amount of caster sugar to coat. Pour some raspberry sauce onto each plate and place 2 or 3 doughnuts on top of the sauce with a raspberry and a mint sprig. Place one cup of mousse with each serving. You could also pipe a small amount of whipped cream on top of the mousse, if you wish.

Gaby's Seafood Restaurant

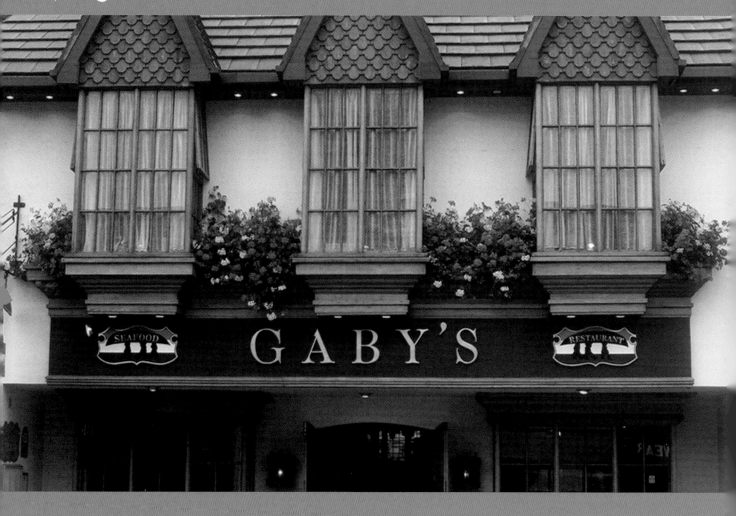

At Killarney's most famous seafood restaurant, chef-proprietor Geert Maes offers well-structured, seasonal, à la carte menus in classic French style. The seafood is ultra fresh and there is an inspiring wine list to match. Culinary skill is assured in this highly regarded establishment which was established in 1976.

27 High Street, Killarney, Co. Kerry
Ph: (064) 32519
www.gabysireland.com

starter

Asparagus wrapped in smoked salmon topped with a hollandaise sauce

main course

Wild Atlantic seabass
with creamed spinach and orange sauce

dessert

Sticky toffee pudding with butterscotch sauce

Asparagus wrapped in smoked salmon topped with a hollandaise sauce

ingredients

For the hollandaise sauce

2 egg yolks
250g/9oz butter
Juice of ½ lemon

For the asparagus

16 asparagus spears
8 slices smoked salmon
Salt and pepper

Fresh flat leaf parsley sprigs, to serve

Serves 4

method

· Preheat the oven to 200°C/400°F/ gas mark 6.

For the hollandaise sauce

· Beat the egg yolks over a pot of hot water until frothy. Melt the butter and add to the egg yolks a little at a time, whilst still whisking, until the mixture becomes thick.

For the asparagus

· Peel and trim the asparagus. Put into a pot of salted water and bring to the boil. Cook for 2-3 minutes when boiled. Remove the asparagus and chill down in cold water to stop it cooking and to retain its colour. Wrap two slices of smoked salmon around a bundle of four chilled spears of asparagus leaving the tips showing. Repeat until you have four bundles.

· Preheat a serving dish. Put the wrapped asparagus bundles on the dish. Cover with the sauce and place in the centre of the oven. Cook for 2-3 minutes just to heat the smoked salmon. Then place under the grill until golden brown.

To serve

· Place the wrapped asparagus bundles on warmed plates, and garnish with parsley sprigs.

Wild Atlantic seabass
with creamed spinach and orange sauce

ingredients

4 x 250g/9oz seabass fillets,
scaled and boned (ask your
fishmonger)
2 teaspoons olive oil
4 shallots, thinly sliced
250ml/9fl oz fish stock
100ml/3½fl oz white wine
225g/8oz butter
Juice of 2 oranges
200ml/7fl oz cream
450g/1lb fresh spinach, tough
stalks removed
4 sun-dried tomatoes, chopped
Salt and pepper

Steamed baby carrots and
chopped fresh flat leaf parsley,
to garnish

Serves 4

method

- Lightly score the skin on the seabass to stop it shrinking.
- Heat a little olive oil in a pan. Sweat the shallots gently until
  softened. Add the fish stock, white wine, salt and pepper and
  reduce by half. Then add half the butter and all the orange juice.
  Leave to reduce slowly to half again. Pass through a fine sieve.
  Keep warm until ready to use.
- Mix the cream and the rest of the butter over a low heat until it
  thickens slightly. Boil the spinach in a little water for 2 minutes,
  then drain. Press out excess juice. Add to the cream and butter
  mixture and stir well.
- Add a little olive oil to a frying pan. Make sure that it is really hot.
  Season the seabass fillets. Place skin side down in the pan for
  3-4 minutes. Turn over and fry the other side for 1-2 minutes until
  golden brown.

To serve

- Place the spinach in the centre of each plate. Drizzle the sauce
  around the spinach. Sprinkle with the sun-dried tomatoes. Place the
  seabass skin side up on the bed of spinach. If you wish you could
  also garnish with flat leaf parsley and steamed baby carrots.

Sticky toffee pudding with butterscotch sauce

ingredients

For the toffee pudding

150g/5oz butter
175g/6oz brown sugar
4 eggs, beaten
1 teaspoon vanilla essence
75g/3oz ground almonds
175g/6oz self-raising flour
75g/3oz blanched almonds,
finely chopped

For the butterscotch sauce

150g/5oz butter
150g/5oz granulated sugar
150g/5oz brown sugar
300ml/10fl oz cream
Juice of ½ lemon

Orange segments, fresh mint
sprigs and pouring cream, to
serve

Serves 10

method

· Preheat the oven to160°C/325°F/
  gas mark 3.

For the toffee pudding

· Cream the butter and sugar until the mixture
  turns a pale shade. Slowly add in the beaten
  eggs and vanilla essence. Mix the ground
  almonds and flour together and fold into the
  mixture. Lastly sprinkle in the finely chopped
  almonds. Poor the mixture into individual
  dariole moulds, or alternatively any cup-
  shaped mould lined with parchment paper.
  Bake in the oven for 30 minutes until well
  risen and lightly golden.

For the butterscotch sauce

· Melt the butter, granulated and brown sugar
  together in a pot over a medium heat until
  the mixture reaches the caramel stage. It
  should look like a soft, light brown, sticky
  mix. This should take approximately 10
  minutes.
· Add in the cream and bring the mixture to
  the boil, stirring well. Stir in the lemon juice
  before serving.

To serve

· Place the pudding on warmed plates and top
  with plenty of hot butterscotch sauce. Add
  the pouring cream. Decorate each plate with
  orange segments and mint sprigs.

Guinea Pig – The Fish Restaurant

The Guinea Pig has been a feature of the culinary landscape of Dalkey since 1957. It offers a timeless atmosphere and good fresh food, with courteous service. Locally sourced fish and meat are prominent on the menu.

17 Railway Road, Dalkey, Co. Dublin
Ph: (01) 285 9055
www.guineapig.dalkey.info

starter
Smokies

main course
Marinated seabass with fennel
served with Pernod-flavoured mayonnaise

dessert
'Eton Mess'

Smokies

ingredients

A little butter, to grease the dish

225g/8oz smoked cod or haddock

Tomato salsa (buy a jar of salsa from your local deli)

4 tablespoons cream

2 tablespoons cheddar, grated

Crusty bread, to serve

Serves 4

method

· Preheat the oven to 220°C/425°F/gas mark 7.

· Grease an ovenproof dish. Put the fish in the dish and cook in the oven for 5 minutes. Remove from the oven and flake the fish equally between 4 ramekins discarding the bones and skin.

· Top the ramekins to three-quarters full with the tomato salsa. Add a tablespoon of cream to each ramekin. Top with the cheese.

· Heat in the oven until bubbling, about 4-5 minutes. (You can prepare this in advance and just pop it into the oven before serving)

To serve

· Serve hot with some crusty bread.

Marinated seabass with fennel served with Pernod-flavoured mayonnaise

ingredients

For the marinade

1 teaspoon chopped fresh coriander
A good pinch of ground mace
1 teaspoon crushed black peppercorns
6 tablespoon olive oil
Salt and pepper

For the fish

8 seabass fillets
4 fennel heads
100g/4oz butter
8 potatoes, cooked and diced
100g/4oz mayonnaise
2 teaspoons Pernod

Mixed green salad leaves, to serve

Serves 4

method

· Preheat the oven to 220°C/425°F/gas mark 7.

For the marinade·

· Mix all the ingredients together in a bowl.

For the fish

· Place the fish in the marinade, turning to ensure an even coating on the fish. Cover and leave to marinate in the fridge for at least 1 hour.
· Slice the fennel thinly, lengthways, trimming and discarding the root. Put one-third aside. Butter an ovenproof dish, put two-thirds of the fennel in the dish. Place the fish on top and bake in the oven for about 8-10 minutes or until cooked.
· Meanwhile, dice the remaining fennel and put in a bowl with the potatoes. Add the mayonnaise and the Pernod. Mix well to ensure the vegetables are well covered. Season with salt and pepper.

To serve

· Transfer the cooked fish onto warm plates. Serve with the fennel and potato salad and a green salad as a side dish.

'Eton Mess'

ingredients

4 meringue nests, crushed
24-30 strawberries, hulled and chopped
100ml/3½fl oz cream, whipped
About 450g/1lb vanilla ice cream

Serves 4

method

· Simply mix the meringues, strawberries and cream together and serve on top of scoops of ice cream. Alternatively, you can place the separate ingredients on the table and allow your guests to mix it themselves!

Harvey Nichols First Floor Restaurant

The sophisticated restaurant at Harvey Nichols offers an exciting fine-dining experience. The menu is a contemporary take on classic dishes, with an emphasis on luxury ingredients. The cooking is clean-flavoured and of an extremely high standard. The restaurant is open for both lunch and dinner.

Dundrum Town Centre, Sandyford Road, Dublin 16
Ph: (01) 291 0488
www.harveynichols.com

starter
Chicken Caesar salad

main course
Seabass with sauce vierge and confit of fennel

dessert
Strawberry cheesecake

Chicken Caesar salad

For the chicken

1litre/1¾ pints chicken stock
2 chicken breasts

For the anchovy dressing

3 egg yolks
1 tablespoon mustard
1 tablespoon white wine vinegar
1 teaspoon sugar
Pinch of cayenne pepper
200ml/7fl oz sunflower oil
2-3 anchovies, drained
50ml/2fl oz olive oil
50g/2oz freshly grated Parmesan
1 tablespoon chopped fresh flat leaf parsley
1 tablespoon snipped fresh chives

For the salad

1 head Cos lettuce
½ baguette
Salt and pepper

Chopped fresh flat leaf parsley, to serve

Serves 4

method

· Preheat the oven to 150°C/300°F/gas mark 2.

For the chicken

· Bring the stock to the boil, then turn down to simmer. Poach the chicken in the stock for 6-8 minutes, then leave to cool in the stock. When cooled, dice the chicken into small pieces. Place in a bowl.

For the anchovy dressing

· Place the egg yolks, mustard, vinegar, sugar, pinch of salt and the cayenne pepper in a blender and liquidise. Gradually add the sunflower oil. Add a little hot water intermittently so the dressing does not become too thick. Add the anchovies and olive oil. Blend again. Add the Parmesan and blend again. Check the seasoning; it may also need a few drops of lemon juice.

· When finished, add some of the dressing to the chicken; make sure the mix is not too wet. Add the parsley and chives and mix well. Place the chicken mixture in small rings or make quenelles with spoons. Keep chilled until ready to serve.

For the salad

· Shred half of the lettuce and toss in some anchovy dressing. Keep 4-8 nice leaves with anchovy dressing and place in shot glasses with the leaves sticking out of the glasses.

· Cut the baguette in thin slices. Brush with a little olive oil and bake in the oven until crisp.

To serve

· Place the dressed shredded leaves on each plate. Put the chicken on top of the leaves. Top with the sliced crisp baguette. Garnish with some parsley. Put the shot glass with the leaves on the side.

Seabass with sauce vierge and confit of fennel

ingredients

For the fish

4 seabass fillets, scaled and boned
1 fennel bulb
Olive oil
3 garlic cloves, chopped
1 fresh thyme sprig
1 fresh rosemary sprig

For the sauce vierge

3 tomatoes, skinned, seeded and diced
1 shallot, diced
1 tablespoon white wine vinegar
Pinch of sugar
3 tablespoons olive oil
½ tablespoon fresh lemon juice
1 tablespoon snipped chives
1 tablespoon chopped fresh flat leaf parsley
6 black olives, stoned and diced
Sea salt and pepper

Serves 4

method

For the fish

· Season the seabass lightly with salt and pepper.
· Meanwhile, trim the fennel and remove the root. Roughly chop into chunks. Heat a little olive oil in a pot and add the fennel, garlic, herbs and a little sea salt. Cook on a low heat for 20 minutes until tender and cooked through but not over cooked. Remove and discard the herbs.
· Heat a little olive oil in a large frying pan and fry the seabass skin side down until nice and caramelised. This should take 2-3 minutes. Turn and finish cooking, about 1-2 minutes.

For the sauce vierge

· Mix the tomatoes, shallot, white wine vinegar, salt and pepper, sugar, olive oil and lemon juice in a bowl. Finish with the chopped herbs and olives.

To serve

· Place the fennel in the centre of warmed plates. Top with the fish, pour some sauce vierge around the plate and a little on the fish.

Strawberry cheesecake

ingredients

For the cheesecake

450g/1lb mascarpone cheese
100g/4oz caster sugar
600ml/1 pint whipping cream

For the sablé Breton

(Alternatively, you can use good quality shortbread biscuits, crumbled)

275g/10oz caster sugar
275g/10oz butter
450g/1lb plain flour
25g/1oz baking powder
3 egg yolks
½ tablespoon salt

For the strawberry coulis

450g/1lb strawberries, hulled
200g/7oz caster sugar
Juice of 1 lemon

Serves 4-6

method

· Preheat the oven to 180°C/350°F/gas mark 4.

For the cheesecake

· Whisk the mascarpone and sugar in a bowl. Whisk the cream in a separate bowl. Add the mascarpone to the cream and mix together.

For the sablé Breton

· Cream the sugar and butter together until you get a smooth paste. Add the flour and baking powder and mix again. Add the yolks and salt and mix again.

· Spread the mixture on a baking sheet. Bake in the oven for 15 minutes. Remove from the oven and break up the mixture. Return to the oven and cook for a further 5-6 minutes. It should be fairly dry. Crumble the mixture and allow to cool.

For the strawberry coulis

· Put all the ingredients in a big pot and bring to the boil. Simmer and allow to reduce a little, then remove from the heat. Using an electric blender, blend until smooth. Strain through a fine sieve into another container. Bottle until ready to serve and keep in the fridge.

To serve

· Place the crumbs in the bottom of a wide glass or individual Martini glasses. Spoon the cheesecake mixture on top. Finally, pour over the coulis.

Il Primo

This very popular restaurant specialises in authentic, rustic, often creative Italian food and Tuscan wines, served in an informal and welcoming atmosphere. Proprietors John Farrell and Anita Thoma offer a range of simple, delicious, Italian dishes, including fresh handmade pastas.

16 Montague Street, Dublin 2
Ph: (01) 478 3373
www.ilprimo.ie

starter
Pan-fried marinated sirloin with rocket and Parmesan

main course
Creamy smoked haddock and chive risotto

dessert
Tiramisù

Pan-fried marinated sirloin with rocket and Parmesan

ingredients

550g/1¼lb sirloin steak,
trimmed
1 tablespoon Dijon mustard
Black pepper
Dash of Tabasco
Dash of Worcestershire sauce
Olive oil
50g/2oz rocket
A little balsamic vinegar

75g/3oz Parmesan shavings, to
serve

Serves 4

method

· Prepare the meat by cutting it into finger-sized thin strips.
· Make the marinade by mixing the mustard, a little black pepper
  and a dash of Tabasco and Worcestershire sauce. Place the strips of
  sirloin in the marinade. You need only enough mustard to coat the
  meat. If you have the time, marinade for a couple of days; if you
  don't, then at least overnight covered in clingfilm in the fridge.
· Heat a little of the oil in a frying pan until very hot. It's important
  that the pan is hot as you want to seal the flavour and juices inside
  the meat. Cook the meat quickly for 1 minute on both sides until
  well sealed and nicely browned.
· Dress the rocket with enough olive oil and balsamic vinegar to just
  coat the leaves.

To serve

· Place a bed of rocket on each plate. Put strips of sirloin on top and
  scatter over the Parmesan shavings.

Creamy smoked haddock and chive risotto

ingredients

50g/2oz butter

1 onion, finely chopped

2 garlic cloves, finely chopped

275g/10oz Arborio rice

Half glass dry white wine

1litre/1¾ pints hot vegetable stock

275g/10oz smoked haddock, skinned, boned and chopped into cubes

85ml/3fl oz cream

Handful snipped fresh chives

50g/2oz freshly grated Parmesan

Salt and pepper

Extra virgin olive oil, to serve

Serves 2

method

· Melt the butter in a heavy-based pan. Cook the onion and the garlic together on a low heat for about 5 minutes. Add the rice, stirring frequently until coated with butter.

· Add the wine and then the stock gradually, ladleful by ladleful. Let the rice grains absorb the liquid before adding more. The rice will take about 16-18 minutes to absorb the liquids and cook.

· After cooking for about 14 minutes, add the chopped haddock with the cream and the chives. Stir in the Parmesan. Season at the end but be careful: smoked fish can often taste salty.

To serve

· Divide the risotto between the warmed plates and drizzle with some good extra virgin olive oil.

Tiramisù

ingredients

3 large egg yolks
4 tablespoons caster sugar
250g/9oz mascarpone cheese
2 large egg whites
150ml/5fl oz strong espresso coffee
3 tablespoons brandy or Tia Maria
About 20 Savoiardi biscuits

50g/2oz plain chocolate, grated, or cocoa powder, to serve

Serves 6

method

· Beat the egg yolks with the sugar until they form soft peaks. Fold in the mascarpone, spoonful by spoonful.

· In a separate bowl, whisk the egg whites until stiff. Add gently to the mascarpone mixture.

· Place the coffee and brandy or Tia Maria in a shallow dish. Dip the biscuits into the coffee and brandy mixture. Don't let the biscuits soak up too much liquid.

· In order to assemble the tiramisù, you can use a deep 20cm/8 inch dish or individual wide-based glasses. Both will work. Place a layer of soaked biscuits on the bottom of the dish or each glass. Then add a layer of the mascarpone mix and another layer of biscuits. Finish with a layer of mascarpone mix and smooth over with a palette knife.

To serve

· Scatter the grated chocolate or cocoa powder over the top.

Isaacs Restaurant

Located in an 18th century warehouse, Isaacs happily combines carefully sourced, high-quality food, a relaxed style and excellent value for money. The cooking is accomplished and the seasonal menus offer a wide range of specials, changed twice every day. The service is top-class.

starter
Pea and coriander soup

main course
American style crab cakes

dessert
Sticky ginger pudding with butterscotch sauce

48 MacCurtain Street, Cork, Co. Cork
Ph: (021) 450 3805

www.isaacsrestaurant.ie

Pea and coriander soup

ingredients

50g/2oz butter
150g/5oz onions, finely chopped
1 green chilli, seeded and finely chopped
2 garlic cloves, finely chopped
450g/1lb frozen peas
900ml/1½ pints chicken stock
2 tablespoons chopped fresh coriander, plus extra to garnish
Pinch of sugar
Salt and pepper

Cream, to serve (optional)

Serves 4

method

· Melt the butter in a heavy pan. Add the onion, chilli and garlic and sweat for 5 minutes. Add the peas and cover with the stock.

· Simmer on a low to medium heat for 8 minutes, stirring occasionally. Add the coriander. Purée the soup in a liquidiser or food processor until smooth. Season with salt and pepper and a pinch of sugar. Reheat gently.

To serve

· Spoon into warm bowls and top with a little cream, if liked, and chopped coriander.

American style crab cakes

ingredients

225g/8oz fresh white crab meat

1 egg, beaten

1 tablespoon mayonnaise

2 teaspoons Dijon mustard

1 tablespoon chopped fresh flat leaf parsley

4 spring onions, finely chopped

75g/3oz fine white fresh breadcrumbs

Plain flour, for dusting

Olive oil

Salt and pepper

Mixed salad leaves, to serve

Serves 4

method

· Preheat the oven to 180°C/350°F/gas mark 4.

· Place the crab meat in a bowl and season with salt and pepper. Add everything else except the breadcrumbs and flour and then mix thoroughly. Add the crumbs and mix again to bind.

· Shape into circles about 2.5cm/1 inch thick and pat with flour. Cover with clingfilm and refrigerate until required for use.

· Heat a little olive oil in a shallow frying pan and fry the crab cakes on both sides until golden. Finish off in the oven for 10 minutes.

To serve

· Place the crab cakes on warmed plates. Garnish with mixed salad leaves.

Sticky ginger pudding with butterscotch sauce

ingredients

For the ginger pudding

175g/6oz self-raising flour
¼ teaspoon baking powder
½ teaspoon bread soda
2 eggs
75g/3oz softened butter, plus extra for greasing
75g/3oz caster sugar
100g/4oz preserved ginger, chopped
½ teaspoon ground cumin
½ teaspoon ground ginger
100g/4oz molasses
1 tablespoon black treacle
1 heaped teaspoon freshly grated root ginger
175g/6oz Bramley apples, peeled, cored and finely chopped
170ml/6fl oz warm water

For the butterscotch sauce

100g/4oz butter
175g/6oz soft brown sugar
100g/4oz granulated sugar
275g/10oz maple syrup
225ml/8fl oz cream
½ teaspoon pure vanilla extract

Whipped cream, to serve

Serves 4-6

method

· Preheat the oven to 180°C/350°F/gas mark 4.

For the ginger pudding

· Sift the flour, baking powder and bread soda into a bowl. Add the eggs, butter and sugar and mix well. Add the rest of the ingredients and blend together well.
· Put into 4-6 buttered ovenproof dishes and bake in the oven for 25-35 minutes. When ready to serve, remove the pudding from the dishes.

For the butterscotch sauce

· Melt the butter, sugars and maple syrup in a pan. Simmer for 10 minutes and remove from heat. Add the cream and vanilla extract and stir for 5 minutes on a low heat. Leave to stand for 10 minutes, stirring occasionally.

To serve

· Place the puddings on warm plates and serve with the warm butterscotch sauce and dollops of whipped cream.

Jacques Restaurant

Long-established and highly regarded for its excellent cooking, comfort and service, Jacques is closely connected to the Cork Slow Food Convivium. An ethos of careful food sourcing is at the heart of its varied menus, created from the output of a network of artisan food producers and fishermen.

Phoenix Street, Cork, Co. Cork
Ph: (021) 427 7387
www.jacquesrestaurant.ie

starter
Asparagus with duck egg, chorizo
and shavings of Gabriel cheese

main course
Castletownbere scallops on a spicy pea mint purée

dessert
Almond and sultana ice cream
with a shot of Pedro Ximenez sherry

Asparagus with duck egg, chorizo and shavings of Gabriel cheese

ingredients

20 asparagus spears, trimmed
Olive oil and butter, for frying
100g/4oz chorizo, preferably
Gubbeen, thinly sliced
4 duck eggs
100g/4oz Gabriel cheese (from
West Cork) or alternatively
Parmesan

Serves 4

method

· Drop the asparagus into some boiling salted water and allow to cook for 5-6 minutes. Remove from the heat.
· Heat a little olive oil in a pan and fry the chorizo for 30-40 seconds until crisp. Remove the chorizo and drain on kitchen paper.
· Fry the eggs in a separate frying pan in some butter.
· Shave the cheese with a potato peeler.

To serve

· Place five asparagus spears on each warmed plate and top with the chorizo and the fried eggs. Finally add the shaved cheese and serve immediately.

Castletownbere scallops on a spicy pea mint purée

ingredients

For the pea purée

450g/1lb frozen peas
2 tablespoons olive oil
Juice of 1 lime
2 tablespoons chopped fresh mint
1 green chilli, seeded and finely chopped
½ teaspoon ground cumin
½ teaspoon ground coriander

For the scallops

20 king scallops, cleaned
Butter, for frying
Lemon juice

Serves 4

method

For the pea purée

· Defrost the peas and put in boiling water for 1 minute. Remove and mix with all the remaining ingredients in a food processor until you have a purée. You can use fresh peas, but frozen are much better unless you have grown them yourself. Heat the pea purée in a pot, stirring occasionally.

For the scallops

· Heat a little butter in a pan and fry the scallops for 1-2 minutes on each side. You may need at least two pans to do this. Squeeze a little lemon juice over the scallops.

To serve

· Put five spots of purée on each plate. Top each with a scallop and serve immediately.

Almond and sultana ice cream with a shot of Pedro Ximenez sherry

ingredients

100g/4oz sultanas
250ml/9fl oz Pedro Ximenez sherry
4 egg yolks
100g/4oz caster sugar
250ml/9fl oz water
100g/4oz flaked toasted almonds
1.2litres/2 pints cream, whipped

Serves 4

method

· Soak the sultanas in one tablespoon of the sherry. Whisk the yolks until light and fluffy.

· Combine the sugar and water until the sugar has dissolved, and heat to 110°C/225°F.

· Pour the mixture into the egg yolks, whisking continuously. Add the almonds and soaked sultanas. Fold the whipped cream into the mixture.

· Turn into an ice cream maker and churn. Freeze until ready to use.

To serve

· Place 2 scoops of ice cream in each tall, wide glass and pour a shot of Pedro Ximenez sherry over each one.

La Bohème Restaurant

La Bohème is clearly serious about food and good service. The cuisine is modern classic French, changes seasonally and is particularly strong on fish and seafood from the nearby port of Dunmore East. There is an all-French cheeseboard, and tempting desserts.

starter
Marinated salmon minute

main course
Poached fillet of seabass à la nage

dessert
Apricot crumble served with basil mascarpone

2 George's Street, Waterford City, Co. Waterford
Ph: (051) 875 645

www.labohemerestaurant.ie

Marinated salmon minute

ingredients

450g/1lb organic salmon fillet, skinned, boned and thinly sliced

About 120ml/4fl oz extra virgin olive oil

Juice of 1 lemon

Drizzle of raspberry vinegar

2 tablespoons chopped fresh dill

40 pink peppercorns, preferably in brine and drained

Salt and freshly ground black pepper

Toasted sourdough bread, mixed salad leaves and lemon slices, to serve

Serves 4

method

· Arrange the salmon in an overlapping layer on chilled plates. Cover with clingfilm and keep chilled until needed.

· Five minutes before you are ready to serve, remove the salmon from the refrigerator and remove the clingfilm.

· Drizzle with a small amount of extra virgin olive oil, lemon juice and raspberry vinegar and disperse all over the salmon using a brush. Sprinkle with the chopped dill and pink peppercorns.

· Season with salt and freshly ground black pepper.

To serve

· Serve with some toasted sourdough bread and mixed salad leaves on the side. Garnish with some lemon slices.

Poached fillet of seabass à la nage

ingredients

For the nage

Olive oil

1 carrot, thinly sliced

1 onion, thinly sliced

4 garlic cloves, thinly sliced

10 coriander seeds

4 star anise

1 fresh thyme sprig

450ml/15fl oz dry white wine

1 tablespoon white wine vinegar

700ml/1¼ pint water

1 bay leaf

For the seabass

4 seabass fillets, each about 2-3cm/1 inch thick, with skin on (ask your fishmonger to remove bones and to scale it)

200g/7oz butter, at room temperature

Juice of 1 lemon

2 tablespoons snipped fresh chives

Salt and freshly ground pepper

Boiled new potatoes or tagliatelle, to serve

Serves 4

method

For the nage

- Heat a little oil in a saucepan. Add the carrot, onion and garlic with the coriander seeds, star anise and fresh thyme. Gently fry for 1 minute. Cover with the wine, white wine vinegar and water. Add the bay leaf, heat gently and cook over low heat for approximately 20 minutes. Do not allow to boil. The carrots should still be al dente when ready. This is called a 'nage.'

For the seabass

- While this cooks, prepare the fish. Place the fish fillets skin side up in a rather flat cooking vessel with sides high enough to hold the liquid. When the fish is ready, boil the nage quickly for 1 minute and immediately pour over the fish and cover with clingfilm very tightly and set aside. This hot liquid is actually going to cook the fish, so depending on the thickness this might take 7-10 minutes.
- Uncover the fish and remove 150ml/5fl oz of the nage and cover again.
- Place the 150ml/5fl oz of the nage in a small pot, keep warm with gentle heat and add the softened butter and whisk until this is completely absorbed. Finish by adding the lemon juice and sprinkle with the snipped chives.

To serve

- Place the seabass in four shallow, warm bowls with the garnish of carrots, onions and garlic and pour the buttered nage over until just under the rim. Season with salt and freshly ground pepper.
- Baby new potatoes or fresh tagliatelle are a perfect accompaniment to this dish to soak up the lovely juices.

Apricot crumble served with basil mascarpone

ingredients

150g/5oz butter
150g/5oz ground almonds
150g/5oz caster sugar
250g/9oz mascarpone cheese
50g/2oz runny honey
½ bunch fresh basil, leaves removed
400g/14oz can apricots halves in natural juice

Serves 4

method

· In a pan, melt the butter, then add the almond powder and caster sugar, cooking slowly until this caramelises slightly. Allow the mixture to cool. This is the crumble.

· Mix the mascarpone with the honey in a food processor. Add the fresh basil leaves (reserving a few to decorate) and blend again briefly. Remove and set aside.

· Again using the food processor, purée the apricot halves without their liquid.

To serve

· Take four martini style glasses and layer first the crumble, then the mascarpone cream and finish with the puréed apricot. Repeat until you have reached the top of the glass finishing with the crumble. Decorate with a fresh basil leaf and enjoy.

L'Ecrivain

Michelin-starred, award-winning l'Ecrivain is an exceptional and much-loved restaurant. Co-owners SallyAnne and chef Derry Clarke and their gifted team have a unique style - classic French with contemporary flair and strong leanings towards modern Irish cooking that uses ingredients carefully sourced from a network of artisan food producers.

109a Lower Baggot Street, Dublin 2
Ph: (01) 661 1919
www.lecrivain.com

starter
Natural smoked haddock risotto with Parmesan and spinach, poached hen's egg and curry froth

main course
Pan-seared ray wing on the bone, Grenobloise with wilted spinach and Parmesan

dessert
Vanilla pannacotta with strawberry compote

Natural smoked haddock risotto with Parmesan and spinach, poached hen's egg and curry froth

ingredients

4 eggs

For the risotto

50g/2oz butter
1 small onion, finely diced
275g/10oz Arborio rice
900ml/1½ pints chicken stock
275g/10oz smoked haddock, skinned, boned and diced
100g/4oz spinach, tough stalks removed and chopped
50g/2oz freshly grated Parmesan

For the curry froth

85ml/3fl oz vegetable stock
50ml/2fl oz double cream
50ml/2fl oz coconut milk
½ teaspoon ground turmeric
½ teaspoon ground cumin
½ teaspoon Thai green curry paste
2.5cm/1 inch lemon grass stalk, broken up to release the flavour
1cm/½ inch piece root ginger, peeled and sliced
½ red chilli, seeded and chopped
50g/2oz butter, diced
Salt and freshly ground pepper

Serves 4

method

For the risotto

· Melt the butter in a medium-sized saucepan and cook the onion gently for 5 minutes until tender. Add the rice, stir, and cook for another 3 minutes. Add the smoked haddock. Meanwhile, heat the stock.

· Add the hot stock to the rice, ladle by ladle, stirring constantly. Continue to stir, allowing the rice to simmer until all the stock is absorbed (15-18 minutes) and the rice is cooked. Add the spinach and allow to wilt down, then add the Parmesan. Keep warm on the stove over a very gentle heat. Season to taste with salt and pepper.

For the curry froth

· Bring the vegetable stock to the boil in a medium-sized saucepan and simmer until it has reduced by half. Add the rest of the ingredients except the butter and bring to the boil with the stock, cream and coconut milk. Then simmer for about 5 minutes until slightly reduced. Pass through a fine sieve and froth the mixture, using a hand blender or whisk. Whisk in the butter and froth the mixture again until you have a good foam.

For the poached eggs

· Bring a large saucepan of salted water to a simmer. Break the eggs into a saucepan, one at a time. Cook for 1 minute before taking off the heat and allowing the eggs to sit in the water for 6 minutes. This gives a translucent egg with a soft, creamy yolk. Remove the eggs with a slotted spoon.

To serve

· Divide the risotto between warm plates and drizzle the curry froth around. Place a poached egg on top of the risotto.

Pan-seared ray wing on the bone, Grenobloise with wilted spinach and Parmesan

ingredients

For the ray

4 ray wings, trimmed (ask your fishmonger to do this)
1 tablespoon sunflower oil

For the Grenobloise

50g/2oz butter, clarified
1 tablespoon baby capers
1 fresh chervil sprig, roughly chopped
1 fresh flat leaf parsley sprig, roughly chopped
1 bunch chives, roughly chopped

For the spinach

25g/1oz butter
100g/4oz spinach, tough stalks removed
2 tablespoons freshly grated Parmesan
Salt and pepper

2 lemons, peeled and pith removed, each cut into 6 segments, to serve

Serves 4

method

For the ray

- Heat the oil in a large, heavy non-stick frying pan. Season the ray wings with salt and pepper and cook them for about 4-5 minutes each side (depending on size, you may have to fry the ray wings one at a time and then keep warm in a low oven). Remove from the frying pan. Keep warm until ready to serve.

For the Grenobloise

- When the fish has been removed from the frying pan, add the clarified butter, capers, chervil, parsley and chives. Warm, allowing the sauce to become a nutty brown colour.

For the spinach

- Melt the butter in a pot and add the spinach. Toss until the spinach is wilted. Add Parmesan and season with salt and pepper.

To serve

- Place the ray wing on warm plates and pour the Grenobloise over it. Arrange three segments of lemon around the fish. Garnish with some spinach.

Vanilla pannacotta with strawberry compote

ingredients

For the strawberry compote
250g/9oz fresh strawberries, hulled and halved
100g/4oz caster sugar

For the vanilla pannacotta
1 vanilla pod
900ml/1½ pints cream
50g/2oz caster sugar
3 gelatine leaves

Mint leaves to serve

Serves 6

method

For the strawberry compote
· Put the sugar and half of the strawberries in a small pot and heat until the sugar is dissolved. Add the rest of the strawberries and leave to cool.

For the vanilla pannacotta
· Split the vanilla pod in half lengthways, scrape out the seeds and place these in a pot with 600ml/1 pint of the cream and the sugar. Heat the cream, stirring to dissolve the sugar. When the cream comes to the boil, remove from the heat.
· Soak the gelatine in cold water. Remove the gelatine from the water and squeeze out excess water. Add the gelatine to the heated cream, whisking until dissolved. Leave to cool but do not refrigerate.

· Meanwhile, whip the remaining cream (300ml/10fl oz) until it forms soft peaks. Fold the whipped cream into the cooled vanilla cream. Pour into greased moulds that hold 150ml/5fl oz of liquid (preferably dariole moulds). Leave to set in the fridge for at least 4 hours.

To serve
· Heat the moulds under a hot tap for a few seconds and turn each onto a plate. Surround each one with some of the strawberry compote. Decorate with some mint leaves.

The Left Bank Bistro

The Left Bank is the top spot in Athlone for informal dining, with a wide-ranging menu, daily specials and a dedicated fish menu. The cooking is precise, the style multicultural, the value good and the welcome warm and relaxed. Blackboard specials add to the impressive regular menu.

starter

Cured gravadlax
with a cucumber and pink peppercorn salsa

main course

Seafood stew with fennel and saffron

dessert

Chocolate truffle torte with Tia Maria and raspberries

Fry Place, Athlone, Co. Westmeath
Ph: (090) 649 4446
www.leftbankbistro.com

Cured gravadlax
with a cucumber and pink peppercorn salsa

ingredients

For the gravadlax

225g/8oz salmon fillet
Bunch fresh dill, finely chopped
(stalks discarded)
1 tablespoons sea salt
1 teaspoon sugar
1 teaspoon vodka
1 teaspoon olive oil
Juice of ½ lemon

For the salsa

1 cucumber
100ml/3½fl oz rice wine
vinegar
1 tablespoon caster sugar
1 teaspoon wholegrain mustard
Some pink peppercorns (freeze
dried, or in brine from a jar and
rinsed)

Lemon quarters, to serve

Serves 4

method

For the gravadlax (prepare 2 days in advance)

· Lay the salmon fillet on a piece of clean cheesecloth or non-stick parchment paper, large enough to wrap around the fillet.

· Mix the dill with the sea salt and sugar. Mix the vodka, olive oil and lemon juice together. Brush this liquid liberally onto the salmon and then pat the herb mixture on top.

· Wrap the paper around the salmon and place on a tray or plate. Then place another plate on top to weigh down the salmon (a couple of cans of baked beans works great). Place in the fridge and leave for 2 days.

For the salsa

· Peel and halve the cucumber and then remove the seeds with a teaspoon. Chop into 2.5cm/1 inch strips. Whisk the vinegar, sugar and mustard together until the sugar is dissolved. Then add to the cucumber and peppercorns.

To serve

· Unwrap the salmon. Drain off any excess liquid and slice thinly with a sharp knife. Place a spoon of the salsa to the side of each plate and then lay 3-4 slices of salmon in a fan shape flat on the plate. Garnish with lemon and serve with the rest of the salsa in a bowl.

Seafood stew with fennel and saffron

ingredients

1½ glasses white wine

16 mussels, washed and beards removed

16 clams, washed and beards removed

Olive oil

2 fennel bulbs, root end removed, thinly sliced lengthways

2 garlic cloves, thinly sliced

225g/8oz monkfish, well trimmed and sliced into medallions

16 cherry tomatoes

Pinch of saffron

A little seafood or fish stock (stock cube may be used)

Salt and freshly ground black pepper

Lemon juice, chopped fresh dill, green salad and crusty rustic white bread, to serve

Serves 4

method

· Add 1 glass of wine to a large saucepan and heat. Add the mussels and clams. Cover and steam for 3-4 minutes or until the shellfish have opened. Strain the shellfish but reserve 225-355ml/8-12fl oz of liquid and set aside. Discard any shellfish that have not opened; reserve the remainder.

· Meanwhile, heat some oil in a large pan over a medium heat and gently fry the fennel, garlic and monkfish for 2-3 minutes until slightly soft but not browned. Add the remaining wine to the pan and cook for about thirty seconds. Add the cherry tomatoes, saffron and reserved liquid. Top up with stock or water if necessary so that all the ingredients are just covered. Simmer gently for approximately 4 minutes or until the monkfish is cooked.

· The dish can be prepared up to this point in advance then gently reheated to serve. Take care not to overcook the fish. Then add the reserved mussels and clams and warm through. Taste and season with salt and pepper.

To serve

· Spoon into warm bowls. Garnish with lemon and fresh dill. Serve with a green salad and lots of crusty rustic white bread to mop up the juices.

Chocolate truffle torte with Tia Maria and raspberries

ingredients

For the pastry

200g/7oz plain flour, plus extra for dusting
1 tablespoon cocoa powder
50g/2oz caster sugar
100g/4oz unsalted butter, diced, at room temperature
1 egg, beaten

For the chocolate filling

350ml/12fl oz cream
350g/12oz good quality dark chocolate drops (70% cocoa solids)
50g/2oz butter, diced
2 tablespoons Tia Maria or any orange or coffee liqueur

Whipped cream and fresh raspberries, to serve

Serves 6-8

method

- Preheat the oven to 180°C/350°F/ gas mark 4.

For the pastry

- Sift the flour and cocoa into a large bowl and then stir in the sugar. Add the butter and work in with your fingertips until well combined. The mixture should resemble fine breadcrumbs. Then mix in the egg to form a firm dough. If it feels a little dry then add a couple of drops of water. Wrap with clingfilm and chill for at least 30 minutes.
- Butter a 23cm/9 inch loose bottomed tart tin. Knead the dough until nice and smooth, then roll out on a floured board so it is large enough to line the tin. Place the dough over the tin and push gently into the sides, trimming down the edges. Prick with a fork and place a piece of baking parchment paper on top. Then fill the tin with baking beans (or any dried beans) to prevent the pastry from rising.
- Bake in the oven for 5-7 minutes, then remove the paper and beans and return to the oven for another 5-7 minutes or until the pastry is cooked.

For the chocolate filling

- Heat the cream in a saucepan over a medium heat until it just comes to the boil. Remove from the heat and gradually whisk in the chocolate and butter until the chocolate is melted and the mixture is nice and smooth. Then add the liqueur and pour the mixture into the tart case. Chill for 2-3 hours until set. The tart is best if made the day before.

To serve

- Remove the tart from the tin and allow it to come up to room temperature. Slice and arrange on plates with freshly whipped cream and raspberries. If you run a knife blade under hot water it will be much easier to slice.

The Lime Tree Restaurant

A lovely period building is home to the ever-popular and extremely pleasant Lime Tree restaurant in Kenmare. The international-style à la carte menu makes a point of featuring local specialty foods and offers plenty of choice, including Kerry lamb and beef and interesting vegetarian dishes, as well as seafood.

Shelbourne Street, Kenmare, Co. Kerry
Ph: (064) 41225
www.limetreerestaurant.com

starter

Celery seed tartlet with creamed leeks, fresh salmon, apple and beetroot salsa and tabouleh salad

main course

Medallions of monkfish tail
with a chorizo and pea risotto, rosemary butter sauce

dessert

Rhubarb tartlet with ginger nut crumble

Celery seed tartlet with creamed leeks, fresh salmon, apple and beetroot salsa and tabouleh salad

ingredients

For the pastry

225g/8oz plain flour
100g/4oz butter, diced, at room temperature
¼ teaspoon celery seeds
½ egg, beaten

For the filling

Olive oil
1 garlic clove, crushed
2 leeks, trimmed and thinly sliced
600ml/1 pint cream
12 thin slices of fresh salmon (your fishmonger will be happy to slice for you)

For the tabouleh salad

300ml/10fl oz hot vegetable stock
225g/8oz cracked wheat (tabouleh)
6 cherry tomatoes
2 spring onions
½ cucumber
6 pitted black olives
4 tablespoons olive oil
Salt and pepper

1 cooked beetroot, 1 Granny Smith apple, a little French dressing and rocket leaves, to serve

Serves 4

method

- Preheat the oven to 180°C/350°F/ gas mark 4.

For the pastry

- Place the flour and butter in a food processor and blitz until they resemble fine breadcrumbs. Add the celery seeds and the egg and combine into dough. Chill for 2 hours before making the tartlets. Roll out the pastry and line 4 x 7.5cm/3 inch individual tartlet tins. Chill again for 1 hour.

- Prick with a fork and place a piece of parchment paper on top. Fill the mould with baking beans (or any dried beans) to prevent the pastry from rising. Bake in the oven for 4-5 minutes. Remove the paper and beans and return to the oven for another 4-5 minutes until golden brown. Cool on a wire rack.

For the filling

- In a heavy-bottomed pot, add a dash of oil and heat before adding the crushed garlic and leeks. Cook without colouring for 1 minute. Then add the cream, bring to the boil and reduce by half. Season with salt and pepper and set aside.

- Fill the tartlets with the creamed leeks and top each with 4 thin slices of fresh salmon. Bake in the oven for 6 minutes.

For the salad

- Add the hot stock to the tabouleh and allow the stock to totally soak into the wheat. Chop the other ingredients into small pieces. Add to the tabouleh once it has cooled down. Add the olive oil to bind everything together and season to taste with salt and pepper.

To serve

- Using the medium side of a grater, grate the beetroot and apple and mix with enough French dressing to barely coat. Place a tartlet on top of the tabouleh with the beetroot salsa and arrange some lightly dressed rocket leaves to the side.

134

Medallions of monkfish tail
with a chorizo and pea risotto, rosemary butter sauce

ingredients

For the chorizo and pea risotto

100g/4oz chorizo, diced
25g/1oz butter
2 shallots, finely chopped
1 garlic clove, crushed
225ml/8fl oz white wine
450g/1lb Arborio rice
2 fish stock cubes dissolved in
700ml/1¼ pints hot water
100g/4oz frozen garden peas,
thawed
100g/4oz freshly grated
Parmesan
50ml/2fl oz cream

For the butter sauce

1 small fresh rosemary sprig,
leaves finely chopped
300ml/10fl oz white wine
vinegar
100g/4oz sugar
50ml/2fl oz cream
200g/7oz butter, diced

For the monkfish

900g/2lb monkfish tails,
well trimmed and cut into
medallions
Olive oil and butter, for frying
Salt and pepper

Serves 4

method

- Preheat the oven to 180°C/350°F/
  gas mark 4.

For the chorizo and pea risotto

- Fry the chorizo until sizzling and set aside.
- Heat the butter in a heavy-bottomed pan
  for 1 minute. Sweat the shallots and garlic
  without colouring. Add the wine and once
  hot add the Arborio rice. Stir constantly over
  a medium heat until the wine is absorbed.
  Then gradually add the stock little by little,
  stirring all the time and softening the rice.
  Once all the stock is absorbed and the rice
  is cooked, add the chorizo and turn off the
  heat.
- When ready to serve, finish the risotto by
  adding the garden peas, grated Parmesan
  and cream.

For the butter sauce

- Add the chopped rosemary leaves, wine
  vinegar and sugar to a pot and reduce by
  half. Add the cream, bring back to the boil
  and whisk in the diced butter. Keep warm
  until ready to serve.

For the monkfish

- Season the monkfish tail medallions with
  salt and pepper. Heat a little oil and butter
  in a pan. Add the monkfish tail and colour
  golden brown on both sides. Finish in the
  oven for 8 minutes.

To serve

- Place the risotto in the middle of warm
  plates. Drizzle the butter sauce around the
  risotto and then place the monkfish tail
  medallions in the butter sauce.

Rhubarb tartlet with ginger nut crumble

ingredients

For the pastry

225g/8oz plain flour
175g/6oz butter, diced, at room temperature
50g/2oz icing sugar
1 egg, beaten

For the rhubarb

1 bunch rhubarb (approximately 8 stalks)
175g/6oz sugar

For the crumble

100g/4oz ginger nut biscuits, crushed
100g/4oz digestive biscuits, crushed
½ teaspoon finely chopped stem ginger
50g/2oz nibbed almonds, chopped
Pinch of ground cinnamon

Raspberry ripple ice cream or custard, to serve

Serves 4

method

- Preheat the oven to 180°C/350°F/ gas mark 4.

For the pastry

- Place the flour, butter and sugar into a food processor and blitz until it resembles fine breadcrumbs. Add the egg and combine to dough. Chill for 4 hours before rolling out to line 4x 7.5cm/3 inch individual tartlet tins. Chill the lined tartlet moulds for 1 hour before they are baked. Prick with a fork and place a piece of parchment paper on top. Fill the mould with baking beans (or any dried beans) to prevent the pastry from rising. Bake in the oven for 4-5 minutes. Remove the paper and beans and return to the oven for another 4-5 minutes until golden brown. Allow to cool and carefully remove from the tins.

For the rhubarb

- Wash the rhubarb and chop into 2.5cm/1inch pieces. Place in an ovenproof dish and cover with the sugar. Cover the dish with foil and place in the oven to cook for 20 minutes until soft but still holding its shape.

For the crumble

- Mix all the ingredients together to make the crumble.
- To assemble the dish, fill each tartlet with some rhubarb, top with crumble mix and place back in the oven for 2-4 minutes to warm through.

To serve

- Place in the middle of a plate and add some custard and/or a scoop of raspberry ripple ice cream.

Locks Restaurant

Locks is a vibrant canal-side restaurant that uses the best of seasonal Irish ingredients to create distinctive bistro-style food. Its popularity with all age groups contributes to its lively 'neighbourhood restaurant' atmosphere.

starter

White bean soup with braised oxtail, rocket and Parmesan

main course

Lamb saddle with aubergine, bulgar wheat and sheep's cheese

dessert

Chocolate beetroot brownie with celery ice cream

1 Windsor Terrace, Portobello, Dublin 8
Ph: (01) 454 3391

www.locksrestaurant.ie

White bean soup with braised oxtail, rocket and Parmesan

ingredients

For the soup

400g/14oz white beans, soaked
(or fresh borlotti)
Olive oil or butter
1 large onion, chopped
1 garlic clove, finely chopped
100g/4oz bacon or pancetta in
one piece, rind removed and
chopped
1 celery heart with fresh thyme
and bay leaf (tied together with
string)
1litre/1¾ pints chicken stock
200ml/7fl oz cream

For the oxtail

Olive oil or butter
1 large onion, chopped
1 large leek, trimmed and
chopped
1 head celery, trimmed and
chopped
50g/2oz can tomato purée
2 teaspoons fresh thyme leaves
1 bottle red wine
900g/2lb trimmed oxtail
Plain flour, to dredge
Sunflower oil
600ml/1 pint chicken stock

Juice of 1 lemon, rocket leaves
and freshly grated Parmesan or
Glebe Brethan, to serve

Serves 6

method

· Preheat the oven to 180°C/350°F/gas 4.

For the soup

· Firstly cook the white beans for
approximately 1 hour or until tender. In a
separate pot, heat the olive oil or butter. Fry
the onion, garlic and bacon for a couple of
minutes or until cooked. When the beans
are almost soft, add to the onion, garlic and
bacon mix. Sweat for a further five minutes
and add the tied celery heart and chicken
stock and simmer for one hour. Remove
the tied celery heart. Add the cream and
transfer the liquid to a blender and blend
until smooth. Return to the pot and keep
warm until ready to serve.

For the oxtail

· Heat the oil or butter in a heavy-bottomed
pan and sweat the vegetables until soft.
Add the tomato purée and thyme and cook
for 5 minutes. Add the bottle of red wine
and stir with a wooden spoon whilst cooking
over a low heat for twenty minutes. Lightly
dust the oxtail with flour. Fry in sunflower
oil until nicely browned, then place in a
casserole dish. Cover with the red wine and
vegetable mix and add the chicken stock
and cook in oven for 2½ hours. Allow to
cool, pick the oxtail off the bones in large
pieces. Strain the cooking liquor and reduce
until a sauce consistency is reached. Pour
over the oxtail and allow to cool.

To serve

· Warm the soup and oxtail separately. Place
the oxtail in the bottom of warmed bowls.
Finish the white bean soup with a squeeze
of lemon. Pour the soup over the oxtail.
Garnish with rocket leaves and grated
Parmesan or Glebe Brethan.

Lamb saddle with aubergine, bulgar wheat and sheep's cheese

ingredients

For the lamb

Olive oil
Saddle of lamb (backbone and both loins of a lamb)

For the aubergine

3 aubergines
Olive oil (infused with thyme)
25g/1oz bulgar wheat
300ml/10fl oz chicken stock
1 bunch fresh coriander
1 courgette, diced and sautéed
100g/4oz Corleggy sheep's cheese, sliced

Slow roast tomatoes and spiced chickpeas, to serve

Serves 6

method

- Preheat the oven to 180°C/350°F/ gas mark 4.

For the lamb

- Heat the olive oil in the pan. Put the saddle of lamb in, fat side down, and cook for 10 minutes. Turn over and seal very quickly on the flesh side. Place in an ovenproof dish and cook in the oven for a further 8-12 minutes. Allow to rest for a further 5 minutes.

For the aubergine

- Halve the aubergines lengthways, score the flesh and drizzle with a little thyme flavoured oil. Roast in the oven for 15 minutes until soft. Then scoop out the flesh, reserving the skins, leaving about 0.5cm/¼ inch of flesh.

- Pour boiling stock over the bulgar wheat and cover with clingfilm. When cool, fluff with a fork. Add the coriander, courgette and aubergine meat. Stuff back into the aubergine shells, top with slices of Corleggy cheese and bake for a further 5 minutes when you are ready to serve.

To serve

- Place half a stuffed aubergine on each warmed plate. Cut the saddle into slices, place on the plate and add a spoonful of the lamb roasting juices on top. Serve it with slow roast tomatoes and spiced chickpeas.

Chocolate beetroot brownie with celery ice cream

ingredients

For the brownie

750g/1¾lb unsalted butter, diced

750g/1¾lb caster sugar

13 eggs

750g/1¾lb plain chocolate, broken into squares (70% cocoa solids such as Palmira)

150g/5oz roasted beetroot, puréed

450g/1lb plain flour

400g/14oz shelled walnuts, chopped

For the celery ice cream

225ml/8fl oz milk

300ml/10fl oz cream

3 celery sticks, trimmed and finely diced

100g/4oz caster sugar

6 egg yolks (free range)

½ vanilla pod, split in half, seeds scraped out

Candied orange or kumquat, to serve

Serves lots!

method

- Preheat the oven to 180°C/350°F/ gas mark 4.

For the brownie

- Cream the butter and sugar together in a bowl. Add the eggs one at a time and beat until smooth.
- Melt the chocolate in a bowl over a pot of boiling water. When melted, add the beetroot purée.
- Fold the chocolate beetroot mix and sieve the flour into the egg mix. Lastly, add the walnuts. Pour into a large tray covered with greaseproof paper and bake in the oven for 18-20 minutes. The tray should be 25cm x 20cm/10 x 12 inches.

For the celery ice cream

- Put the milk, cream and half of the celery into a heavy pot and infuse over a low heat.
- Beat the sugar and yolks with the scraped vanilla pod seeds until smooth. Add to the cream mixture and slowly heat at a very low heat, stirring continuously. The cooked anglaise should coat the back of a wooden spoon and leave a mark when you run your finger over it. Allow to cool. Remove the celery trimmings.
- Pour into an ice cream machine to churn and, towards the end, add the rest of the finely diced celery.

To serve

- Place the warm brownie on a nice plate with a scoop of the ice cream. Garnish with a little candied orange or kumquat.

The Lodge at Doonbeg Golf Club

Good food is the priority at all three dining options in this luxury golf resort and hotel. The fine-dining restaurant is the Long Room, an intimate venue with its own bar and with windows overlooking Doughmore Bay. It has a well-earned reputation for high standards, with a wide-ranging menu and attentive service.

Doonbeg, Co. Clare
Ph: (065) 905 5600
www.doonbeggolfclub.com

starter

Dublin Bay prawns
with couscous and tomato and caper dressing

main course

Fillet of John Dory with white beans,
globe artichoke and smoked bacon velouté

dessert

Valrhona chocolate pod, raspberry jelly
and ginger ice cream

Dublin Bay prawns
with couscous and tomato and caper dressing

ingredients

Olive oil, for frying
8 large Dublin Bay prawns,
peeled and veins removed

For the couscous

100g/4oz couscous
85ml/3fl oz hot water
1 tablespoon chopped fresh
coriander
1 tomato, finely diced
1 tablespoon olive oil

For the tomato and caper dressing

1 tomato, chopped
½ shallot, finely diced
1 teaspoon capers
50ml/2fl oz olive oil
Salt and pepper

Baby salad leaves, to serve

Serves 2

method

For the couscous

· Pour the hot water over the couscous and keep it covered with clingfilm for 20 minutes, until fluffy. When ready to serve, mix the coriander, tomato and olive oil into the couscous. Season well with salt and pepper.

For the tomato and caper dressing

· Mix the tomatoes with the shallots and the capers and the olive oil.

For the prawns

· Heat a little olive oil in a pan and gently sauté the prawns, approximately 1 minute until they have turned pink.

To serve

· Place the couscous, shaped in a circle or square, on each plate. Put the sauté prawns on top. Drizzle over a little dressing. Finally, place some nice salad leaves on top and drizzle a little more of the dressing around the plate.

Fillet of John Dory with white beans, globe artichoke and smoked bacon velouté

ingredients

For the sauce

25ml/1fl oz olive oil
2 shallots, cut in strips
50g/2oz bacon lardons
2 fresh thyme sprig
100ml/3½fl oz white wine
100ml/3½fl oz chicken stock
50ml/2fl oz double cream
Salt and pepper

For the fish

2x150g/5oz John Dory fillets, skin on
25ml/1fl oz olive oil
100g/4oz cooked white beans (such as cannellini or haricot)
1 tablespoon softened butter
50g/2oz baby spinach leaves
100g/4oz leeks, trimmed and cut in julienne
2 tomatoes, skinned, seeded and finely diced
2 marinated artichoke hearts
2 sun-dried tomatoes, cut into quarters

Serves 2

method

For the sauce

· Heat the oil in a pan. Sauté the shallots, bacon lardons and the thyme until soft, being careful to avoid colouring. Add the white wine and reduce it until nearly all gone. Add the chicken stock, season to taste and reduce by half. Add the cream to the stock and simmer gently for 3 minutes. Pass through a sieve and return to the pot and keep warm.

For the fish

· Lightly season the John Dory with salt and pepper. Heat a little oil in a pan. Fry the John Dory fillets, flesh side down, for 3-4 minutes. Then remove from the heat, turn the fish over to the skin side and leave in a warm place until ready to serve.

· Then add the beans to the pan and sauté them lightly. Add the butter, then the spinach and the leeks and continue to sauté until the spinach is melted. Add the tomatoes and season with salt and pepper.

· Cut the artichokes into wedges. Heat the remaining oil in a frying pan and sauté the artichokes until you have a golden colour on both sides.

To serve

· Spoon the beans and spinach mix onto deep plates. Arrange the artichokes and the sun-dried tomatoes around the beans. Put the fish on top and pour over some sauce.

Valrhona chocolate pod, raspberry jelly and ginger ice cream

ingredients

For the chocolate

1 gelatine leaf
2 egg yolks
25g/1oz caster sugar
100ml/3½fl oz milk
100ml/3½fl oz cream
25g/1oz Valrhona chocolate

For the jelly

3 gelatine leaves
100g/4oz caster sugar
Juice of 2 limes
Juice of 1 orange
250ml/9fl oz water
250g/9oz raspberries

For the ice cream

75g/3oz caster sugar
4 egg yolks
150ml/5fl oz milk
200ml/7fl oz cream
25g/1oz glucose
1 teaspoon freshly grated root ginger

Chocolate biscuits, to serve

Serves 4

method

For the chocolate

· Soak the gelatine in 4 tablespoons of cold water. Mix the egg yolks with the sugar. Put the milk and cream in a pot and bring to the boil. Add some of this into the egg yolk mix and stir. Then put this back into the cream mix and stir again. Put back on the heat for 1 minute stirring all the time.

· Melt the chocolate in a bowl over a pot of boiling water. Add the chocolate to the cream and egg mixture. Remove the gelatine from the water. Squeeze out excess water. Add to the chocolate and stir again. Spoon the chocolate into 4 ramekins and refrigerate for about 2-3 hours until set, or overnight is best.

For the jelly

· Soak the gelatine in 4 tablespoons of cold water. Put the sugar, juices and water in a pot. Add the raspberries. Bring to the boil and then simmer for 5 minutes. Pass through a sieve. Allow to cool. Remove the gelatine from the water. Squeeze out excess water. Add to the raspberry mixture and mix well. Place in a bowl and refrigerate for 2 hours until set, or overnight is best.

For the ice cream

· Mix the sugar with the egg yolks. Put the milk, cream, glucose and ginger in a pot and bring to the boil. Add some to the egg mix. Then put this back into the cream mix and stir again. Put back on heat for 2 minutes stirring continuously. Put through a sieve. Pour into an ice cream maker and churn until frozen.

To serve

· Remove the chocolate pods from the ramekins by dipping briefly in hot water and put on each plate. (Alternatively, you can leave the chocolate in the ramekin). Place a chocolate biscuit on the side with a scoop of ice cream on top. Cut a square of jelly and place it on top of the ice cream.

MacNean House & Restaurant

Winner of Food & Wine magazine's prestigious 'Restaurant of the Year' award, MacNean House and Restaurant offers the ultimate dining experience, created by award-winning chef Neven Maguire. Maguire's outstanding cooking makes a meal here an event to remember. Choose from a range of excellent value menus.

Blacklion, Co. Cavan
Ph: (071) 985 3022
www.macneanrestaurant.com

starter
Roasted red pepper soup

main course
Peppered duck breast with spinach and mushrooms

dessert
Pear Belle-Hélène

Roasted red pepper soup

ingredients

6 red peppers, halved, cored
and seeded
5 tablespoons olive oil
1 tablespoon balsamic vinegar
½ teaspoon chopped fresh
thyme
2 onions, finely chopped
2 garlic cloves, crushed
2 tablespoons tomato purée
1.2litres/2 pints chicken or
vegetable stock
2 tablespoons torn fresh basil
Maldon sea salt and freshly
ground black pepper

Basil oil or pesto and freshly
baked ciabatta, to serve

Serves 4–6

method

· Preheat the oven to 190°C/375°F/gas mark 5.

· Arrange the pepper halves in a baking tin, cut side up. Drizzle over
  4 tablespoons of the olive oil, then sprinkle the vinegar, thyme
  and 1 teaspoon of salt on top. Place in the oven and roast for 20
  minutes, until softened and lightly golden. Allow to cool.

· When the peppers are cool enough to handle, slip the skins off and
  discard; then roughly chop the flesh, reserving as much of the juice
  as possible. Set aside until needed.

· Heat the remaining tablespoon of oil in a pan, add the onions
  and garlic and sweat for 10 minutes until lightly golden, stirring
  occasionally. Add the reserved pepper flesh with the tomato purée
  and stock and bring to the boil. Reduce the heat and simmer for
  10–15 minutes, until slightly reduced. Add the basil and then blitz
  with a hand blender until smooth. Season to taste with salt and
  pepper.

To serve

· Ladle the soup into warmed bowls and drizzle with a little basil oil
  or pesto, then serve with some ciabatta bread.

Peppered duck breast with spinach and mushrooms

ingredients

4 duck breasts
Black pepper
25g/1oz butter
2 tablespoons olive oil
4 garlic cloves, unpeeled
1 tablespoon balsamic vinegar
150ml/5fl oz red wine
Pinch of brown sugar
1 tablespoon chopped thyme
100ml/3½fl oz duck or beef stock
100g/4oz fresh spinach
100g/4oz mixed mushrooms
Salt and pepper

Chopped fresh mixed herbs and potatoes, to serve

Serves 4

method

· Grind the black pepper onto the duck and press down well. Season the duck breasts with salt.
· Heat half the butter and oil in a frying pan. Place the duck breast on the pan skin side down. Add the garlic. Fry for 4 minutes either side for medium rare or 7 minutes either side for well-done. Keep warm. Deglaze the pan with balsamic vinegar and add red wine, sugar, thyme and stock. Reduce heat and simmer to a sauce consistency; season to taste.
· Fry the spinach with the mushrooms in the rest of the butter and oil until just cooked. Season with salt and pepper and stir well.

To serve
· Spoon spinach and mushrooms onto the centre of warmed plates. Slice the duck and arrange on top of the spinach mixture. Drizzle the sauce over, garnish with herbs and serve with your favourite potatoes.

Pear Belle-Hélène

ingredients

For the pears

6 ripe conference pears, peeled, cored and halved
300ml/10fl oz apple juice
1 cinnamon stick
½ vanilla pod
2 whole star anise (optional)
50g/2oz caster sugar
1 orange, sliced

For the chocolate mousse

225g/8oz plain chocolate, broken into squares (minimum 55% cocoa solids)
3 eggs
2 tablespoons Baileys Irish cream liqueur
300ml/10fl oz cream

For the chocolate fudge sauce

350ml/12oz plain chocolate, broken into squares
300ml/10fl oz cream
75g/3oz caster sugar
50g/2oz unsalted butter

50g/2oz toasted flaked almonds and fresh mint sprigs, to serve

Serves 6

method

For the pears

· Place the pear halves in a pan with the apple juice, cinnamon stick, vanilla pod, star anise, if using, the sugar and orange slices. Bring to the boil, then reduce the heat and simmer for 15-20 minutes until the pear halves are tender. Remove from the heat and leave to cool in the syrup. Remove the cooled pears with a slotted spoon. (Reserve the cooking juices to use in a fresh fruit salad.)

For the chocolate mousse

· Melt the chocolate in a heatproof bowl set over a pan of simmering water. Whisk the eggs with the Baileys in a separate bowl over a pan of simmering water until doubled in volume. It is very important to ensure the water does not boil or it will cook the eggs.

· Fold the melted chocolate into the egg mixture, then leave to cool for 5 minutes. Meanwhile, whisk the cream in a bowl and then fold into the chocolate mousse. Cover with clingfilm and refrigerate for 2-3 hours or overnight.

For the chocolate fudge sauce

· Melt the chocolate very gently in a heatproof bowl set over a pan of gently simmering water. Set aside. Place the cream in a separate pan with the caster sugar and butter. Bring to a simmer, stirring until the sugar has dissolved.

· Remove the cream mixture from the heat and leave to cool down a little, then whisk

in the melted chocolate until you have achieved a smooth sauce. Pour into a jug and cover with clingfilm. This sauce keeps very well in the fridge and can be warmed gently when needed.

To serve

· Scoop some of the chocolate mousse into each bowl. Carefully fan out the pear halves, and place two beside each portion of mousse. Drizzle some of the chocolate fudge sauce over the fanned out pears. Sprinkle with the toasted almonds and decorate with the mint.

Mary Ann's Bar and Restaurant

Seafood is the star at Mary Ann's, a traditional establishment in the beautiful fishing village of Castletownshend in West Cork. Whether you eat in the Vine Room; al fresco in the pretty garden; or in the cosy traditional bar, you'll enjoy - in addition to brilliantly cooked seafood - a wide choice of local, seasonal foods, including farmhouse cheeses.

Castletownshend, Skibbereen, Co. Cork
Ph: (028) 36146
www.westcorkweek.com/maryanns

starter
Mussels à la crème

main course
Scallops Mary Ann

dessert
Pear and almond frangipane tart

Mussels à la crème

ingredients

900g/2lb mussels
120ml/4fl oz white wine
3 shallots, finely sliced
150ml/5fl oz double cream
2 garlic cloves, finely chopped
1 tablespoon chopped fresh parsley
Juice of 1 lemon
Salt and pepper

4-8 slightly toasted slices of bread, to serve

Serves 4

method

· Rinse the mussels and throw away any that will not close when tapped on the sink, then remove the beards. Put them in a large saucepan with the wine and shallots. Bring to the boil, cover and steam for 3-4 minutes. Shake the pan from time to time until the mussels have all opened; throw away any that are still closed.

· Add the cream, garlic and parsley. Reheat gently without letting it boil. Season well with salt and pepper. Pour the lemon over the sauce to taste.

To serve

· Divide the mussels among the bowls and pour over the sauce. Serve with the toasted bread on the side to mop up the sauce.

Scallops Mary Ann

ingredients

150g/5oz butter
25g/1oz plain flour
120ml/4fl oz white wine
150ml/5fl oz single cream
A little sunflower oil
16 scallops, cleaned
2 courgettes

550g/1¼lb mashed potatoes and snipped fresh chives, to serve

Serves 4

method

· Put the butter in a pan and heat until melted. Add the flour and stir into the melted butter making a roux. Then add the white wine and the cream and stir again. Bring to the boil, stirring all the time. Remove from the heat.

· In a slightly oiled frying pan, sear the scallops on both sides until golden. This will take less than a minute per side depending on thickness.

· Slice the courgettes in thin slices and put in boiling water for 1 minute. Remove and make 4 rolls.

To serve

· Reheat the sauce and pour some onto each plate. Put the mashed potato in the middle and top with the courgette rolls. Add the seared scallops. Garnish with chives.

Pear and almond frangipane tart

ingredients

For the frangipane

200g/7oz butter, softened
200g/7oz caster sugar
4 eggs, beaten
200g/7oz ground almonds
1-2 teaspoons vanilla extract
85ml/3fl oz white rum

For the tart

450g/1lb short crust pastry
(shop bought is fine)
A little plain flour
8 canned pear halves, in natural
juices
Honey or apricot jam, to glaze

Icing sugar and either whipped
cream or vanilla ice cream, to
serve

Serves 6

method

· Preheat the oven to 180°C/350°F/gas mark 4.

For the frangipane

· Cream the butter and sugar together in a mixing bowl. Gradually add the eggs. Then add the ground almonds, vanilla and rum and mix together until combined well. Leave in the fridge until required.

For the tart

· Roll out the pastry in a lightly floured work surface and line a loose bottomed flan tin that is 25cm/10 inches in diameter. Prick the base with a fork all over. Chill for 30 minutes in the fridge. Cut out a circle of parchment paper to cover the pastry case, then fill with baking beans and cook for 10 minutes. Remove the paper and cook for a further 5 minutes to dry out a little. Cool for 10 minutes.

· Spoon the frangipane mixture onto the pastry. Arrange the pears, fanned out in a circle, on the frangipane. Bake in the oven for 25-30 minutes until the mixture is firm to touch and nicely brown on top. Leave to cool slightly and then glaze with melted honey or apricot jam.

To serve

· Dust with icing sugar. Serve warm, cut into slices, on plates with fresh whipped cream or ice cream.

Matz at the g Hotel

Designed by internationally famous milliner, Philip Treacy, the décor in the g Hotel is remarkable and great fun. The restaurant, Matz at the g, is both stylish and comfortable, with an extensive menu that combines international cuisine with Italian-style dishes.

Wellpark, Galway, Co. Galway
Ph: (091) 865 200
www.theghotel.ie

starter
Chilled mushroom and mature cheddar duxelles cake, vinaigrette of fresh herbs

main course
Steamed black sole fillets and crabmeat, in a velvet crab bisque sauce

dessert
Apple and clove tarte tatin with caramel ice cream

Chilled mushroom and mature cheddar duxelles cake, vinaigrette of fresh herbs

ingredients

For the cake

150g/5oz butter

1.5kg/3lb mushrooms, finely diced

200g/7oz shallots, finely diced

2 small garlic cloves, finely chopped

2 tablespoons truffle oil, optional

25g/1oz chopped fresh flat leaf parsley

1 teaspoon chopped fresh rosemary

1 teaspoon chopped fresh thyme

7 soft flour tortilla wraps, cut to fit a 25cm/10 inch cake tin

200g/7oz mature Cheddar, grated

For the herb dressing

85ml/3fl oz extra virgin olive oil

25ml/1fl oz white wine vinegar

1 tablespoon honey

2 tablespoons snipped fresh chives

2 tablespoons chopped fresh flat leaf parsley

Salt and pepper

Mixed salad leaves, to serve

Serves 6

method

For the cake

- Heat the butter in a pot and gently cook the mushrooms until soft. Add the shallots and garlic. Continue cooking gently for 20 minutes until the mix is very dry. Season with salt, pepper and truffle oil, if using. Add the herbs and correct the seasoning.

- Line a cake tin (approx 25cm/10 inch diameter) with parchment paper. Cover the base with a layer of the tortillas cut to size. Then cover with a couple of tablespoons of the mushroom mixture and sprinkle some cheese on top. Repeat the layers of tortilla, mushroom mixture and cheese, finishing with the last tortilla. Place the cake tin in the fridge for at least 1 hour with some weight on top to press it down tightly.

For the herb dressing

- Gently combine the olive oil, white wine vinegar, honey and herbs with a spoon until the honey is dissolved. Correct the seasoning. The dressing should not be fully mixed through. The balsamic should stay separate from the oil.

To serve

- Slice the cake in 6 portions. Serve each slice of cake with some tossed salad leaves. Drizzle with the balsamic and olive dressing.

Steamed black sole fillets and crabmeat, in a velvet crab bisque sauce

ingredients

For the sauce

25g/1oz butter
1 large onion, chopped
1 small leek, chopped
1 celery stick, chopped
2 carrots, chopped
450g/1lb fresh velvet crabs
(see note below)
25g/1oz tomato purée
1litre/1¾ pints chicken stock,
or water
120ml/4fl oz cream

For the fish

12 black sole fillets, trimmed
and skinned (about 50g/2oz
each)
900g/2lb fresh white crabmeat
25g/1oz butter
150ml/5fl oz dry white wine
12 fresh crab toes
Salt and pepper

Sautéed spinach and creamed
potatoes, to serve

Serves 6

Note:
Velvet crabs are soft-shelled crabs
much smaller in size and more
delicate in flavour than regular
crabs. The velvet crab needs to be
very fresh and may only be cooked
within 24 hours of catching. For
this recipe the whole crabs are
used, extracting the flavours during
cooking.

method

- Preheat the oven to 180°C/350°F/
  gas mark 4.

For the sauce

- Heat the butter in a pot. Add the vegetables
  and gently cook until slightly browned. Add
  the velvet crabs and continue cooking for
  another 5 minutes. While still cooking, crush
  the crab into smaller pieces using the side
  of a cylindrical rolling pin or a heavy-duty
  potato masher. Add the tomato purée and
  sweat for 1 minute.
- Add the chicken stock or water and cook for
  a maximum of 20-25 minutes. Strain and
  reduce the liquid by two-thirds. Add the
  cream, return to the boil and strain again.
  Keep hot and correct the seasoning.

For the fish

- Season each sole fillet with salt and pepper
  and place equal amounts of crabmeat
  on each fillet. Roll up each fillet with the
  crabmeat and secure with a cocktail stick,
  if required. Place the fillets in a shallow
  buttered oven dish and pour over the white
  wine. Add the crab toes. Cover with tin foil
  and cook in the oven for 10-12 minutes.
  Remove the fillets and add the cooking
  juices/wine to the velvet crab sauce. Heal
  and reduce again.

To serve

- Arrange the sautéed spinach on warmed
  plates with two stuffed fillets on top. Serve
  with the creamed potatoes. Garnish each
  portion with 2 crab toes and pour over a
  generous amount of sauce.

Apple and clove tarte tatin with caramel ice cream

ingredients

200g/7oz caster sugar
100ml/3½fl oz water
175ml/6fl oz custard
85ml/3fl oz cream
6 apples
50g/2oz unsalted butter
6 whole cloves
50g/2oz caster sugar
6 discs puff pastry, each about
12.5cm/5 inches in diameter

Caramel ice cream, 6 fresh mint
sprigs, 25g/1oz pistachio nuts,
chopped, to serve

Serves 6

method

· Preheat the oven to 180°C/350°F/
  gas mark 4.
· Carefully bring the sugar and water to the
  boil. Clean down the sides of the pot with
  water and a brush to prevent crystallisation.
  When the mixture is caramelised pour the
  caramel into tarte tatin moulds (round
  baking moulds 12.5cm/5 inches in diameter
  and 1cm/½ inch deep).
· Combine the custard and cream and keep
  chilled.
· Peel and core each apple and slice into 8
  wedges. Melt the butter in a pan. Place
  the apple, cloves and sugar in the pan.
  Gently cook until the apples are slightly soft.
  Remove from the heat and cool. Remove
  the cloves.

· Arrange 8 apple wedges neatly on the
  caramel in the moulds and cover with a disc
  of puff pastry. Place the tarts in the oven
  for 7-8 minutes until the pastry is a golden
  brown colour. Remove from the heat and
  turn the tart upside down.

To serve

· Pour a pool of cream custard on each plate
  and place a tart in the centre. Place a scoop
  of caramel ice cream on the centre of the
  tart. Garnish with mint, then sprinkle with
  pistachio nuts and serve immediately.

Monart

There is nothing spartan about the dining experience in the restaurant at Monart, the splendid, luxurious destination spa. Although spa-type dishes are highlighted for those seeking healthier options, there is a very creative approach to all the food, which is beautifully cooked and presented and served with panache.

The Still, Enniscorthy, Co. Wexford
Ph: (053) 923 8999
www.monart.ie

starter
Honey-roast duck breast,
exotic fruit chutney and mâche salad

main course
Roast herb-crusted rack of Slaney lamb,
aubergine caviar, balsamic and poached garlic jus

dessert
Bread and butter pudding Monart style

Honey-roast duck breast, exotic fruit chutney and mâche salad

ingredients

For the duck

2 duck breasts
Sunflower oil, for frying
½ teaspoon honey

For the chutney

Olive oil
¼ teaspoon finely chopped root ginger
½ red chilli, seeded and very finely chopped
25g/1oz sugar
50ml/2fl oz Muscatel vinegar (alternatively, use rice wine vinegar)
150ml/5fl oz passion fruit purée
200g/7oz can lychees, diced (keep the liquid)
1 mango, peeled, stoned and cut into small 1cm/½ inch cubes
½ pineapple, peeled, centre removed, cut into small 1cm/½ inch cubes
4 passion fruit, scooped out flesh

Dressed mixed leaves, to serve

Serves 2

method

· Preheat the oven to 190°C/375°F/ gas mark 5.

For the duck

· Score the skin with a sharp knife. Season with salt and pepper. Heat the oil and place the duck breasts in the hot pan and get a good colour on both sides. Take off the pan and transfer to a baking dish. Brush with the honey. Allow to finish cooking in the oven for approximately 6-8 minutes for medium rare to medium and up to 10 minutes for well cooked. Allow to cool before slicing.

For the chutney

· In a pot, heat a little oil. Add the ginger and chilli and cook a little. Add the sugar and allow to caramelise. Then deglaze the pan with the vinegar. Allow to reduce a little, then add the passion fruit purée and the lychee juice and reduce by half.

· When the liquid has reduced, add the fruit and cook until soft but not a purée. When cooked put the chutney into a sieve, retaining the liquid. Then spread the fruit out onto a flat tray to allow it to cool quickly. Place the liquid in a pot, bring to the boil and reduce until slightly thick. Keep this for the sauce.

To serve

· Slice the duck thinly allowing 5 slices per person. Place the duck beside some dressed mixed salad. Pour some of the sauce from the chutney beside the duck. Take the fruit of the chutney and shape into a quenelle between 2 spoons and place on the plate.

Roast herb-crusted rack of Slaney lamb, aubergine caviar, balsamic and poached garlic jus

ingredients

For the herb crust

50g/2oz white breadcrumbs
50g/2oz butter, softened
1 tablespoon chopped fresh flat leaf parsley
1 tablespoon chopped rosemary
Juice of 1 lemon

For the lamb

2 racks of lamb
2 garlic cloves, roughly chopped
1 tablespoon roughly chopped fresh rosemary
1 tablespoon roughly chopped fresh thyme
85ml/3fl oz olive oil

For the aubergine caviar

4 aubergines
1 garlic clove, cut into slivers
8 small fresh thyme sprigs
4 tablespoons olive oil

For the jus

Olive oil
1 red onion, finely chopped
½ carrot, finely chopped
½ celery stick, finely chopped
2 garlic cloves, chopped
1 teaspoon fresh mixed herbs
150ml/5fl oz balsamic vinegar
85ml/3fl oz red wine
1 teaspoon tomato purée
700ml/1¼ pint lamb stock
Salt and pepper

Serves 4

method

· Preheat the oven to 190°C/375°F/ gas mark 5.

For the herb crust

· Combine all the ingredients in a food processor. Place the mixture between 2 sheets of parchment paper and roll out thinly.

For the lamb

· Cut the racks of lamb in half. Mix the garlic, rosemary and thyme with the olive oil and marinate the lamb in this overnight in a non-metallic dish. Heat a little oil in a pan and seal the lamb on all sides. When browned, put in a roasting tin. Place the herb crust on the skin side of the lamb before placing it in the oven for 8 minutes for medium, 12–13 minutes for well done. Allow to rest for 5 minutes before slicing.

For the aubergine caviar

· Slice the aubergines in half lengthways, put a few slits in the flesh and place some garlic and thyme in each piece. Brush with olive oil and season with salt and pepper. Put in an ovenproof dish and cook in the oven for 25-30 minutes until soft. Scoop out the flesh and mix well. Season again with salt and pepper and keep warm until ready to serve.

For the jus

· Heat a little oil in the pan. Add the vegetables and herbs and sweat until soft. Add the vinegar and reduce by two-thirds, stirring occasionally. Add the tomato purée and cook a little. Add the red wine and reduce by two-thirds, again stirring occasionally. Add the stock and reduce until

a thick sauce consistency is reached. Pass the sauce through a sieve. Return to the pot and keep warm.

To serve

· Cut the lamb into individual cutlets. Warm the plates and arrange three cutlets on each one. Add a spoonful of the aubergine caviar to the side and pour around the jus.

Bread and butter pudding Monart style

ingredients

4 croissants
3 eggs
175g/6oz caster sugar
85ml/3fl oz rum
250ml/9fl oz cream
250ml/9fl oz milk
Fresh or frozen berries (fresh in season)

Vanilla ice cream or freshly whipped cream, to serve

Serves 4

method

· Preheat the oven to 150°C/300°F/gas mark 2.
· Cut the croissants into small bite size pieces. Place in four 250ml/9fl oz ramekins (soup bowls or a suitable ovenproof equivalent).
· Beat the eggs, sugar and rum together until smooth. Then add the cream and milk and mix gently again.
· Sprinkle the berries on top of the croissants. Then add the sauce (for best results leave to soak overnight in the fridge).
· Bake in the oven for 30-35 minutes or until set. Leave to cool for five minutes.

To serve
· Serve with vanilla ice cream or freshly whipped cream on the side.

The Mustard Seed at Echo Lodge

The Mustard Seed offers exceptional hospitality in a country-house ambience, with wonderful cooking in an individual contemporary Irish style. Menus are seasonal, based on local artisan products and organic home-grown vegetables, fruit and herbs from an extensive kitchen garden. A walk in the garden is a must before dinner.

Ballingarry, Co. Limerick
Ph: (069) 68508

www.mustardseed.ie

starter
Pan-fried seabass with celeriac purée, roast wild mushroom and a basil and lemon dressing

main course
Loin of lamb with baby leeks wrapped in Parma ham, roast cherry tomatoes and pea sauce

dessert
Vanilla pannacotta
with strawberries and shortbread crumble

Pan-fried seabass with celeriac purée, roast wild mushroom and a basil and lemon dressing

ingredients

For the celeriac

250g/9oz celeriac, peeled and diced
100ml/3½fl oz cream
100ml/3½fl oz water
½ vegetable stock cube
1 bay leaf

For the mushrooms

Olive oil
150g/5oz mixed wild mushrooms, trimmed and sliced if large

For the dressing

25ml/1fl oz olive oil
Juice of 1 lemon
15 fresh basil leaves, chopped
Salt and pepper

For the seabass

4 x 75g/3oz seabass fillets (ask your fishmonger to clean and scale)
Knob of butter

Serves 4

method

For the celeriac

- Put the celeriac, cream, water, stock cube and bay leaf in a small saucepan and bring to the boil and then simmer until the celeriac is soft. Remove half of the liquid and the bay leaf and blitz the celeriac and remaining liquid in a food processor until puréed. Set aside.

For the mushrooms

- Preheat a frying pan until quite hot. Put a drizzle of oil in the pan and fry the mushrooms until golden brown. Remove from the heat and season with salt and pepper.

For the dressing

- Whisk together the oil and lemon juice and add the chopped basil. Season with salt and pepper.

For the seabass

- Heat a non-stick frying pan until hot. Season the fish with salt and pepper and rub oil on the fish, and not in the pan. Place the fish skin side down into the pan and reduce heat to a medium temperature. Let the fish cook for at least 4-5 minutes. Then remove the pan from the heat and turn the fish over, add the butter, swirling it around the pan and leave to rest for a couple of minutes.

To serve

- Heat the celeriac purée in a small pan and put into the centre of warmed plates. Place the mushrooms around the purée. Put the fish on top of the purée, drizzle with dressing and tuck in.

Loin of lamb with baby leeks wrapped in Parma ham, roast cherry tomatoes and pea sauce

ingredients

For the lamb

4 x 175g/6oz loins of lamb, well trimmed
Olive oil
4 cherry tomatoes
Salt and pepper

For the leeks

1½ litres/2½ pints of chicken stock
8 baby leeks trimmed into 7.5cm/3 inch lengths
4 slices Parma ham

For the pea sauce

50g/2oz butter
2 shallots, finely chopped
1 garlic clove, finely chopped
200g/7oz frozen peas

4 fresh rosemary sprigs, to serve

Serves 4

method

· Preheat the oven to 200°C/400°F/ gas mark 6.

For the lamb

· Season the lamb with salt and pepper. Heat some oil in a pan and brown off the meat. Then place it on a tray with the tomatoes and roast in the oven for about 5 minutes for pink lamb (8 minutes for medium or 10 minutes for well done). Let the meat rest for 3 minutes.

For the leeks

· Bring the stock to the boil. Drop in the leeks and cook for 4 minutes. Remove the leeks from the pot and plunge into cold water and set aside. Reserve the stock. While the lamb is resting, wrap two leeks in a slice of ham and roast in the oven in a small roasting tin for 2 minutes.

For the pea sauce

· Melt the butter in the pan. Add shallots and garlic and sweat until soft. Bring the stock to the boil again. Drop the peas into the boiling stock for 2-3 minutes until soft. Drain the peas and reserve some of the stock. Put the pea, shallot and garlic mixture in a food processor and blitz. Add some of the remaining stock when the motor is running until you get the consistency of cream. Set the sauce aside.

To serve

· Reheat the pea sauce in a small pan, if necessary. Place some pea sauce on the side of each warmed plate. Slice the lamb and place beside the sauce. Finally, put the tomato and Parma ham wrapped leeks on the plate and garnish with rosemary.

Vanilla pannacotta
with strawberries and shortbread crumble

ingredients

2 gelatine leaves
1 vanilla pod
120ml/4fl oz milk
300ml/10fl oz cream
100g/3oz caster sugar

200g/7oz strawberries, 4
shortbread biscuits, crushed, and
4 fresh mint sprigs, to serve

Serves 4

method

· Soak the gelatine in a bowl of cold water until it is soft. Split the vanilla pod in half lengthways, scrape out the seeds and place these in a pot with the milk, cream, and sugar. Bring to the boil, making sure the sugar is dissolved. Remove from the heat.

· Remove the gelatine from the water, squeeze dry and drop into the cream and whisk the mixture until smooth.

· Pour the mix into 4 x 150ml/5fl oz moulds or cups and place in the fridge for 4 hours until set.

To serve

· Dip the moulds into a basin of hot water to loosen them and then tip them onto 4 plates. Place the strawberries around the pannacotta. Sprinkle the crushed biscuits over the top. Decorate with the mint sprigs.

Nuremore Hotel and Country Club

The exceptionally talented chef Raymond McArdle has earned a national reputation for the restaurant at the Nuremore. Consistent and innovative, the cooking style is elegant: a meeting of modern Irish and classic cuisine. Expect great food and a great wine list; caring service; and value for money.

Carrickmacross, Co. Monaghan
Ph: (042) 966 1438
www.nuremore.com

starter
Honey-roast pigeon
with grilled Parma ham and Madeira gravy

main course
Shepherd's pie with roast root vegetables

dessert
Lasagne of pineapple and Asian fruits
with pina colada sorbet

Honey-roast pigeon
with grilled Parma ham and Madeira gravy

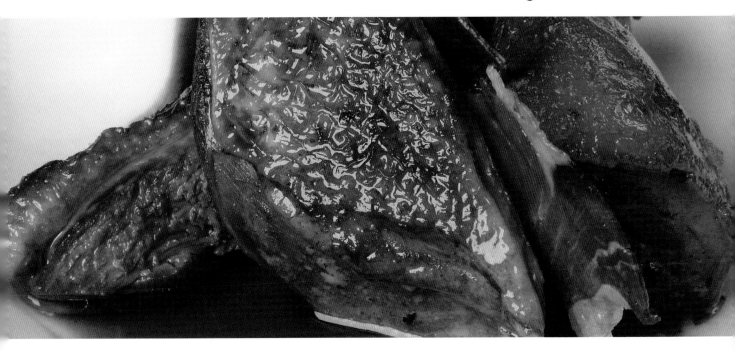

ingredients

For the pigeons

1 tablespoon olive oil
2 oven-ready pigeons
1 tablespoon honey

For the Madeira gravy

1 tablespoon olive oil
1 shallot, chopped
1 garlic clove, sliced
1 fresh thyme sprig
300ml/10fl oz Madeira
300ml/10fl oz gravy (good quality)
4 thin slices Parma ham
Salt and pepper

Serves 4

method

· Preheat the oven to 180°C/350°F/ gas mark 4.

For the pigeons

· Heat the olive oil in a non-stick pan. Season the pigeons with salt and pepper. Put in the pan and colour on all sides. Remove from the pan and brush with the honey. Put on a small tray and roast in the oven for 8-10 minutes. Take out and rest. They should be nice and pink. For well done, roast for a further 5 minutes.

For the Madeira gravy

· Heat a pan with the oil. Add the shallot and garlic to the hot pan and cook over a low heat until they soften and caramelise to a golden brown. Stir regularly. Add the thyme followed by the Madeira. Bring to the boil and then reduce by half. Then add the gravy.

· Bring the sauce to a simmer and skim off any fat. Cook for 10 minutes on a medium heat and pass through a fine sieve into a clean pot and reheat gently to finish.

· Grill the Parma ham until crispy.

To serve

· Remove the legs and breasts of the pigeons and put a leg and breast on each warmed plate. Spoon over a little Madeira sauce and place a piece of the crisp Parma ham on top of each one.

Shepherd's pie with roast root vegetables

ingredients

For the pie

4 large potatoes
1½ tablespoons softened butter
½ tablespoon olive oil
1 onion, finely chopped
1 carrot, finely diced
900g/2lb lean minced lamb
600ml/l pint gravy or stock
1 teaspoon chopped fresh rosemary
2 tablespoons Worcestershire sauce
1 egg
1 tablespoon milk (optional)

For the root vegetables

Butter and oil, to fry
1 celeriac, diced into large pieces
2 carrots, thickly sliced
2 parsnips, thickly sliced
½ turnip, diced into large pieces
1 fresh thyme sprig
Salt and pepper

Serves 4

method

- Preheat the oven to 180°C/350°F/ gas mark 4.

For the pie

- Peel and halve the potatoes. Put them in a pot of boiling, salted water and cook until tender. Drain, mash with some butter and season to taste. Add milk depending on your preferred consistency.

- Heat a deep pot and add ½ tablespoon butter and the oil. When the butter is melted, add the onion and carrot. Cook slowly until soft. Add the minced lamb and cook until well coloured.

- Add the gravy or stock to the mince and cook on a low heat for 45 minutes. Add the rosemary and season well with salt and pepper. Add the Worcestershire sauce.

- Beat the egg and milk. Place the mince into an ovenproof dish. Cover with the mash and brush with the egg and milk mixture. Place the pie in the oven until the mash is glazed and crisp. This will take 10-15 minutes.

For the root vegetables

- Heat the butter and the oil in a hot pan. Add the root vegetables and season well. Brown the vegetables all over. Then put in a roasting tray or casserole dish, add the thyme and cook in the oven until tender and lightly caramelised. This will take approximately 20-25 minutes depending on personal taste.

To serve

- Place a portion of the pie on each warm plate and serve with the roast root vegetables on the side.

Lasagne of pineapple and Asian fruits with pina colada sorbet

ingredients

For the lasagne

300ml/10fl oz water
100g/4oz caster sugar
3 vanilla pods, each split in half
12 very thin slices pineapple
1 passion fruit
1 paw paw
1 mango
6 lychees
1 papaya
1 pomegranate

For the pina colada sorbet

250ml/9fl oz coconut milk
250ml/9fl oz vanilla custard
(shop-bought or home-made)
1 tablespoon white rum
150ml/5fl oz pineapple juice

Serves 4

method

For the lasagne

· Make a stock syrup by boiling the water with the sugar and one vanilla pod until it forms a syrup consistency. Marinate the pineapple slices in the stock syrup and another of the vanilla pods. Scrape the seeds from the remaining vanilla pod and the passion fruit.

· Finely dice all the other fruits, discarding all the skin and stones, and mix together in a bowl. Layer up the lasagne on plates, starting with the pineapple slices then the diced fruits to create three layers. Cover with clingfilm and reserve any excess fruits in a separate covered bowl. Put in the fridge until ready to serve.

For the pina colada sorbet

· Mix the coconut milk, custard, rum and pineapple juice. Pour into an ice cream machine and churn until ready.

To serve

· Remove the lasagnes of pineapple and Asian fruits from the fridge and take off the clingfilm. Spoon the sorbet on top. Decorate with the reserved excess fruits.

The Old Convent

The Old Convent, Dermot and Christine Gannon's luxurious 'gourmet hideway', is located in one of the most unspoilt and lovely parts of the country. It offers an exceptional eight-course set menu that changes daily, featuring innovative, stunning, precise cooking that emphasises local organic food. The very fair price for this feast makes it great value.

Mount Anglesby, Clogheen, Co. Tipperary
Ph: (052) 746 5565

www.theoldconvent.ie

starter
Air-dried lamb and goat's cheese salad

main course
Seared scallops
with sweet potato and coconut velouté

dessert
Irish mint ice cream martini

Air-dried lamb and goat's cheese salad

ingredients

1 cantaloupe melon
1 tablespoon sugar
2 tablespoons white wine vinegar
½ tablespoon chopped fresh mint
Mixed salad leaves
1 packet thinly sliced air-dried lamb (McGeough's, available in delicatessens). Alternatively use 8 slices prosciutto or Parma ham
4 tablespoons soft goat's cheese (preferably Ardsallagh)
Balsamic vinegar
Olive oil

Crusty bread, to serve

Serves 4

method

· Scoop the flesh of the melon into balls with a small scoop or melon baller. Mix the melon balls with sugar, vinegar and mint leaves in a non-metallic bowl and leave to marinate for 1 hour.

To serve

· Divide salad leaves onto 4 plates and top with the air-dried lamb, goat's cheese and pickled melon, draining off any excess liquid. Drizzle with balsamic vinegar and olive oil. Serve with crusty bread.

Seared scallops
with sweet potato and coconut velouté

ingredients

For the sweet potato

2 large sweet potatoes, peeled and cubed

Olive oil

600ml/1 pint chicken stock

40g/1½oz butter

1 lime leaf

½ lemon grass stick, bruised

150ml/5fl oz coconut milk

For the scallops

2 tablespoons peanut oil

12 large scallops, cleaned and roes removed

Salt and freshly ground pepper

Serves 4

method

· Preheat the oven to 190°C/375°F/ gas mark 5.

For the sweet potato

· Place the potatoes into a roasting dish and coat with a little olive oil. Roast the potatoes for approximately 40-45 minutes until soft. Remove the potatoes from the oven. When cool, chop and place into a pot with chicken stock over a medium high heat. Stir in the butter until melted. Add the lime leaf, lemon grass and coconut milk and heat.

· Remove from the heat and remove the lime leaf and lemon grass stick. Place the mixture into a blender and whizz until smooth. Pour the mixture through a sieve. Season to taste with salt and pepper. Keep warm until the scallops are ready.

For the scallops

· Heat a heavy-based frying pan over a high heat until smoking. Add the peanut oil to the pan. Add the scallops and sear for 1 minute on each side. The scallops should be warm in the middle. Remove the scallops from the pan.

To serve

· Spoon the sweet potato and coconut velouté into each warmed bowl. Place 3 scallops on top.

Irish mint ice cream martini

ingredients

About 350g/12oz vanilla ice cream (good quality)

About 6 tablespoons Baileys Irish Cream

About 4 tablespoons Crème de Menthe

Flavoured sugar, fresh mint leaves, chocolate shavings or cocoa powder, to decorate.

Serves 4

method

· Put the vanilla ice cream in a blender and blend to taste with the Baileys Irish Cream and Crème de Menthe. Of course you can adjust the quantity of ice cream according to how many you are serving, and add liqueurs to taste. Pour the mixture into martini glasses.

To serve

· For an extra touch coat the rim of the glass with flavoured sugar or decorate with mint leaves, chocolate shavings or cocoa powder.

One Pico

One Pico is among Dublin's most popular fine-dining restaurants. Under the supervision of Chef Patron Eamonn O'Reilly, a previous winner of the Irish 'Chef of the Year' award, it has been critically acclaimed by all major food writers and guide books and awarded a '3-star exceptional' rating by Frommer's Guide. The cooking is excellent and the style up to the minute: sophisticated classic French, with a twist.

5-6 Molesworth Place, Schoolhouse Lane, Dublin 2
Ph: (01) 676 0300

www.onepico.com

starter

Beetroot and goat's cheese salad
with red chard and caramelised walnuts

main course

Butter-roasted turbot
with caramelised duck and Puy lentils

dessert

Vanilla cheesecake mousse with berry compote

Beetroot and goat's cheese salad with red chard and caramelised walnuts

ingredients

25g/1oz butter
1 teaspoon sugar
1 tablespoon chopped walnuts
100g/4oz fresh goat's cheese
25ml/1fl oz cream
1 tablespoon chopped fresh basil, chive and flat leaf parsley, plus extra to garnish
25g/1oz honey
1 teaspoon fresh lemon juice
4 cooked beetroots
1½ tablespoons red wine vinegar
6 tablespoons extra virgin olive oil
Salt and pepper

1 tablespoon toasted pine nuts, 12 red chard leaves and 12 wild rocket leaves, to serve

Serves 4

method

· Melt the butter and sugar in a pan until it turns a blond caramel colour. Add the walnuts and stir until coated, then remove from the pan and allow to cool, preferably on a silicone mat to prevent sticking.

· Crumble the goat's cheese into the blender. Slowly add the cream. When smooth, add in the herbs, honey and lemon juice, and mix again. Season to taste and place in a piping bag.

· Thinly slice the beetroot into 24 slices. Finely dice the end pieces of the beetroot and retain 1 tablespoon of diced beetroot.

· Pipe little mounds of the goats cheese sandwiched between two slices of beetroot. Place 3 per person on a plate.

· Mix the vinegar, olive oil and diced beetroot for the dressing. Season to taste with salt and pepper.

To serve

· Drizzle the dressing around the beetroot sandwiches. Scatter some pine nuts and herbs over the plates and garnish with the red chard and rocket leaves.

Butter-roasted turbot
with caramelised duck and Puy lentils

ingredients

For the sauce

Olive oil
2 shallots, finely chopped
1½ garlic cloves, finely chopped
½ teaspoon chopped fresh thyme
85ml/3fl oz red wine
25ml/1fl oz chicken stock

For the lentils

2 shallots, finely chopped
1½ garlic gloves, finely chopped
1 teaspoon chopped fresh thyme
100g/4oz Puy lentils, cooked
Squeeze of lime juice
2 teaspoons chopped fresh mixed flat leaf parsley, tarragon and chive

For the turbot

4 x 200g/7oz turbot fillets, skinned and boned
1 teaspoon fresh lemon juice
50g/2oz butter
Pinch of curry powder

For the duck

Olive oil
1 duck leg or 12 little pieces of duck confit
1 teaspoon honey

Serves 4

method

For the sauce

- In a hot pan, heat a little oil. Cook the shallots, garlic and thyme until translucent. Add the red wine and stock. Reduce the sauce by two-thirds. Simmer until it is the required consistency.

For the lentils

- In a separate pan sauté the shallots and garlic. Add the thyme and the cooked Puy lentils. Add a squeeze of lime and the chopped herbs. Keep warm until ready to serve.

For the turbot

- In a hot non-stick pan, place the turbot and cook for 2 minutes on each side, presentation side down first. Adjust the seasoning and add the lemon juice and butter plus a pinch of curry powder and continue to baste the turbot for 1 minute with the butter spices. Take out of the pan. Rest for 1 minute.

For the duck

- Heat a little oil in a heavy-based frying pan. Fry the pieces of duck confit with the honey in a very hot pan until caramelised.

To serve

- Arrange the Puy lentils in the middle of warmed plates. Place the turbot on top of each one and garnish with the duck. Spoon over the sauce.

Vanilla cheesecake mousse with berry compote

ingredients

For the biscuit topping

6 plain Hobnob biscuits (or other biscuits of your choice)
25g/1oz caster sugar

For the berry compote

100g/4oz frozen mixed berries
50g/2oz caster sugar

For the filling

150g/5oz cream cheese
25g/1oz caster sugar
1 vanilla pod, split and seeds scraped out
50g/2oz double cream
1 teaspoon fresh lemon juice

Serves 4

method

· Preheat the oven to 200°C/400°F/ gas mark 6.

For the biscuit topping

· Crush the biscuits to a rough crumble texture. Sprinkle with sugar and place on a baking sheet. Put in the oven for 5-10 minutes to caramelise. Cool and set aside, then break up.

For the berry compote

· Heat the berries and sugar in a pan for 10 minutes until the mixture is reduced to a thick compote. Set aside and allow to cool.

For the filling

· Put the cream cheese, sugar and the seeds from the vanilla pod into a mixing bowl. Whisk on a low setting until it is mixed well. Now add the cream, a little at a time, mixing all the time to ensure there are no lumps. Then add the lemon juice and whisk until the mixture starts to thicken. As soon as the mixture becomes thick turn the machine off. Spoon into a piping bag ready to pipe.

To serve

· Put some compote into each martini glass, then pipe in the cheesecake mousse. Finally, sprinkle over the caramelised biscuit.

Park Hotel Kenmare

The magnificent classical dining room at the Park Hotel Kenmare is exquisite, and the kitchen is widely regarded as distinguished. The cooking here is superb: with the emphasis on simplicity, it ensures that the flavours of good-quality, locally sourced raw materials are merely enhanced. It all adds up to an exceptional dining experience.

Kenmare, Co. Kerry
Ph: (064) 664 1200
www.parkkenmare.com

starter
Warm salad of St Tola goat's cheese,
balsamic glaze strawberries, pear and rocket salad

main course
Coffee-rubbed fillet of Irish beef
on glazed pearl onions and baby spinach

dessert
Glazed lemon tart with raspberry sorbet

Warm salad of St Tola goat's cheese, balsamic glaze strawberries, pear and rocket salad

ingredients

300ml/10fl oz balsamic vinegar
150g/5oz sugar
4 brioche slices, toasted
4 x 100g/4oz slices of St Tola goat's cheese
50g/2oz sliced almonds
12 fresh strawberries, hulled and halved
1 pear
200g/7oz fresh rocket
3-4 tablespoons French dressing

Serves 4

method

· Preheat the oven to 180°C/350°F/gas mark 4
· In a small pot, bring the balsamic vinegar and sugar to the boil and reduce to a syrup texture. Leave to cool.
· Place the toasted brioche slices on a baking sheet, place the goat's cheese slices on top and sprinkle with the sliced almonds. Bake in the oven for approximately 8-10 minutes until golden brown.
· In a small bowl, mix the fresh strawberries with the cold balsamic glaze. De-core the pear and cut into thin segments.
· Mix the rocket leaves with a little French dressing.

To serve

· Divide the rocket leaves among the plates. Scatter over the pear and balsamic strawberries. Top with the warm goat's cheese toasts and serve immediately.

Coffee-rubbed fillet of Irish beef on glazed pearl onions and baby spinach

ingredients

4 x 225g/8oz Irish beef fillets

For the onion and spinach

250g/9oz pearl onions
200ml/7fl oz red wine
100g/4oz honey
1 fresh rosemary sprig
1 fresh thyme sprig
200g/7oz baby spinach
200ml/7fl oz port jus

For the coffee rub

1 teaspoon dried thyme
1 teaspoon paprika
1 teaspoon freshly ground coffee
1 teaspoon dried red chilli flakes

For the port jus

1 garlic clove, finely chopped
1 onion, chopped
1 fresh rosemary sprig, chopped
1 fresh thyme sprig, chopped
1 tablespoon tomato purée
25g/1oz plain flour
400ml/14fl oz beef stock
100ml/3½fl oz port
Salt and black pepper

Serves 4

method

- Preheat the oven to 180°C/350°F/ gas mark 4.

For the onions and spinach

- In a hot pan, heat the oil and fry the pearl onions. Add the red wine, honey, rosemary and thyme. Place the onion mixture in an ovenproof dish and cover. Braise in the oven for 15-20 minutes until tender. Remove the herb sprigs and leave to cool.

- When ready to serve, mix the baby spinach into the onions and cook for another 2-3 minutes until the spinach has wilted and the pearl onions have warmed through.

For the coffee-rubbed steaks

- In a small bowl, combine all the ingredients for the coffee rub and mix well. Season the fillet steaks with the salt and pepper. Rub the coffee mix on the steaks and rest for 2 minutes.

- On a hot, oiled griddle pan, seal the steaks quickly on both sides. Transfer to a baking tin and cook in the oven for 8-10 minutes until cooked medium. Rest for 3-4 minutes before serving.

For the port jus

- In a pot sauté the garlic, onion and herbs until soft. Add the tomato purée. Remove from the heat, add the flour and cook out the flour. Heat the stock and add to the mixture. Reduce by half. Add the port and reduce further to a sauce consistency. Strain and keep warm.

To serve

- Place some onion and spinach in the middle of warmed plates and put the steaks on top. Serve with the port jus.

Glazed lemon tart with raspberry sorbet

ingredients

For the sweet pastry

175g/6oz butter, at room temperature
175g/6oz caster sugar
275g/10oz plain flour, plus extra for dusting
1 egg

For the raspberry sorbet

200g/7oz caster sugar
200ml/7fl oz water
450g/1lb fresh raspberries, plus extra to decorate

For the lemon mix

200ml/7fl oz fresh lemon juice
175g/6oz caster sugar
300ml/10fl oz cream
6 eggs
Zest of 2 lemons
Icing sugar

Serves 6-8

method

- Preheat the oven to 180°C/350°F/ gas mark 4.

For the sweet pastry

- In an electric mixer, cream the butter and sugar together until smooth. Add the flour and egg and blend again. Do not over-mix. Wrap in clingfilm and chill for at least two hours.
- Roll out the pastry and line a 23cm/9 inch loose-bottomed tart tin. Prick with a fork and place a piece of baking parchment paper on top. Then fill the tin with baking beans (or any dried beans) to prevent the pastry from rising. Bake in the oven for 8 minutes, then remove the paper and beans and return to the oven for another 7 minutes or until the pastry is cooked.

For the raspberry sorbet

- Combine the sugar, water and raspberries together and purée in a food processor until smooth. Pass through a fine sieve. Turn the mixture into an ice cream machine and churn according to the manufacturer's instructions. Keep frozen until ready to serve.

For the lemon mix

- In a pot, heat the lemon juice and sugar, boil and reduce to a syrup.
- In another pot, heat the cream. Do not let boil.
- In a bowl, whisk the eggs, add the hot syrup and the hot cream, and then the lemon zest.

- Pour into the pre-baked tartlet case. Reduce the oven temperature to 150°C/300°F/gas mark 2 and bake for about 20 minutes until jelly-like in the centre.
- Remove from the oven and chill for 4 hours. With a blow-torch, glaze with some icing sugar on top. Cut into slices.

To serve

- Place a piece of tart on each plate, decorate with the fresh raspberries and serve each one with a scoop of the raspberry sorbet.

Pearl Brasserie

Sophisticated yet friendly and relaxed, Pearl Brasserie is one of Dublin's leading restaurants. Here, the gifted Michelin-recommended chef-patron Sebastian Masi cooks with flair and offers unusual and beautifully presented dishes. He is loved for the assured, contemporary spin he brings to his classic French training and wide experience.

20 Merrion Street Upper, Dublin 2
Ph: (01) 661 3572
www.pearl-brasserie.com

starter
Fresh and smoked salmon tartare
with horseradish vinaigrette

main course
Baked loin of rabbit stuffed with prawns

dessert
Lemon tart

Fresh and smoked salmon tartare with horseradish vinaigrette

ingredients

For the salmon

275g/10oz fresh salmon, skinned and boned

150g/5oz smoked salmon slices

1 apple, peeled, cored and diced

1 red onion, diced

1 tomato, peeled, seeded and diced

1 celery stick, diced

1 teaspoon snipped fresh chives

1 teaspoon chopped fresh dill

A little fresh lemon juice

Drop of Tabasco sauce

A little olive oil

For the horseradish dressing

1 tablespoon mascarpone cheese

½ tablespoon maple syrup

½ tablespoon sherry vinegar

½ tablespoon freshly grated horseradish

Salt and pepper

Lightly dressed mixed salad leaves, to serve

Serves 4

method

For the salmon

· Dice the fresh and smoked salmon as small as possible and mix. Add all the remaining ingredients to the salmon and season to your liking with lemon juice, Tabasco, olive oil and pepper. Do not add salt as the smoked salmon can be salty enough.

For the horseradish dressing

· Simply mix all the ingredients together, season with salt and pepper and leave to rest for 1 hour.

To serve

· Place spoonfuls of the salmon in rounds on a plate and drizzle the dressing around the salmon tartare. Serve garnished with a salad of mixed leaves.

Baked loin of rabbit stuffed with prawns

ingredients

For the rabbit jus

Olive oil
1 carrot, chopped
1 celery stick, chopped
1 onion, chopped
1 garlic clove, chopped
1 leek, chopped
½ teaspoon fresh thyme leaves
2 glasses red wine

For the rabbit

2 whole rabbits, including the kidneys (ask your butcher to remove all bones and give them to you for the jus)
1 egg
4 jumbo prawns
Salt and pepper

Boiled potatoes and a green vegetable, to serve

Serves 4

method

- Preheat the oven to 190°C/375°F/ gas mark 5.

For the rabbit jus

- Heat a little oil in a pot. Add the vegetables and thyme with the rabbit bones. Add the red wine and enough water to cover the vegetables. Bring to the boil and then reduce by half. Reduce the heat and cook slowly on a low heat for 30 minutes. Pass through a sieve and strain. Put back on the heat, bring to the boil and reduce to a jus.

For the rabbit

- Make a farce (stuffing) using the meat from the legs and kidneys. Put the leg meat and kidneys into a food processor. Add the egg. Blend to a smooth paste.
- Open the rabbit loins and season with salt and pepper. Divide the farce on the loins

and on the lap of the rabbits (the lap is the skin above the cutlets).

- Place 2 prawns on top of each one. Roll the loin back over the farce and let the lap make a seal. Butter one long sheet of foil and roll the loin in it tightly until sealed and refrigerate for 30 minutes. Do the same with the other loin.
- In a hot, large ovenproof pan, lightly seal the rabbit in tin foil parcels and then put into the hot oven for 12 minutes.
- Remove from the oven and leave to rest. Remove the foil and carve.

To serve

- Heat the jus and drizzle over warmed plates. Place several slices of the rabbit on top. Serve with the boiled potatoes and a green vegetable.

Lemon tart

ingredients

For the pastry

250g/9oz plain flour, plus extra
for dusting

75g/3oz caster sugar

50g/2oz ground almonds

175g/6oz butter, softened

1 egg yolk, beaten

1 egg, beaten

Zest of 1 lemon

For the filling

3 eggs, beaten

100g/4oz caster sugar

100ml/3½fl oz lemon juice

Zest of 1 lemon

100g/4oz crème fraîche

175g/6oz fresh raspberries, and
icing sugar, to serve

Serves 6

method

- Preheat the oven to 160°C/325°F/
gas mark 3.

For the pastry

- In a bowl, mix together all the dry
ingredients. Add the butter and mix
thoroughly. Finally, add the egg yolk, beaten
egg and lemon zest. When the pastry is
done, rest in the fridge for 1 hour before
rolling on a lightly floured surface.

- Line a 23cm/9 inch loose-bottomed tart tin
with the pastry. Prick with a fork and place
a piece of baking parchment paper on top.
Then fill the tin with baking beans (or any
dried beans) to prevent the pastry from
rising. Bake in the oven for 5 minutes, then
remove the paper and beans and return to
the oven for another 5 minutes or until the
pastry is cooked. Allow to cool.

For the filling

- Mix the eggs and the sugar together into
a smooth paste. Add all the rest of the
ingredients and mix again.

- Pour the mix into the pre-baked pastry. Cook
in the oven for 20 minutes until just set
but still with a slight wobble in the middle.
Allow to cool for 1 hour.

To serve

- Decorate the top of the tart with some of
the raspberries. Lightly sprinkle icing sugar
on top. Serve with the remaining raspberries
on the side.

Peploe's

Stylish and sophisticated, Peploe's is one of Dublin's most talked-about establishments, serving great food and seriously good wine at reasonable prices. This is a good place to eat at any time of the afternoon or evening, offering à la carte, pre-concert and small plate menus.

16 St. Stephen's Green, Dublin 2
Ph: (01) 676 3144
www.peploes.com

starter
Gravadlax with dill-mustard sauce and brown toast

main course
Roast venison with confit root vegetables, seasonal mushrooms and blackberry sauce

dessert
Rhubarb and strawberry crumble with vanilla ice cream

Gravadlax with dill-mustard sauce and brown toast

ingredients

For the gravadlax

150g/5oz coarse sea salt
225g/8oz sugar
12 black peppercorns
12 juniper berries
1 tablespoon mustard seeds
900g/2lb salmon fillets (centre piece, pin boned, skin on)
100g/4oz fresh dill, chopped
3 bay leaves

For the dill-mustard sauce

2 tablespoons Dijon mustard
1 tablespoon caster sugar
1 tablespoon honey
½ tablespoon white wine vinegar
150ml/5fl oz sunflower oil
4 tablespoons chopped fresh dill
Salt and pepper

Mixed lettuce leaves, boiled egg quarters (optional), and toasted good quality brown bread, to serve

Serves 8

method

For the gravadlax

- Combine the salt, sugar, peppercorns, juniper berries and mustard seeds in a food processor and blend for 30 seconds. Wash and dry the salmon fillet, making sure that it is free of any bones.
- Spread half of the salt and sugar mixture onto the bottom of a deep dish. Place the salmon on top, skin side down and cover with the dill and bay leaves. Spread the remainder of the salt and sugar mixture over the salmon and cover tightly with clingfilm.
- Keep the salmon for 24 hours in the fridge, then turn over the fillet and marinate for a further 24 hours.
- At the end of the two days, remove the salmon from the marinade and soak for 10 minutes in cold water. Pat the salmon dry, rub with a little oil and wrap tightly in clingfilm.
- The salmon will keep for 2 weeks in the fridge.

For the dill-mustard sauce

- Combine the mustard, sugar, honey and vinegar in a bowl and whisk together. Add the oil slowly, whisking all the time until you have a smooth mixture. Add the dill and season with salt and pepper.

To serve

- Slice the salmon thinly with a long sharp knife and arrange on the plates. Drizzle with the mustard sauce. Garnish each plate with some lettuce and quarter of a boiled egg (optional). Serve with a basket of the brown bread.

Roast venison with confit root vegetables, seasonal mushrooms and blackberry sauce

ingredients

1 small turnip
1 small celeriac
2 large carrots
200g/7oz duck or goose fat
Oil and butter for frying
900g/2lb venison, boneless
(loin or rump)
1 fresh rosemary sprig
10 juniper berries
175g/6oz wild mushrooms,
trimmed, and sliced if large
25ml/1fl oz fruit-based vinegar
(e.g. raspberry or redcurrant)
100ml/3½fl oz red port
100ml/3½fl oz red wine
200ml/7fl oz chicken or beef
stock
Pinch of sugar
20 fresh blackberries
Salt and freshly ground black
pepper

Roast or mashed potatoes, to
serve

Serves 4

method

· Peel and cut the root vegetables into similar sized cubes. Heat the duck or goose fat in a medium sized saucepan. Gently cook the vegetable cubes in the fat. They should be completely submerged. When soft, drain the vegetables and put aside in a warm place. Keep the duck or goose fat for future use.

· Heat some oil and a knob of butter in a frying pan. Season the venison with salt and pepper and fry with the rosemary and the juniper berries on a medium heat for 6-8 minutes on each side for medium rare/medium.

· When cooked, remove from the pan and leave to rest in a warm place.

· Reheat the pan again with a little more oil and butter. Sauté the mushrooms until cooked. Keep warm until ready to serve.

· Deglaze the pan with the vinegar, port and red wine and reduce by three quarters. Add the stock and reduce until the sauce slightly thickens. Season with a little salt, pepper and sugar and pass through a sieve into a clean saucepan. Add the blackberries. Heat up, but do not allow to boil.

To serve

· Season the root vegetables with salt and pepper and reheat for 2 minutes in a hot oven. Arrange neatly on pre-warmed plates together with the carved venison slices, sautéed wild mushrooms and the sauce. Simple roast or mashed potatoes are a perfect accompaniment for this dish.

Rhubarb and strawberry crumble with vanilla ice cream

ingredients

For the crumble

200g/7oz butter, at room temperature
150g/5oz plain flour
125g/4½oz caster sugar
75g/3oz ground almonds
100g/4oz ginger nut biscuits

For the rhubarb and strawberry filling

400g/14oz rhubarb, trimmed
50g/2oz unsalted butter
75g/3oz caster sugar
250g/9oz strawberries, hulled

Vanilla ice cream, to serve

Serves 4

method

- Preheat the oven to 180°C/350°F/ gas mark 4.

For the crumble

- Combine the butter, flour, sugar, almonds and ginger nut biscuits in a food processor and grind to a fine mixture. Line a baking sheet with parchment paper or greaseproof paper.
- Spread the mixture onto the sheet to a depth of about 1cm/½ inch. Bake for 5-10 minutes until golden brown, occasionally turning the mixture with a spatula until evenly coloured. Remove from the oven and allow to fully cool down.
- Once cool, the mix will harden again. Break it into sizeable chunks and blend it once again in the food processor until it is ground into small pieces.

For the rhubarb and strawberry filling

- Peel the rhubarb and chop into 2.5cm/1 inch pieces. Heat the butter in a large frying pan. When the butter is hot and foaming, add the rhubarb and fry over a high heat until it is soft and lightly coloured, constantly moving the pieces around. Add the sugar and toss until dissolved, then drain over a small colander and allow to cool.
- Spread the rhubarb into the bottom of an ovenproof dish. Cut the strawberries into quarters or halves and place on top of the rhubarb. Cover the rhubarb and strawberries with a generous layer of the crumble and bake in the oven for 10 minutes.

To serve

- Spoon the crumble into warmed bowls and serve with vanilla ice cream.

Rathsallagh House

Rathsallagh House Hotel & Golf Club is owned and run by the hospitable O'Flynn family. The beguiling Kitchen Bar is an ideal place to peruse a menu that changes daily and is based on local seasonal produce, much of it from Rathsallagh's own farm and kitchen garden. The working kitchen is in the skilled hands of head chef John Kostuik, and provides Irish country-house cooking at its best: fresh, visually attractive and served with a smile.

Dunlavin, Co. Wicklow
Ph: (045) 403 112
www.rathsallagh.com

starter
Tartare of tuna spiked with lime and sesame, with lime crisps and mango-basil vinaigrette

main course
Lime, honey and soy marinated chicken supreme with pak choi and coriander sauce

dessert
Ginger pudding
with banana sorbet and chocolate sauce

Tartare of tuna spiked with lime and sesame, with lime crisps and mango-basil vinaigrette

ingredients

For the tuna

400g/14oz fresh tuna, finely diced
1 shallot, finely diced or minced
½ cucumber, peeled, seeded and finely diced or minced
1 celery stick, finely diced or minced
Zest of 1 lime
½ teaspoon sesame oil
Small pinch of sesame seeds

For the lime crisps

225g/8oz plain flour
3 tablespoons caster sugar
3 tablespoons Wasabi powder
2 tablespoons melted butter
6 tablespoons fresh lime juice
Water

For the mango-basil vinaigrette

1 ripe mango, peeled, stoned and chopped
5 fresh basil leaves
25ml/1fl oz sherry vinegar
40ml/1½fl oz olive oil
Salt and pepper

Baby green leaves and baby or chopped pickled vegetables, to serve

Serves 4-6

method

- Preheat the oven to 160°C/325°F/ gas mark 3.

For the tuna

- Mix all the ingredients together in a bowl. Season with salt and pepper.

For the lime crisps

- Mix the flour, sugar and Wasabi powder, then stir in the butter and lime juice to make a paste. Add just enough water to make the paste spreadable. Allow to stand for 10 minutes. Add a little more water if the paste is too thick to spread evenly.
- Spread the paste thinly on a silicone mat or a greased baking sheet in circles of 7.5cm/3 inches in diameter, allowing 3 per portion. Bake for 6 minutes. Leave in the oven with the door open for 5 minutes to crisp them up.

For the mango-basil vinaigrette

- Blend the mango and basil with the vinegar. Slowly pour in the olive oil and blend again. Strain through a fine sieve into a clean bowl.

To serve

- For each portion, place some salad leaves in the centre of the plate. Place one crisp on top. Cover with tuna and repeat the process. Top off with a crisp and garnish with a spoonful of pickled vegetables. Drizzle the mango vinaigrette around the plate.

Lime, honey and soy marinated chicken supreme with pak choi and coriander sauce

ingredients

For the sauce

100g/4oz butter, softened
25g/1oz fresh coriander, stalks removed and chopped
Juice of ½ lemon
150ml/5fl oz white wine
250ml/8½fl oz dark chicken stock, good quality

For the chicken

175ml/7fl oz honey
Juice and zest of 2 limes
150ml/5fl oz sweet soy sauce
4 x 200g/7oz chicken breast fillets, skin on
2-3 tablespoons vegetable oil

For the pak choi

4 baby pak choi, split lengthwise
2 tablespoons vegetable oil
1 teaspoon sesame oil (optional)
1 thumb-sized piece fresh root ginger, peeled and cut into very thin strips
1 tablespoon butter, softened
Salt and pepper to season

Fried mushrooms, to serve (optional)

Serves 4

method

- Preheat the oven to 180°C/350°F/ gas mark 4.

For the sauce

- In a food processor blend the butter, coriander and lemon juice until fully mixed. Spread out in log form on a piece of clingfilm and roll. Refrigerate until firm. You will only need a small portion of this. It will stay good for about 6 months in the freezer. Whenever you need it, just take a hot knife and cut what you require.
- Put the wine in a pot, bring to the boil and reduce slightly. Add the chicken stock, bring back to the boil and reduce by half. Remove from the heat and whisk in some of the coriander butter until the sauce thickens. Do not put back on the heat or the sauce will split. Keep warm.

For the chicken

- Mix the honey with the lime juice and zest. Whisk in the soy sauce. Cover the chicken breasts in the marinade for 1-4 hours.
- Pour the vegetable oil into a heavy-bottomed frying pan on a medium heat. Pat the chicken breasts until dry and lightly season with pepper. Place the chicken, skin side down, in the pan. Fry to crisp the skin (about 1-2 minutes) being careful not to burn. Turn over and brown the bottom for 1 minute.
- Put in a roasting tin lined with parchment paper, skin side up, and cook in the oven for about 15 minutes or until the juices run clear. Check it every few minutes to make sure the honey is not burning. Turn it twice during this period.

For the pak choi

- Blanch the pak choi for 1 minute in salted boiling water. Drain. Heat a wok or deep-sided pan. Add the vegetable oil and sesame oil and then add the ginger and butter. Carefully add the pak choi and stir fry for 1 minute.

To serve

- Put the chicken on warmed plates add some pak choi. Scatter mushrooms on the chicken and around the plate (optional). Drizzle around the sauce.

Ginger pudding
with banana sorbet and chocolate sauce

ingredients

For the ginger pudding

75g/3oz butter, plus extra for greasing

75g/3oz brown sugar

100g/4oz honey

100g/4oz treacle

½ teaspoon ground ginger

¼ teaspoon ground cinnamon

120ml/4fl oz milk

1 egg, lightly beaten

150g/5oz plain flour

½ teaspoon bicarbonate of soda

For the banana sorbet

(or use your favourite ice cream or sorbet)

1kg/2¼lb bananas, weight after peeling

Juice of 4 lemons

600ml/1 pint milk

1 cinnamon stick

450g/1lb sugar syrup or glucose

For the chocolate sauce

170ml/6fl oz water

40g/1½oz caster sugar

100g/4oz cocoa

Serves 12

method

· Preheat the oven to 150°C/300°F/gas mark 2.

For the ginger pudding

· Heat the butter, brown sugar, honey, treacle, ginger and cinnamon in a pot. When just boiled, take off the heat and allow to cool. Then add the milk and egg. Sieve the flour and bicarbonate of soda and add to the mixture. Mix well with a hand whisk.

· Pour into buttered ramekins to half fill them. Arrange on a baking sheet and bake for 15 minutes until well risen and firm to the touch.

For the banana sorbet

· Slice the bananas into quarters long ways and remove the seeds. Slice into small pieces and place in the lemon juice.

· Bring the milk to the boil with the cinnamon stick and allow to cool. Blend the banana and lemon juice, sugar syrup or glucose and milk until smooth. Churn in an ice cream machine until set. Store in the freezer.

For the chocolate sauce

· Bring the water, sugar and cocoa to the boil, stirring until the sugar has dissolved. Cool and blitz in a blender until smooth.

To serve

· Place the pudding in the centre of each plate and put a scoop of sorbet next to it. Drizzle around the chocolate sauce.

Restaurant 23

Restaurant 23 is a popular downtown restaurant offering an enticing menu created from the finest quality foods. It offers an eclectic mix of traditional and cutting-edge modern fare, cooked with flair, presented with style and served in a comfortable and elegant room.

starter
Prawn and asparagus chowder

main course
Honey-roast duck with potato fondant and glazed fig

dessert
Banana tarte tatin

23 Church St, Warrenpoint, Co. Down
Ph: +44 (0)28 4175 3222
www.restaurant23.com

Prawn and asparagus chowder

ingredients

600ml/1 pint fish stock
1 carrot, diced
2 shallots, sliced
1 garlic clove, sliced
1 celery stick, diced
1 leek (white part only), diced
1 bunch asparagus, trimmed
600ml/1 pint double cream
20 Dublin Bay prawns, peeled
and veins removed
1 tablespoon snipped fresh
chives
Salt and pepper

Crusty bread, to serve

Serves 4

method

· Bring the fish stock to the boil and reduce to a quarter of its original volume. Add the carrot, shallots, garlic, celery and leek. Cook for 5 minutes or until soft.
· Cook the asparagus in boiling salted water for 2 minutes.
· Add the cream to the vegetables and fish stock and simmer until slightly thickened. Add the prawns and cook for 1 minute.
· Cut the blanched asparagus in half and add to the vegetables and cream mixture to finish. Season with salt and pepper.

To serve

· Spoon the chowder into each bowl, and sprinkle with the snipped chives. Serve with crusty bread.

Honey-roast duck
with potato fondant and glazed fig

ingredients

For the duck

4 breasts Gressingham or
Peking duck
2 tablespoons honey

For the potato fondant

4 baking potatoes
100g/4oz butter, plus a little
extra
300ml/10fl oz chicken stock
1 garlic clove
1 fresh thyme sprig
1 fresh rosemary sprig

For the figs

2 fresh figs
1 tablespoon brown sugar
Sea salt and pepper

Serves 4

method

- Preheat the oven to 190°C/375°F/
  gas mark 5.

For the duck

- Score the duck breast fat with a sharp knife
  and season with salt and pepper. Heat
  a non-stick frying pan and add the duck
  breasts, skin side down. Fry quickly for a
  minute or two on each side.
- Remove the duck from the pan and season
  again with sea salt and pepper. Brush on the
  honey and put into a roasting tin.
- Cook the duck breasts skin side up in the
  oven for 8-10 minutes for medium or 15
  minutes for well done.

For the potato fondant

- Peel and cut the potatoes into a cylinder
  shape with a cutter. In a deep pot, combine
  the butter, stock, garlic and herbs. Bring to
  the boil and add the potatoes. Simmer until
  soft but still keeping their shape. Remove
  from the stock and drain.
- Glaze the potatoes in a non-stick pan with a
  little butter until golden. Season well.

For the figs

- Cut the figs in half, sprinkle with the brown
  sugar and grill until caramelised.

To serve

- Carve the duck breasts and arrange the
  duck slices on warm plates. Add the potato
  fondants and caramelised figs.

Banana tarte tatin

ingredients

50ml/2fl oz water
150g/5oz caster sugar
4 bananas
250g/9oz readymade puff
pastry, thawed if frozen

50g/2oz melted chocolate,
vanilla ice cream and vanilla
pods, to serve

Serves 4

method

- Preheat the oven to 190°C/375°F/gas mark 5.
- Put the water and sugar into a shallow non-stick frying pan and reduce, without stirring, until it turns a caramel colour and has a sauce consistency. Then peel the bananas and add to the pan. Cook for 1-2 minutes, tossing gently to coat.
- Remove the bananas from the pan onto a sheet of greaseproof paper on a baking sheet. Cool the bananas. Roll out the puff pastry until quite thin. Cut the pastry in the shape of the banana and cover each banana with the pastry.
- Put the banana tarts in the oven for 8-10 minutes, until the pastry is crisp and golden.

To serve

- Brush the plates with the melted chocolate. Invert the tarts and place banana-side up on each plate. Add a scoop of vanilla ice cream to each one and decorate with a dried vanilla pod.

Restaurant Patrick Guilbaud

Restaurant Patrick Guilbaud is one of Ireland's most highly regarded fine-dining venues. Head chef Guillaume Lebrun has presided over the achievement and retention of two Michelin stars over many years. Lebrun and his team always strive for excellence – in terms of locally sourced top-quality ingredients, meticulous preparation and skilled execution of their immaculate and imaginative dishes. This is a vibrant, art-filled modern space in which to enjoy marvellous food.

21 Upper Merrion Street, Dublin 2
Ph: (01) 676 4192

www.restaurantpatrickguilbaud.ie

starter
King scallops
with mango chutney and red wine reduction

main course
Roast turbot on the bone with sweet onion purée,
tomato caramel and asparagus

dessert
Strawberries with rhubarb and mascarpone cream

King scallops
with mango chutney and red wine reduction

ingredients

For the mango chutney

1 mango, chopped finely
2 spring onions, chopped finely
½ chilli, seeded and sliced
10 coriander leaves
4 tablespoon flaked almonds, toasted

For the red wine reduction

300ml/10fl oz red wine
150ml/5fl oz port
75g/3oz sugar
1 star anise
½ bunch dill

For the scallops

8 12 scallops depending on size
Curry powder
Olive oil, for frying
Salt and pepper

Coriander leaves, to serve

Serves 4

method

For the mango chutney

· Mix all the ingredients, except the almonds, together in a bowl. When ready to serve, add the almonds.

For the red wine reduction

· Put the wine, port, sugar and star anise in a pot. Bring to the boil. Reduce slowly until you have a syrup consistency. Add the dill and allow to infuse for 10 minutes in a warm place. Remove the dill before serving.

For the scallops

· Cut the scallops in half. Mix equal amounts of curry powder and salt. Season the scallops with this mixture. Heat a little oil in the pan. Fry the scallops for 30 seconds on both sides.

To serve

· Spoon the chutney onto the middle of a warmed plate. Place the scallops on top. Drizzle the wine reduction around. Put some coriander leaves on top of the scallops.

Roast turbot on the bone with sweet onion purée, tomato caramel and asparagus

ingredients

For the tomato caramel

900g/2lb tomatoes, chopped
4 drops of Tabasco
1 garlic clove
½ bunch of basil
A good pinch of sugar

For the onion purée

4 silver skinned onions, sliced
50ml/2fl oz cream
Olive oil

For the turbot

50g/2oz clarified butter
4 pieces turbot on the bone, approximately 200g/7oz per portion
4 pieces asparagus, trimmed
Salt and pepper

Serves 4

method

For the tomato caramel

- Put all the ingredients in the food processor. Blitz until you have a purée. Pass through a sieve. Transfer to a pot and bring to the boil. Reduce the liquid to about one-tenth of its original volume, until the tomato mixture is syrupy and somewhat caramelised.

For the onion purée

- Sprinkle salt on the onions and leave for 30 minutes. This will remove excess water and part-cook the onions. Heat olive oil in the pan. Add the onions and sweat without colouring them. When soft, transfer to the food processor. Add the cream and blitz to a purée. Season with salt and pepper. Keep warm until ready to serve.

For the turbot

- Heat the butter in the pan. Fry the turbot quickly on both sides to give a nice golden colour. Cook for a further 8 minutes – 4 minutes on each side – continuously basting the turbot with the foam of the butter. This will keep the fish lovely and moist.

- Meanwhile, blanch the asparagus in boiling, salted water for 2-3 minutes.

To serve

- Put drops of onion purée and tomato caramel on warmed plates. Place the fish in the middle of the plate and garnish with the asparagus on top.

Strawberries with rhubarb and mascarpone cream

ingredients

For the strawberries

550g/1¼lb strawberries, hulled
Juice of 1 lemon
25g/1oz icing sugar
25ml/1fl oz balsamic vinegar
25g/1oz brown sugar

For the rhubarb

400g/14oz rhubarb
75g/3oz sugar

For the mascarpone cream

150ml/5fl oz cream
250g/9oz mascarpone cheese
50g/2oz icing sugar
Zest and juice of 1 lime
Juice of 1 lemon

Almond biscuits, to serve
(optional)

Serves 4

method

For the strawberries

· Put half of the strawberries in the blender
  and blitz. Pass through a sieve. Add the
  lemon juice and icing sugar and mix again.
· Mix the balsamic vinegar and the brown
  sugar together. Marinate the remaining
  strawberries in this mixture.

For the rhubarb

· Remove the skin on the rhubarb and cut into
  small pieces. Put in a pot with the sugar.
  Heat and stir continuously to avoid sticking.
  Cook until you have a compote.

For the mascarpone cream

· Whip the cream. Mix the mascarpone
  with the icing sugar and the rest of the
  ingredients. Add part of the cream to the
  mascarpone and mix again. Fold in the
  remaining cream until just combined.

To serve

· Put the strawberry purée in the bottom
  of four wide glasses. Add the marinated
  strawberries. Put the rhubarb on top in a
  neat circle. Top with the mascarpone cream.
  If you like, you can put an almond biscuit
  beneath the mascarpone cream for extra
  crunch.

The Ritz-Carlton, Powerscourt

With its sweeping views across the Wicklow Mountains, the Sugar Loaf restaurant offers an enjoyable venue for lunch or an informal dinner in this luxury hotel. The restaurant is in the charge of head chef Cihan Cetinkaya, who prefers local suppliers as a source for the highest-quality foods, allowing menus to reflect the seasons.

starter
Salmon phyllo, dill cream, Guinness reduction

main course
Tipperary beef fillet, chunky chips, king mushrooms, Cabernet sauce

dessert
Vanilla cheesecake, poached pears and cinnamon

Powerscourt Estate, Enniskerry, Co. Wicklow
Ph: (01) 274 8888

www.ritzcarlton.com/Powerscourt/

Salmon phyllo, dill cream, Guinness reduction

ingredients

25ml/1fl oz red wine vinegar

25ml/1fl oz olive oil

1 teaspoon Dijon mustard

½ teaspoon salt, plus an extra pinch

250g/9oz Irish salmon fillet, boneless and skinless

4 spring roll wrappers, thawed if frozen (each about 20cm/8 inches)

1 carrot, thinly sliced (julienne)

100g/4oz radish, thinly sliced (julienne)

½ bunch scallions, thinly sliced (julienne)

½ bunch fresh coriander

Olive oil

50ml/2fl oz cream

1 tablespoon chopped fresh dill

Squeeze of lemon

250ml/9fl oz Guinness

Serves 4

method

· Preheat the oven to 180°C/350°F/gas mark 4.

· Mix the red wine vinegar, olive oil, Dijon mustard and salt in a non-metallic bowl.

· Cut the salmon fillet into 12 very thin slices. Add the salmon slices to the marinade and make sure they are fully covered. Keep in the marinade for at least 10 minutes and no longer than 30, or the marinade will start to "cook" the fish.

· Cut the spring roll wraps into triangles of approximately 10cm/4 inches and roast them in the oven on baking sheets for about 5 minutes or until crispy. You will need 4 triangles per portion.

· Mix the carrot, radishes and scallions in a bowl. Pick the coriander leaves and mix in. Season with some olive oil and salt.

· Whip the cream and add the chopped dill and lemon juice.

· Put the Guinness in a saucepan. Bring to the boil and reduce until it is of a syrup consistency.

To serve

· Put one full tablespoon of the dill cream in the middle of each flat, round plate and spread it with a spoon in a round shape. Place some of the vegetable salad on top of the triangle crisps and put a piece of salmon on top. Make three layers for every portion and place it in the middle of the plate on top of the cream sauce. Put the Guinness reduction on the edge of the cream sauce as very small dots.

Tipperary beef fillet, chunky chips, king mushrooms, Cabernet sauce

ingredients

For the beef

900g/2lb Tipperary beef fillet
25g/1oz butter
3 garlic cloves, not peeled
½ bunch fresh thyme

For the chunky chips

900g/2lb baking potatoes, peeled
100g/4oz cornflour
Vegetable oil, for deep frying

For the mushrooms

25g/1oz butter
200g/7oz trumpet or porcini mushrooms, trimmed and cut in half
2 garlic cloves, finely chopped
2 tablespoons chopped fresh flat leaf parsley

For the Cabernet sauce

200ml/7fl oz Cabernet wine
50ml/2fl oz demi-glace or beef stock
Salt and black pepper

Serves 4

method

· Preheat the oven to 180°C/350°F/ gas mark 4.

For the beef fillet

· Cut the beef fillet into 4 portions. Season with salt and black pepper. In an ovenproof pan heat half the butter, the garlic cloves and the thyme. Add the beef and sear on both sides. Transfer to the oven and cook for 15-20 minutes for medium (10-15 minutes for rare, or 20-25 minutes for well done).

For the chunky chips

· Boil the potatoes and drain well. Add salt and pass through a fine sieve or mash until really smooth. Layer it in a tray to 2.5cm/1 inch thickness. Cover with the corn starch and cool down. Clean the starch from the potato with a brush and cut into 2.5cm x 15cm (1 inch x 6 inch) pieces. Fry in a deep fat fryer until crispy and golden.

For the mushrooms

· Heat the butter in a pan and sauté the mushrooms in the butter with the garlic and parsley until tender.

For the Cabernet sauce

· Reduce the wine in a saucepan until it reaches syrup consistency and then pour in the boiling demi-glace/beef stock and reduce again.

To serve

· Put the chunky chips in the middle of each plate. Place the beef fillet beside the chips and pour the sauce on top of the beef fillet. Spread the mushrooms on the other side of the potatoes.

Vanilla cheesecake, poached pears and cinnamon

ingredients

For the base

100g/4oz digestive biscuits
40g/1½oz butter, melted

For the cheesecake

275g/10oz cream cheese
225ml/8fl oz fresh cream
100g/4oz caster sugar
1 vanilla pod, split in half and
seeds scraped out

For the pears

450ml/15fl oz water
250g/9oz sugar
2 cinnamon sticks
2 pears, peeled
10 fresh mint leaves

Serves 4

method

· Preheat the oven to 180°C/350°F/
  gas mark 4.

For the base

· Crumble the biscuits. Add the melted butter
  and mix with the crumbled biscuits. Spoon
  into an ovenproof dish and cook in the oven
  for 6 minutes until toasted.

For the cheesecake

· Whip the cream cheese, cream, sugar and
  vanilla pod until the consistency becomes
  soft and smooth.

For the pears

· Heat the water, sugar and cinnamon sticks
  in a pot until they become soft. Add the
  pears and poach until the pears become
  soft. Cool down and then dice the pears,
  discarding the cores. Fold half of the diced
  pears into the cheesecake mix. Mix the rest
  with 6 of the mint leaves that have been
  finely chopped.

To serve

· For each portion, put some crumble in the
  middle of the plate or wide glass. Place
  some of the cream cheese mix on top.
  Sprinkle the pear and mint mix around and
  on top of the cake. Decorate with one fresh
  mint leaf on top.

Roly's Bistro

Roly's is an institution; much appreciated for its buzzing atmosphere and relaxed style as well as for its good service, good value and consistently good food. The menu style is 'classic-French-meets-modern-Irish,' with a few global detours.

7 Ballsbridge Terrace, Dublin 4
Ph: (01) 668 2611

www.rolysbistro.ie

starter
Tian of Castletownbere crab and tomato with apple dressing

main course
Roast fillet of cod with minted peas à la française

dessert
Roly's biscuit cake

Tian of Castletownbere crab and tomato with apple dressing

ingredients

200g/7oz white Castletownbere crab meat
50g/2oz mayonnaise
50g/2oz snipped fresh chives
100g/4oz apple, peeled, cored and diced
8 tablespoons olive oil
3 tablespoons cider vinegar
4 firm, ripe tomatoes
Salt and freshly ground pepper

Serves 4

method

· Mix the crab meat, mayonnaise, chives and half of the diced apple. Season to taste with salt and pepper.

· Mix the remaining apple with the olive oil and cider vinegar to make the dressing.

· Cut a cross into the top of each tomato and plunge them into boiling salted water, one at a time. Remove after 30 seconds and then plunge briefly into ice cold water. The skin should now remove easily. Cut each tomato into four and fully remove the seeds so that just the flesh of the tomato is left.

To serve

· Place a 5cm/2 inch pastry cutter on each plate. Arrange four tomato quarters in the base of each one. Top with the crab mixture and press down gently, then carefully remove the cutters. Top with the diced apple in the cider vinegar dressing.

Roast fillet of cod with minted peas à la française

ingredients

For the chicken stock

450g/1lb chicken carcasses, chopped up
1 litre/1¾ pints water
50g/2oz celery, chopped
50g/2oz onions, chopped
50g/2oz leeks, chopped
1 garlic clove
½ fresh thyme sprig
1 bay leaf

For the fish

1 onion, finely diced
50g/2oz butter
8 tablespoons white wine
¼ head iceberg lettuce, shredded
150g/5oz cooked peas
4 x 175g/6oz cod fillets, scaled and boned (nearly all types of fish work with this dish)
8-10 mint leaves, torn into pieces
Oil, for frying

Serves 4

method

For the chicken stock

· Put the chicken carcasses with the water in a large pot and bring to the boil. Skim off all the foam, add the remaining ingredients, return to the boil, and then simmer for 1½ - 2 hours, skimming off any fat that rises to the top. Pass the stock through a colander and then through a fine strainer.

For the fish

· Sweat the onion in the butter until soft but without colour. Add the white wine and allow to reduce by half, then add the chicken stock and reduce by one third. Add the lettuce and peas and warm through.

· Heat some oil in a frying pan and put the fish in skin side down. Fry for about 4 minutes on each side.

To serve

· Add the mint to the pea mixture and then divide among the plates. Top with the cod.

Roly's biscuit cake

ingredients

250g/9oz plain chocolate,
broken into squares
400g/14oz milk chocolate,
broken into squares
200g/7oz white chocolate,
broken into squares
150g/5oz unsalted butter
275g/10oz golden syrup
275g/10oz digestive biscuits

For the ganache (icing)

40g/1½oz liquid glucose
175ml/6fl oz cream
25g/1oz unsalted butter
175g/6oz good quality Belgian
chocolate chips, minimum 70%
cocoa solids

Icing sugar and redcurrants, to
decorate (optional)

Serves 10-12

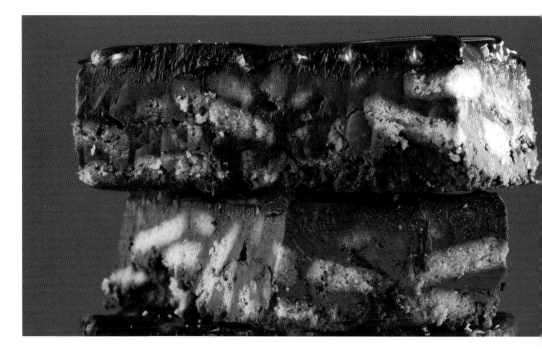

method

- Melt all the chocolates, butter and golden syrup in a bowl over a
  pot of hot water. In a separate bowl, roughly break up the biscuits,
  though not too small. When the chocolate is fully melted with the
  butter, add the biscuits into the melted chocolate mixture and stir
  until everything is combined.
- Line a 15cm/6 inch square (or 18cm/7 inch round) cake tin or
  a flat tray with parchment or greaseproof paper. Fill with the
  chocolate biscuit mixture and allow to set in the fridge for 2 hours.
  Remove the parchment or greaseproof paper.

For the ganache (icing)

- In a saucepan, bring the glucose, cream and butter to the boil,
  sprinkle in the chocolate and whisk until a sauce is formed. If it
  sets, it can be micro-waved down again.
- After 2 hours, remove the biscuit cake from the fridge and cover
  the top with the ganache. Then, return to the fridge to set.

To serve

- Cut into slides and arrange on plates. You could dust with some
  icing sugar and decorate with redcurrants.

Rosso Restaurant

In a comfortable, stylish and ultra-modern space, Rosso has built a reputation for excellent food at reasonable prices, and very friendly service. Head chef Conor Mee presents cutting-edge menus; his cooking blends unexpected spins on classic dishes and traditional Irish fare.

5 Roden Place, Dundalk, Co. Louth
Ph: (042) 935 6502
www.rossorestaurant.com

starter
Bruschetta of Irish goat's cheese, pistachio and creamed rocket salad

main course
Roast monkfish and spices with lobster, crab and potato chowder

dessert
Creamed vanilla rice pudding with toffee apples and ginger ice cream

Bruschetta of Irish goat's cheese, pistachio and creamed rocket salad

ingredients

For the goat's cheese cream

25ml/1fl oz milk
25ml/1fl oz cream
1 bay leaf
½ fresh thyme sprig
2 white peppercorns
4 x 50g/2oz goat's cheese

For the tomato fondue

25ml/1fl oz white wine vinegar
15g/½oz caster sugar
25ml/1fl oz olive oil
½ shallot, finely diced
1 garlic clove, ground
½ teaspoon coriander seeds, crushed
½ tablespoon tomato purée
3 tomatoes, skinned, seeded and chopped

For the bruschetta

4 large slices sourdough bread (cut on the diagonal)
50ml/2fl oz olive oil
1 garlic clove, halved (not peeled)
25g/1oz pistachio nuts, chopped

For the salad

100g/4oz rocket salad
Sea salt and pepper

Serves 4

method

· Preheat the oven to 180°C/350°F/ gas mark 4.

For the goat's cheese cream

· Put the milk, cream, bay leaf, thyme and peppercorns into a small pot and bring to the boil. Cut the rind of the goat's cheese. Place the rind trimmings into the liquid. Allow to simmer very gently until the cheese has become soft. Then strain through a sieve. Return to a clean pot and add salt and pepper as appropriate. Allow to cool.

For the tomato fondue

· In a small pot, combine the vinegar and sugar. Boil until reduced to a syrup consistency.

· Heat a pot and add olive oil. Add the shallots and fry without colouring until soft. Next add the garlic and coriander and cook for a further 1 minute. Add the tomato purée and cook slowly for 3 minutes. Add the chopped tomatoes and allow it to simmer. Add the vinegar syrup and cook until thick and darker in colour. Check for seasoning.

For the bruschetta

· Brush the bread with olive oil, rub with a little garlic and sprinkle a little salt. Toast or bake on a baking sheet until slightly crisp and coloured. Place a spoonful of tomato fondue onto the bruschetta. Place a piece of goat's cheese on top of each bruschetta and sprinkle over the pistachios. Bake in the oven for 5-6 minutes.

For the salad

· Place the rocket in a bowl, add a little salt and four spoonfuls of the cooled goat's cheese cream and gently mix.

To serve

· Place the baked bruschetta on warm plates. Divide the salad into four portions and serve on top of the bruschetta.

Roast monkfish and spices with lobster, crab and potato chowder

ingredients

For the fish

450g/1lb monkfish fillet, trimmed
Pinch of salt
2 teaspoons mild curry powder
Olive oil

For the chowder

(You can substitute all fish and shellfish with what is fresh and available)
Olive oil
1 shallot, diced
2 garlic cloves, diced
4 cardamom pods, crushed
1 tablespoon Thai green curry paste (less if you prefer milder)
400g/14oz coconut milk
200ml/7fl oz cream
1 lemon grass stick
100ml/3½fl oz fish stock
675g/1½lb lobster, cooked and meat removed
6 small waxy potatoes, cooked and cut in small cubes
100g/4oz pak choi, chopped coarsely
4 spring onions, chopped
25g/1oz fresh coriander, chopped
400g/14oz fresh white crab meat
1 teaspoon Thai fish sauce (Nam Pla)
Juice of ½ lime
Salt and pepper

Serves 4

method

- Preheat the oven to 180°C/350°F/ gas mark 4.

For the fish

- Season the monkfish with salt and curry powder and allow to rest for 10 minutes.
- Heat a little olive oil in a frying pan. Once the pan is smoking, place the monkfish in the pan (do not overcrowd) and fry to colour evenly. Remove the fish from the pan and place in a roasting tin. Bake in the oven for 6-7 minutes.

For the chowder

- Heat a little olive oil in a pan. Gently fry the shallot for 3 minutes. Then add the garlic and cardamom and cook for another 1 minute. Add curry paste and cook for 2 minutes, stirring. Add the coconut milk, cream and lemon grass.
- Add the fish stock and bring the sauce to the boil, then reduce the heat and simmer for a few minutes until slightly reduced. Add the lobster, potatoes, pak choi and spring onion and cook for 2 minutes. Finish the sauce with the fresh coriander, crab meat, a dash of fish sauce, lime juice, salt and pepper. Heat thoroughly again.

To serve

- Divide the chowder equally between warmed bowls and place the monkfish on top.

Creamed vanilla rice pudding with toffee apples and ginger ice cream

ingredients

For the ginger ice cream

1 teaspoon freshly grated root ginger
150ml/5fl oz milk
300ml/10fl oz cream
6 egg yolks
75g/3oz caster sugar

For the vanilla rice pudding

400ml/14fl oz milk
1 vanilla pod, split in half
50g/2oz pearl rice
75g/3oz caster sugar
100ml/3½fl oz fresh cream

For the toffee apples

100g/4oz caster sugar
25g/1oz butter
2 Granny Smith apples, peeled, cored and sliced

Serves 6

method

For the ginger ice cream

- Put the ginger, milk and cream in a pot and heat very gently for 10-15 minutes, allowing the ginger to infuse (the longer the better). Then bring the milk and cream mixture to the boil.

- Using an electric mixer, combine the yolks and sugar and whip until white and creamy. Pour all of the milk and cream liquid onto the yolk mixture and stir well to combine. Pour this back into the pot and stir vigorously over low to medium heat (about 78°C if you have a thermometer) until the liquid has slightly thickened and coats the back of the spoon. Do not boil as it will curdle.

- Strain the mixture through a sieve and allow to cool (TIP: Preparation a day in advance is best as it gives more flavour). Transfer to an ice cream machine and churn until ready. Store in the freezer.

For the rice pudding

- Put the milk into a pot and scrape the vanilla seeds into the milk. Bring the milk and vanilla mixture to the boil.

- Wash the rice well under cold water. Add the rice to the milk, then reduce the heat and allow to cook gently until the rice is soft, stirring frequently. It will be much thicker. Stir in the sugar and allow to stand.

- Just before serving, add the cream and re-heat the rice, gently stirring occasionally.

For the toffee apples

- Place the sugar in a frying pan and heat until it becomes golden brown, without stirring. Add the butter and mix well. The mixture will crystallise initially but the sugar crystals will dissolve back into a toffee again if heated gently. Being careful, quickly add the apples to the heated toffee. Toss until evenly coated. Reduce heat and cook for 3-4 minutes.

To serve

- Divide the rice into warm bowls and place the toffee apples on top. Finally, finish off with a generous scoop of the ginger ice cream.

Salt Restaurant at Lisloughrey Lodge

Salt occupies an elegant space on the first floor of Lisloughrey Lodge, with stunning views out over Lough Corrib. Chef Wade Murphy's outstanding cooking and the varied and imaginative menus ensure that a visit to Salt is a memorable dining experience. Wade is passionate about using local produce and presenting it with style and flair, and because of this the awards keep on coming.

The Quay, Cong, Co. Mayo
Ph: (094) 954 5400
www.lisloughrey.ie

starter
Spice-roasted butternut squash soup
with toasted pumpkin seed croûtons

main course
Irish Angus fillet of beef with warm rocket, watercress and baby potato salad and Béarnaise vinaigrette

dessert
Classic raspberry fool with orange biscuits

Spice-roasted butternut squash soup with toasted pumpkin seed croûtons

ingredients

For the harissa

(this can be bought in most supermarkets if you wish)
10-12 dried red chilli peppers
3 garlic cloves, crushed
½ teaspoon salt
2 tablespoons olive oil
1 teaspoon ground coriander
1 teaspoon ground caraway seeds
½ teaspoon ground cumin

For the croûtons

French baguette, cut into thin slices
Olive oil
A little Spanish paprika
25g/1oz pumpkin seeds, toasted
Salt and pepper

Snipped fresh chives, to serve

Serves 4-6

For the butternut squash soup

1 large or 2 small butternut squash, halved and seeded
3 tablespoons softened unsalted butter
¼ teaspoon ground cumin
¼ teaspoon ground coriander
¼ teaspoon chopped fresh chilli
Pinch of cloves
2 teaspoons olive oil
½ onion, roughly chopped
2 carrots, roughly chopped
1 celery stick, trimmed and roughly chopped
¼ leek, trimmed and roughly chopped
250ml/8½fl oz vegetable stock (from a stock cube is fine)
50ml/2fl oz hot water
50ml/2fl oz crème fraîche

method

· Preheat the oven to 200°C/400°F/gas mark 6.

For the harissa

· Soak the dried chillies in hot water for 30 minutes. Drain. Remove stems and seeds. In a food processor combine chilli peppers, garlic, salt and olive oil. Add the remaining spices and blend to form a smooth paste. Store in an airtight container. Drizzle a small amount of olive oil on top to keep fresh. It will keep for a month in the refrigerator.

For the butternut squash soup

· Place the squash in a baking dish and brush the cut side with the softened butter. Season with salt and pepper to taste and sprinkle with a small amount of each spice. Cover with tinfoil and bake in the oven for 20 minutes. Remove the foil and continue baking for another 15-20 minutes, or until tender. Remove the squash from the oven and scoop out the pulp from the skin.

· In a heavy-bottomed saucepan, heat the olive oil and the rest of the softened butter. Fry the onion, carrots, celery and leek with the remaining spices without colouring. Place the squash in the saucepan, gently fry a little and then add the stock. Bring to the boil and simmer for 20 minutes.

· Transfer in batches to a blender and, for a really smooth finish, strain through a fine sieve into a medium saucepan. Season and cook for 10 minutes, adding more hot water, if necessary. Remove from the heat and whisk in the crème fraîche and 1 teaspoon of the harissa. Season with salt and pepper to taste.

For the croûtons

· Turn the oven down to 160°C/325°F/gas mark 3. Brush the bread slices with olive oil and sprinkle with paprika on 1 side. Bake in the oven on a baking sheet for 5-10 minutes, or until lightly golden brown. Remove from the oven and sprinkle with the seeds.

To serve

· Ladle the soup into warmed bowls, float a few croûtons on top. Garnish with the chives.

Irish Angus fillet of beef with warm rocket, watercress and baby potato salad and Béarnaise vinaigrette

ingredients

For the Béarnaise vinaigrette

25ml/1fl oz dry white wine
25ml/1fl oz white wine vinegar
25g/1oz finely chopped shallots
2 tablespoons fresh chopped tarragon (keeping the stalks)
2 large egg yolks
½ teaspoon fresh lemon juice
1 teaspoon English mustard
225ml/8fl oz grapeseed oil

For the salad

100g/4oz wild mushrooms
2 tablespoons softened butter
50ml/2fl oz extra virgin olive oil
200g/7oz new season baby potatoes, quartered
¼ teaspoon chopped thyme
¼ teaspoon chopped rosemary
¼ teaspoon chopped oregano
200g/7oz rocket leaves
200g/7oz watercress, good leaves only
100g/4oz red onion, thinly sliced
100g/4oz cucumber, peeled, quartered, seeded and sliced
Squeeze of lemon juice
Salt and pepper

For the steak

4 x 175g/6oz beef fillets (a less expensive steak can be used, such as rib-eye or sirloin, if you like)
Olive Oil

Serves 4

method

- Preheat the oven to 150°C/300°F/ gas mark 2.

For the Béarnaise vinaigrette

- Put the white wine, white wine vinegar, shallots and tarragon stalks in a saucepan. Bring to the boil and reduce by two-thirds. Allow to cool slightly but not totally.

- Place the reduction in a food blender and blitz quickly. Add the egg yolks and blend slowly for 2 minutes. Add the lemon juice and mustard and blend again. Leaving the blender running, slowly add the oil. It is vital you add this slowly, as the vinaigrette could split. Once you have added enough oil and the vinaigrette is thick enough to coat the back of a spoon, add the chopped tarragon and season to taste with salt and pepper.

For the salad

- Trim the mushrooms and cut into halves or quarters depending on size. Using a heavy-duty frying pan melt the butter and add a touch of olive oil in order to stop the butter burning. Add the potatoes and sauté them until golden brown. Finish in the oven for 10 minutes.

- After 5 minutes add the mushrooms to the potatoes and mix. Return to the oven for another 5 minutes. Finally add the chopped herbs and season to taste. Leave somewhere warm and do not allow them to cool down fully as you want the potato and mushroom mix to slightly wilt your salad before serving.

- In a mixing bowl, place the rocket leaves, watercress, onion, cucumber, potatoes and mushrooms. Add the rest of the olive oil and the lemon juice and season to taste with salt and pepper.

For the steak

- Turn up the oven to 180°C/350°F/gas 4.

- Season the fillet steaks with sea salt and fresh ground black pepper. Heat a frying pan or griddle pan. Add a little oil. When the oil is smoking hot, add the beef. Brown evenly on all sides for about 1 minute at a time and then place in the oven for about 9-10 minutes. This should give a good medium. If you like it less cooked or more well done then just place it in the oven for about 6 minutes for medium rare and about 18-19 minutes for well done.

To serve

- Place the warm salad in the centre of large bowls. Slice the fillet steaks into two medallions each and place on top of the salad. Drizzle with the Béarnaise vinaigrette and serve. Have the rest of the Béarnaise vinaigrette in a jug to hand around separately.

Classic raspberry fool with orange biscuits

ingredients

For the fond

300g/11oz fresh raspberries
(or frozen, if out of season),
reserving 4 for decoration
100g/4oz granulated sugar
1 tablespoon cornflour
Zest and juice of ½ an orange
¼ vanilla pod split, or dash of
vanilla essence

For the raspberry fool

150g/5oz fresh raspberries
1 tablespoon sifted icing sugar,
plus extra for dusting
1 tablespoon raspberry liqueur
(optional)
300ml/10fl oz cream

For the orange biscuits

1 egg
150g/5oz caster sugar
150g/5oz strong white flour,
plus extra for dusting
75g/3oz butter, diced, at room
temperature
1 teaspoon baking powder
75g/3oz almonds
Zest of 1½ oranges

Strawberries or raspberries, to
decorate

Serves 4

method

- Preheat the oven to 160°C/325°F/
gas mark 3.

For the fond

- In a heavy bottomed saucepan combine all
the ingredients. Cook over a medium heat,
stirring continuously until the sauce thickens
and is bubbly. Remove from the heat and
allow to cool. Taste and add more sugar if
needed. Cover and refrigerate.

For the raspberry fool

- In a bowl, mash the raspberries, sugar and
liqueur with a fork. Whip the cream until it
forms firm peaks. With a spatula, fold into
the raspberry mixture and chill.

For the orange biscuits

- Using a mixer, cream the egg and sugar.
Sift the flour into a bowl and crumb in the
butter. Add the remainder of the ingredients
and finally fold the egg and sugar into the
butter and flour mix. Chill the mix for about
30 minutes. On a floured surface, roll out the
dough to your desired thickness, preferably
around 2cm/¾ inch. Using a round or
square cutter, cut the dough in shapes
around 2.5cm/1 inch in diameter. Place on
baking sheets lined with non-stick baking
parchment and cook for 15-16 minutes until
golden brown. Remove. Allow to cool and
store in an airtight container.

To serve

- Use pre-chilled cocktail glasses. Place 2
spoonfuls of the fond on the bottom and
then cover with 2 spoonfuls of the fool and
repeat 2 or 3 times. Crumble a few of the
biscuits on top and decorate with a fresh
berry. Serve the orange biscuits on the side,
lightly dusted with icing sugar.

Sha-Roe Bistro

The picturesque and historic village of Clonegal may be off the beaten track, but the many fans of this delightful family-owned and run bistro know that eating here is a dining experience well worth a detour. Offering a menu in tune with the seasons, meticulously sourced ingredients, faultless cooking, and the pleasure of dining in a beautifully restored 18th century building, Sha-Roe is superb value for the quality of food, culinary skill and service.

Main Street, Clonegal, Co. Carlow
Ph: (053) 937 5636

starter
Tapas plate

main course
Braised beef cheeks

dessert
Lemon posset with butter biscuits

Tapas plate

ingredients

For the gazpacho

900kg/2lb tomatoes, chopped
1½ garlic cloves
2 red peppers, chopped
2 medium-sized cucumbers, halved, seeded and chopped
½ red onion, chopped
¼ chilli (depending on strength)
8 tablespoons olive oil
6 tablespoons red wine vinegar

For the toasted almonds

250g/9oz skinned, whole almonds
2 teaspoons olive oil
3 teaspoons sea salt
2 teaspoons smoked paprika

For the potato and sweet onion tortilla

1 large onion, sliced
350g/12oz boiled potatoes, peeled
6 eggs
Olive oil
Salt and pepper

For the marinated black olives

400g/14oz black olives
3 garlic cloves, finely chopped
2 tablespoons chopped fresh flat leaf parsley
½ teaspoon chopped fresh rosemary
Olive oil

Crispy bread, to serve

Serves 4

method

- Preheat the oven to 140°C/275°F/ gas mark 1.

For the gazpacho

- Blend the tomatoes, garlic, red peppers, cucumbers, red onion and enough chilli to taste in a food processor to a purée. Remove and whisk in olive oil and red wine vinegar. Pass through a sieve and chill in the refrigerator.

For the toasted almonds

- Mix all the ingredients together. Then place in a roasting tin and roast in the oven for 15-20 minutes, until golden brown.

For the potato and sweet onion tortilla

- Heat some olive oil in a pot. Place the onions in the pot and cook slowly until they begin to caramelise. Remove from the heat and leave to cool. Slice the cooked potatoes.

- Whisk the eggs with the salt and pepper. Add the cooked onions and sliced potatoes to the egg mixture. Heat some olive oil in an ovenproof pan. Add the mixture and place in the oven for 15-20 minutes or until the tortilla is set. Remove from the oven and allow to cool. Cut into 2.5cm/1 inch cubes.

For the marinated black olives

- Put the olives, garlic, parsley and rosemary in a bowl. Add enough olive oil to coat and marinate for 1 hour.

To serve

- Arrange the tapas on plates and in bowls in the middle of the table and serve with crispy bread.

Braised beef cheeks

ingredients

For the beef

2 x 400g/14oz beef cheeks
(may need to be pre-ordered
from your butcher)
Plain flour for dusting
1 tablespoon vegetable oil
200ml/7fl oz red wine
2 celery sticks, chopped
1 leek, trimmed, halved and
sliced
2 carrots, chopped
Small bunch fresh thyme
1litre/1¾ pints beef stock

For the mashed potatoes

900g/2lb Rooster or Maris Piper
potatoes
50ml/2fl oz milk
200g/7oz butter
Sea salt and freshly ground
white pepper

Serves 4

method

· Preheat the oven to 150°C/300°F/gas mark 2.

For the beef

· Trim down the beef cheeks and remove any skin. Dust evenly with the flour, shaking off any excess.
· Heat the oil in a frying pan. Add the meat and brown on all sides. Remove the meat and deglaze the pan with the red wine.
· Then pour the wine into a large saucepan or casserole dish. Add the meat with the celery, leek, carrots and thyme. Season with salt and pepper. Cover with the beef stock and bring to boil.
· Transfer to the oven and let simmer gently for about 3–4 hours or until the meat is tender and falling apart. Remove the beef cheeks and keep warm.
· Strain the stock and boil until the sauce has thickened. Season to taste.

For the mashed potatoes

· Boil the potatoes in salted water. When cooked, drain the water and, using a potato masher, mash the boiled potatoes. Add the milk and butter and mash again until you get a creamy consistency. Add sea salt and pepper to taste.

To serve

· Place the beef cheeks on warmed plates. Pour over the sauce. Serve with the mashed potatoes.

Lemon posset with butter biscuits

ingredients

For the lemon posset

450ml/15fl oz double cream
125g/4½oz caster sugar
Juice of 1½ lemons

For the butter biscuits

100g/4oz butter, at room
temperature
50g/2oz icing sugar, plus extra
to dust (optional)
Juice of ½ lemon
150g/5oz plain flour

Serves 4

method

- Preheat the oven to 180°C/350°F/
  gas mark 4.

For the lemon posset

- Put the cream and sugar in a pot and bring
  to the boil, stirring frequently. Then add the
  lemon juice, stirring to combine. Remove
  from the heat and leave the mixture to
  cool slightly. Pour into 4 tall, wide-rimmed
  glasses and chill in the refrigerator for at
  least 1-2 hours before serving.

For the butter biscuits

- Mix the butter and icing sugar together until
  you have a smooth paste. Then add lemon
  juice and mix well. Add the flour, mixing
  well until smooth.
- Roll into sausage shape and refrigerate for
  at least 15 minutes or overnight is fine.

- Cut into round biscuit shapes and bake in
  the oven for 10 minutes until lightly golden.

To serve

- Place each glass on a plate. Place one biscuit
  in the glass of lemon posset and serve more
  biscuits on the side. Dust with icing sugar, if
  you wish.

Shanahan's on the Green

Set in a classic Georgian building with many of its original features, Shanahan's on the Green is a luxurious American-style steakhouse and seafood restaurant. It features specially chosen, certified Irish Angus beef, along with the freshest of seafood and other produce from Irish nature's bounty. Quality and attention to detail are evident in both the food and the service.

119 St. Stephen's Green, Dublin 2
Ph: (01) 407 0939
www.shanahans.ie

starter
Garlic shrimp

main course
Bone-out rib of beef with bourguignon garnish

dessert
Bread and butter pudding

Garlic shrimp

ingredients

10-12 tiger shrimps

Plain flour, to dust

50ml/2fl oz white wine

1 tablespoon fresh lemon juice

1 tablespoon cream

1 tablespoon shallots, finely chopped

1 teaspoon garlic purée

1 teaspoon rinsed capers

40g/1½oz garlic butter

Olive oil

Pinch of snipped chives

Mixed salad leaves, to serve

Serves 2

method

· Heat a heavy-based frying pan with a little olive oil. Dust the shrimps lightly with flour. Place the shrimps in the heated pan and colour on both sides.

· Add the white wine, lemon juice, cream, shallots, garlic purée and capers, stirring to combine. Reduce the heat, then whisk in the garlic butter.

· Toss the salad leaves in a teaspoon of olive oil.

To serve

· Place a small mound of mixed salad leaves in the centre of each plate. Stand the sautéed shrimps around the lettuce. Drizzle the sauce over the shrimp. Sprinkle with chives.

Bone-out rib of beef with bourguignon garnish

ingredients

200g/7oz small silverskin onions

200g/7oz piece pancetta

200g/7oz very small button mushrooms

25g/1oz butter

450ml/15fl oz red wine

4 x 275g/10oz rib steaks

Olive oil

200ml/7fl oz veal jus, or a good quality beef stock

Salt and pepper

Potatoes and green vegetables, to serve

Serves 4

method

· Peel the outer skin off the onions. Slice the pancetta into thin lardons or strips. Remove the root from the mushrooms. Put the butter in a hot frying pan and add the mushrooms straight away. Strain off any excess juice from the mushrooms and put the pan back onto a hot heat. Add the onions and pancetta lardons and cook until golden and crisp.

· Remove all the ingredients from the pan and keep warm. Add the red wine to the pan and reduce by half. Add the veal jus or stock and put all the ingredients back in.

· Meanwhile, season the rib steaks with salt and pepper. Heat a heavy-based griddle pan, then brush with a little oil. For a medium cooked steak cook for 6-8 minutes on both sides on the pan. Adjust the timing for rare or well done steaks. Allow to rest for a few minutes before serving.

To serve

· Place the beef on warmed plates and spoon the mushrooms on top. Serve with your favourite potatoes and some green vegetables.

223

Bread and butter pudding

ingredients

5 croissants (day old is best)

50ml/2fl oz milk

75g/3oz caster sugar

200ml/7fl oz cream

½ vanilla pod, halved and seeded

3 egg yolks

25ml/1fl oz whiskey

75g/3oz plain or milk chocolate drops

Whipped cream, to serve

Serves 6-8

method

· Preheat the oven to 160°C/325°F/gas mark 3.

· Cut each croissant into 4-6 slices.

· Whisk the milk, sugar, cream, vanilla seeds and egg yolks together. Pour over the croissants. Add the whiskey and chocolate drops and mix until the croissants have absorbed all the liquid.

· Place into an oven-proof dish, preferably 12.5cm/5 inch deep and cover tightly with tinfoil. Then put in a roasting tin and half fill with hot water. Bake for 35 minutes, remove the tinfoil and cook for a further 10 minutes or until golden.

To serve

· Serve warm. Spoon some pudding onto each warm plate and serve with a little whipped cream.

The Strawberry Tree

The Strawberry Tree is Ireland's only certified organic restaurant. All the food reflects Evan Doyle's philosophy of using only ingredients that are wild, organic, or produced by 'Slow Food' methods. It's a relaxed place. Menus are not too long and the cooking style - a modern take on classic Irish - features many ultra slow-cooked dishes. Dining here is a unique and enjoyable experience.

Brooklodge & Wells Spa, Macreddin Village, Co. Wicklow
Ph: (0402) 36444
www.brooklodge.com

starter
Wild crab and Dillisk bread and butter pudding

main course
Slow cooked wild venison shank
with baby potatoes and baby carrots

dessert
White chocolate passion fruit tart

Wild crab and Dillisk bread and butter pudding

ingredients

For the crab mix

15g/½oz Dillisk (seaweed), chopped

275g/10oz fresh white crab meat (preferably wild Irish crab), cooked

½ organic red chilli, seeded and finely chopped

1 organic onion, finely chopped

Juice and zest of 1 organic lemon

For the bread mix

½ loaf or 6-8 slices organic Irish white sliced bread

100g/4oz organic butter

450ml/15fl oz organic cream

10 organic egg yolks

Olive oil for frying

Salt and pepper

Lightly dressed organic mixed green salad, to serve

Serves 6-8

method

· Preheat the oven to 150°C/300°F/gas mark 2.

For the crab mix

· Soak the Dillisk for 10 minutes in warm water, then drain and chop. Combine all the ingredients for the crab mix and season with salt and pepper to taste.

For the bread mix

· Butter both sides of the bread. Mix the cream and egg yolks and season with salt and pepper.

· Line a 1kg/2lb loaf tin with clingfilm. Alternate layers of crab, bread and cream/egg mix until full. Let stand for 10 minutes.

· Put into a bain marie in the oven and bake for 45 minutes. (If you do not have a bain marie just put the loaf tin in a roasting tin half filled with water.) Leave to cool overnight in the fridge.

To serve

· Slice the pudding into 6-8 slices, discarding the ends. Heat a large, non-stick frying pan with a little olive oil and fry one side to a light golden colour. You will have to do this in batches. Place each slice on a large plate, golden side up, and accompany with a mixed green salad.

Slow cooked wild venison shank with baby potatoes and baby carrots

ingredients

6 wild venison shanks, each about 450g/1lb
900g/2lb organic baby potatoes
450g/1lb organic baby carrots
Plain flour
Olive oil

For the marinade

1 bottle organic red wine
½ organic garlic clove
300ml/10fl oz water
1 organic onion, chopped
2-3 organic celery sticks, chopped
2-3 organic carrots
3 organic bay leaves
5 organic juniper berries
1 organic star anise
A few organic peppercorns
1 tablespoon organic tomato purée

Organic crème fraîche, to serve

Serves 6

method

· Preheat the oven to 160°C/325°F/gas mark 3.
· Mix all the ingredients for the marinade together. Place the venison shanks in a deep non-metallic dish or pot. Pour over the marinade and leave in a fridge overnight.
· Take the shanks out of the marinade and lightly flour. Heat enough oil in a pan and brown the venison on all sides until golden brown. Replace the shanks back into the marinade and cover with tin foil. Cook in the oven for about 2½ - 3 hours or until the meat is tender and comes easily off the bone.
· Take the shanks out of the sauce and allow to settle. Keep warm. Strain the liquid into a saucepan and reduce a little. Taste, and season if necessary.
· Boil the baby potatoes in salted water. Steam the baby carrots. Take the venison meat off the bone, discarding all the bones and fat, and reheat in the sauce.

To serve

· Place the venison on warmed plates with the baby carrots and potatoes. Top with a dollop of crème fraîche (optional).

White chocolate passion fruit tart

ingredients

For the chocolate pastry

150g/5oz organic butter,
unsalted

75g/3oz organic caster sugar

1 organic egg

1 organic egg yolk

50g/2oz organic plain chocolate

175g/6oz organic plain flour,
plus extra for dusting

40g/1½oz organic cocoa
powder

For the passion fruit chocolate filling

300g/11oz organic white
chocolate (Green and Black's)

150ml/5fl oz organic cream

2 organic passion fruits

Serves 8

method

· Preheat the oven to 150°C/300°F/gas 2.

For the chocolate pastry

· Beat the butter and sugar together until you
have a smooth paste. Beat in the whole egg
and the egg yolk. Melt the plain chocolate
in a bowl over a pot of boiling water. Allow
to cool a little and quickly whisk into the
eggs. Finally mix in the flour and cocoa
powder. When the mixture is well mixed
together, wrap in clingfilm. Leave in the
fridge for one hour, then roll out on a lightly
floured surface.

· Line a 25cm/10 inch loose-bottomed tart
tin with the chocolate pastry. Prick with a
fork and place a piece of baking parchment
paper on top. Then fill the tin with baking
beans (or any dried beans) to prevent the
pastry from rising. Bake in the oven for
10-15 minutes, then remove the paper and

beans and return to the oven for another
10-15 minutes or until the pastry is cooked.
Allow to cool fully before adding the filling.

For the passion fruit chocolate filling

· Melt the white chocolate in a bowl over a
pot of boiling water. Allow to cool a little.
Bring the cream to the boil and pour over
the melted white chocolate. Whisk both
together until it is a smooth consistency. Cut
the passion fruits in half. Take out the pulp
and add to the chocolate mixture. Whisk
together.

· Pour the white chocolate passion fruit filling
into the tart case and allow to set in the
fridge for at least one hour.

To serve

· Carefully remove the tart from the tin and
cut into slices. Arrange on plates.

The Tannery

Owned and run by innovative chef Paul Flynn and his wife Maire, the Tannery is one of Ireland's leading restaurants. Expect the best of local seasonal food. While menus may appear simple, the accomplished cooking, inspired by global trends as well as regional (particularly Mediterranean) cuisine, delivers meals that are always exciting and served with style.

Dungarvan, Co. Waterford
Ph: (058) 45420
www.tannery.ie

starter
Seared salmon with raisin and caper butter

main course
Turf-roasted belly of pork

dessert
Banana gingerbread

Seared salmon with raisin and caper butter

ingredients

100g/4oz butter
50g/2oz raisins, soaked for a few hours in 120ml/4fl oz water
50g/2oz capers
Zest of 1 lemon
Handful snipped fresh chives
4 x 75g/3oz salmon fillets, boned and scaled
Salt and pepper

Lightly dressed, mixed salad leaves, to serve

Serves 4

method

· Using a food processor, blitz together the butter, drained raisins, capers and lemon zest, and then stir in the chives. Chill this in a piece of parchment squeezed together to make a cracker shape and, after a few hours, cut into chilled butter coins. Alternatively, place as much butter as you need in a saucepan, bring to the boil, and then leave to settle for 2-3 minutes for the flavours to absorb.

· Season the salmon fillets with salt and pepper and grill under a blisteringly hot grill until charred but still moist inside. This should take approximately 3-4 minutes depending on thickness, turning once.

To serve

· Arrange the charred salmon fillets, crispy side up, on warmed plates. Pour around the butter sauce. Serve with some mixed salad leaves to the side.

Turf-roasted belly of pork

ingredients

1 piece of turf, cut into pieces to fill the bottom of a roasting tin
1 large onion, sliced into rings
4 garlic cloves, finely chopped
1 bunch fresh sage, finely chopped
100ml/3½fl oz water
900g/2lb pork belly, rind removed
150ml/5fl oz dry cider
8 whole cloves
Pinch of ground allspice
Pinch of ground cinnamon
75g/3oz demerara sugar
Salt and freshly ground black pepper

Potatoes and a green vegetable, to serve

Serves 4

method

· Preheat the oven to 160ºC/325°F/gas mark 3.
· Break up the turf, using a hammer and chisel, or a very sharp, heavy knife. Place the turf in a single layer in the base of a roasting tin, and top with the slices of onion.
· Sprinkle with the garlic and half the sage, then pour in the water. Sit the pork belly on top, then splash with the cider.
· Sprinkle with the remaining sage, the spices and seasoning, then cover the whole dish tightly with foil. Cook in the oven for 3 hours.
· Remove from the oven, take away the foil, pour off any liquid, and sprinkle the sugar on top of the pork.
· Increase the oven temperature to 200ºC/400°F/gas mark 6 and return the pork to the oven, sitting on top of the turf, for 30 minutes or until glazed and golden and infused with the aroma of the turf.
· Remove the pork to a warm plate and leave to rest for about 30 minutes.

To serve

· Cut the turf-roasted belly of pork into thick slices and serve with potatoes and a green vegetable.

Banana gingerbread

ingredients

225g/8oz self-raising flour
1 teaspoon ground ginger
100g/4oz treacle
100g/4oz butter
100g/4oz demerara sugar
175g/6oz golden syrup
1 egg
3 ripe bananas

Whipped cream and maple
syrup, to serve

Serves 8

method

- Preheat the oven to 160°C/325°F/gas mark 3.
- Mix the flour and ginger in a bowl.
- Melt together the treacle, butter, sugar and golden syrup.
- Beat the egg and mash the bananas well. Mix all the ingredients together in a bowl.
- Turn into a 900g/2lb loaf tin. Bake for 45 minutes to 1 hour. Leave to rest for 10 minutes in the tin before turning out onto a wire tray.

To serve
- Serve this banana gingerbread cut into slices with some whipped cream and a dash of maple syrup. For an extra touch, you could add some caramelised bananas and sprinkle with sesame seeds. This dessert also freezes superbly.

Thornton's Restaurant

Gifted chef Kevin Thornton has been thrilling diners for years. His cuisine is based on fantastic ingredients, beautifully presented and with an emphasis on flavour. At his Michelin-starred restaurant, you experience fine dining and impeccable service in a peaceful, elegant space.

128 St. Stephen's Green, Dublin 2
Ph: (01) 478 7008
www.thorntonsrestaurant.com

starter
Sautéed Dublin Bay prawns
with prawn bisque and sabayon

main course
Grilled yellow-fin tuna with soy and ginger dressing

dessert
Fresh fig tartlet with lavender ice cream

Sautéed Dublin Bay prawns with prawn bisque and sabayon

ingredients

For the bisque

900g/2lb prawn shells
100g/4oz mirepoix (1 carrot, 2 celery sticks, 1 Spanish onion, 1 leek, all roughly chopped)
½ garlic bulb
1 dessertspoon whole white peppercorns
2 bay leaves
1 small bunch fresh thyme
25ml/1fl oz brandy
200ml/7fl oz dry white wine
1litre/1¾ pints fish or vegetable stock
450g/15fl oz cream
25g/1oz unsalted butter
Olive oil, for frying

For the sabayon

3 free range eggs
20ml/1fl oz dry martini
2 tablespoons spring water

For the prawns

20 raw Dublin Bay prawns, peeled and veins removed (use shells for bisque, see above)
Olive oil, for frying
Dash of brandy
Juice of 1 lemon
1 teaspoon snipped fresh chives
Sea salt and freshly ground white pepper

Serves 4

method

For the bisque

- Heat a little olive oil in a large saucepan and add the prawn shells. Cook the shells for 10 minutes on a medium heat, stirring all the time. Add the mirepoix, garlic, peppercorns and herbs and continue to mix well. Add a dash of brandy and flambé. Add another 2 dashes of brandy, allowing them also to flambé.

- Add the white wine and bring the mixture to the boil. Simmer and reduce the liquid by three-quarters. Add the fish stock or vegetable stock and bring to the boil again. Reduce the heat to simmer and cook for 4 hours, skimming the surface of any impurities from time to time.

- Remove from the heat. Pass through a fine strainer and return to the pot. Add the cream and bring to the boil. Simmer and reduce by three-quarters. Taste and season with salt and pepper. Add unsalted butter. Remove and blitz the sauce with a hand blender. Keep in a warm place until ready to serve.

For the sabayon

- Break the eggs into a stainless steel bowl and mix with a stainless steel whisk. Season with salt and pepper. Add the dry martini and water. Sit the bowl over a saucepan of boiling water and whisk until it forms a peak.

For the prawns

- Season the prawns lightly with sea salt and freshly milled white pepper. Drizzle olive oil over the prawns and place them in a hot Teflon frying pan over a high heat for about 10 seconds. Turn the prawns and flambé with a dash of brandy. Squeeze the lemon juice over the prawns and sprinkle the chives on top. Remove from the heat.

To serve

- Spoon the bisque into the base of a warm shallow soup plate. Place a spoon of sabayon on top and add the prawns.

Grilled yellow-fin tuna with soy and ginger dressing

ingredients

For the tuna

4 tuna steaks
Olive oil
Juice of 1 lemon
100g/4oz girolle mushrooms
cleaned and cut in half
(optional)
1 shallot, diced

For the dressing

15ml/1 tablespoon rice wine
25ml/1fl oz soy sauce
1 teaspoon sesame oil
50ml/2fl oz sunflower oil
1 shallot, finely diced
1 teaspoon fresh chopped dill
Juice of 1 lime
5 slices preserved pickled
ginger, finely diced
Juice of 1 lemon
Sea salt and freshly ground
pepper

Diced roasted peppers, to serve

Serves 4

method

- Pre-heat the oven to 160°C/325°F/
  gas mark 3

For the tuna

- Heat a griddle pan. Season the tuna steaks
  with salt and pepper and drizzle with olive
  oil. Lay them on the hot griddle. After 2
  minutes turn the steaks over (they should
  be nicely marked at this point) and cook the
  other side for 2 minutes. Squeeze the juice
  of a lemon over the steaks.

- The fish is ready to serve at this stage,
  although if you like your tuna well done
  place the steaks in a hot oven for a further 5
  minutes.

For the dressing

- Place all the ingredients in a Pyrex bowl
  and mix well. Season with salt and pepper
  and mix again. Correct the seasoning if
  necessary.

- Heat the olive oil in a pan until hot. Sauté
  the girolles, if using. Add the shallot and
  cook until the liquid from the mushrooms
  has evaporated.

To serve

- Spoon the mushrooms into the middle of
  the warmed plates, if using, and place the
  tuna steak on top. Arrange the diced roasted
  peppers around the tuna. Dot the plate with
  the dressing.

Fresh fig tartlet with lavender ice cream

ingredients

For the lavender ice cream

25g/1oz lavender flowers
½ vanilla pod, split in half and seeds scraped out
225ml/8fl oz cream
225ml/8fl oz milk
A little still water
5 egg yolks
65g/2½oz icing sugar

For the frangipane

15g/½oz plain flour
50g/2oz caster sugar
50g/2oz unsalted butter, at room temperature
50g/2oz ground almonds
Zest of 1 orange
1 large egg, preferably free range

For the tart

8 fresh figs, thinly sliced
100g/4oz puff pastry (bought is fine)

Caramelised blanched almonds, to serve

Serves 4

method

· Preheat the oven to 180°C/350°F/ gas mark 4.

For the ice cream

· Infuse the lavender flowers and vanilla seeds in the milk and cream in a bowl and leave overnight in the fridge. The next day, remove the lavender flowers and vanilla seeds. Line the base of a stainless steel pot with a little water and add the milk and cream. Bring to the boil and remove from the heat.

· In a bowl whisk the egg yolks and add the sugar. Whisk well. Pour half the milk and cream into the egg and sugar and mix well with a whisk. Pour the mixture back into the pot containing the rest of the milk and cream and stir. Bring the heat to just before boiling point, stirring all the time with a wooden spoon. Remove from the heat and place in an ice bath to cool it quickly.

· Once it has cooled down you can turn it into an ice cream machine and churn until frozen. Alternatively, put the mixture into a stainless steel bowl and freeze until frozen, beating occasionally to prevent ice crystals forming.

For the frangipane

· Sieve the flour into a bowl, add the caster sugar, butter, ground almonds, orange zest and mix with a hand blender. Beat the egg and add it to the mixture and mix again.

For the tart

· Roll out the pastry on a lightly floured worktop until very thin and then cut into rectangular shapes (around 7cm x 13cm/3 inch x 6 inch) and place on lightly greased

baking sheets. Prick with a fork to ensure it does not rise too much. Spread each pastry piece lightly with the frangipane mixture and bake in the oven for 10 minutes. Remove from the oven and layer the fig slices on top. Turn the oven down to 150°C/300°F/gas mark 2 and return the tarts to bake for a further 5 minutes, until cooked through.

To serve

· Place the tarts in the centre of large plates. Spoon some ice cream on the side with the rest of the fresh figs on top. Finish by sprinkling with caramelised blanched almonds.

Town Bar & Grill

'Town' is a New York style restaurant featuring a range of menus to suit every time of day and every occasion - including a children's menu based on 'real' food! The dishes are eclectic and interesting, Beautifully cooked and served by cheerful, well-informed staff.

21 Kildare Street, Dublin 2
Ph: (01) 662 4800
www.townbarandgrill.com

starter

Zuppa de pesce with langoustine, mussels and clams

main course

Grilled whole seabream
with cherry tomatoes and spinach

dessert

Pavlova

Zuppa de pesce with langoustine, mussels and clams

ingredients

Olive oil

4 red peppers, cored, seeded and diced

½ chorizo sausage, diced

1 tablespoon finely chopped garlic

4 whole langoustines (Dublin Bay prawns)

16 mussels, cleaned and beards removed

16 clams, cleaned

8 fresh crab claws

450g/1lb cod, boned, skinned and diced

1 glass white wine

400g/1lb can diced tomatoes

Salt and pepper to taste

1 tablespoon chopped fresh flat leaf parsley, to serve

Serves 4-6

method

- Heat some olive oil in a pan. Fry the peppers, chorizo and garlic at a low heat for 20 minutes until the peppers are softened.
- In a large pot, heat some olive oil. Add the seafood, cover with a lid and shake the pot while cooking for one minute. Add the chorizo-red pepper mix and stir. Add the white wine, tomatoes and season with salt and pepper.
- Cook for 4-5 minutes until the seafood is cooked through.

To serve

- Pour the soup into warm bowls. Garnish with the chopped parsley.

Grilled whole seabream
with cherry tomatoes and spinach

ingredients

2 seabream, approximately
450g-550g/1lb-1¼lb
Olive oil, for frying
1 tablespoon finely chopped
garlic
200g/7oz cherry tomatoes,
halved
100g/4oz fine green beans,
trimmed
200g/7oz spinach, tough stalks
removed and chopped
2 glasses white wine
150g/5oz unsalted butter
1 tablespoon chopped fresh flat
leaf parsley
Salt and pepper

Boiled new potatoes, to serve

Serves 4

method

· Heat the grill. Chargrill the seabream for 10 minutes, turning once;
then allow to rest.

· In a deep pan, heat the olive oil. Add the garlic and fry until soft.
Add the cherry tomatoes, fine beans and spinach. Add the white
wine. Cook for about 12-15 minutes to reduce by one-third, then
add the unsalted butter and keep stirring until the sauce is nice and
thick. Add salt and pepper to taste and stir in the parsley.

To serve

· Place the fish in the dish with the tomatoes and spinach and
bring to the table with the boiled potatoes in a separate dish.
Alternatively, cut the seabream into four pieces, removing all bones
and the head and tail. Spoon the vegetables onto warm plates.
Place the seabream on top. Serve with potatoes as you like.

Pavlova

ingredients

For the pavlova

3 egg whites
130g/4½oz caster sugar

For the filling

200ml/7fl oz whipping cream
50g/2oz caster sugar
½ vanilla pod, split in half and
seeds scraped out
100g/4oz mascarpone cheese

Fresh strawberries and mint
sprigs, to serve

Serves 6

method

· Preheat the oven to 110°C/225°F/gas mark ¼.

For the pavlova

· Line a baking sheet with greaseproof paper. Whisk the egg whites
and sugar until stiff and shining. Scoop the meringue into six nests
on the lined baking sheet. Make an indentation in each one. Bake
for 1½ hours. Remove and allow to cool.

For the filling

· Whisk the cream, sugar and scraped out vanilla seeds until soft
peaks form. Fold in the mascarpone cheese.

To serve

· Spoon the filling on each of the meringue nests. Decorate with
strawberries (or any fruits you like) and mint sprigs.

Via Veneto

Via Veneto is an authentic Italian restaurant run by Paolo Fresilli,
President of the Irish delegation of the Italian Chefs' Federation.
A warm, family-friendly place and a hive of activity, it offers great
regional and traditional dishes that you won't see elsewhere. The
food is all cooked to order from honest ingredients. The all-Italian
wine list is well worth exploring.

58 Weafer Street, Enniscorthy, Co. Wexford
Ph: (053) 923 6929
www.viaveneto.ie

starter
Skewers of Parma ham with melon

main course
Medallions of beef Bolognese and tomato cups
with mascarpone cheese

dessert
Chocolate pannacotta with Grand Marnier sauce

Skewers of Parma ham with melon

ingredients

900g/2lb ripe honeydew melon
Small glass port
100g/4oz Parma ham slices
Fresh mint leaves
Extra virgin olive oil
Pepper

Serves 4

method

- Cut the melon in half, remove the seeds and use a scoop to create melon balls. Place in a bowl with the port, cover and put in the fridge for 10 minutes. Drain the melon.

To serve

- Cut the Parma ham slices in four, then thread onto the skewers, alternating with the melon balls and mint leaves. Season with pepper and extra virgin olive oil. Arrange on plates.

Medallions of beef Bolognese and tomato cups with mascarpone cheese

ingredients

For the beef

50g/2oz butter

4 x 100g/4oz beef fillet, cut into slices

200g/7oz Fontina cheese or similar (Gruyère, Emmental, Gouda or Edam)

1 tablespoon capers, rinsed

For the tomato cups

100g/4oz long grain rice

4 large round tomatoes, or 8 small ones

½ cucumber, seeded and finely chopped

100g/4oz cooked shrimp, chopped

125g/4½oz natural yogurt

1 teaspoon mild curry powder

150g/5oz mascarpone cheese

Salt and pepper

Serves 4

method

For the beef

· Warm the butter in a pan. Add the beef fillets and brown on both sides. Season with the salt. Cover the beef fillets with the slices of cheese and the capers. Cover with a lid and cook on a low heat for another 5 minutes.

For the tomato cups

· Boil the rice al dente. Meanwhile halve the tomatoes and scoop out the pulp. Sprinkle them with salt and allow them to stand. Chop up the pulp and remove the seeds. Mix the rice, the pulp of the tomatoes and the cucumber, shrimp, yogurt, curry powder and salt in a bowl and mix in the mascarpone. Rinse the tomato halves and dry them with kitchen paper. Fill them with the mixture and keep cool until ready to serve.

To serve

· Serve the beef on warmed plates with the tomato cups on the side.

Chocolate pannacotta with Grand Marnier sauce

ingredients

For the pannacotta

2 gelatine leaves
150g/5oz plain chocolate (at least 55% cocoa solids)
150ml/5fl oz milk
50ml/2fl oz cream
75g/3oz caster sugar
1 vanilla pod, split in half and seeds scraped out
A little butter, to grease
Cocoa powder, for dusting

For the Grand Marnier sauce

4 egg yolks
4 tablespoons caster sugar
1 generous tablespoon cornflour
450ml/15fl oz milk
5 tablespoons Grand Marnier

Wafer or sponge finger biscuits and candied orange peel, to serve

Serves 6

method

For the pannacotta

- Place the gelatine leaves in cold water to soften.
- Break the chocolate into squares and place in a pot with the milk, cream, sugar and vanilla seeds. Bring to the boil, stirring with a wooden spoon, to ensure the sugar is dissolved and the chocolate is melted and the mixture is well combined. Remove from the heat and allow to cool a little.
- Remove the gelatine from the water and squeeze out any excess water. Add the gelatine to the mixture and stir well to dissolve fully.
- Lightly butter the individual moulds (120ml/4fl oz) and fill with the mixture. Allow to cool and then put in the refrigerator for at least 3-4 hours, or overnight if possible.

For the Grand Marnier sauce

- Whip the egg yolks with the sugar until you have a smooth paste. Combine the cornflour with the milk, then add to the egg mixture and mix well.
- Transfer the mixture to a pot and bring gently to the boil, stirring often. When it starts to boil, lower the temperature and continuing stirring for a few more minutes. Remove from the heat, add the Grand Marnier and leave to cool.

To serve

- Dip the moulds in hot water to loosen the pannacotta. Invert onto individual plates. Sprinkle with cocoa. Spoon around the Grand Marnier sauce. Serve with wafers or sponge finger biscuits and decorate with candied orange peel.

Wineport Lodge

Wineport Lodge is beautifully located overlooking a lake. Skillful cooking here does justice to a well-balanced, strongly seasonal menu that tends towards international dishes, based on gorgeous Irish artisan ingredients. The extensive wine list charts a wine connection with the area going back to 1542 and offers special treats, many wines by the glass, and plenty of affordable choices.

Glasson, Athlone, Co. Westmeath
Ph: (090) 643 9010
www.wineport.ie

starter
Pan-roasted Lough Ree pike on sweet chilli orzo with sun-dried pepper and onion marmalade

main course
Pappardalle pasta with Boilie cheese, spicy chorizo sausage and roast peppers

dessert
Late summer berries
with Baileys Irish cream and crushed Amaretti biscuits

Pan-roasted Lough Ree pike on sweet chilli orzo with sun-dried pepper and onion marmalade

ingredients

For the marmalade

150g/5oz red onion, sliced thinly

75g/3oz sun-dried peppers, chopped

50g/2oz caster sugar

2 tablespoons white wine vinegar

1 pinch of fennel seeds

For the fish

Olive oil for frying

2 x 100g/4oz pike fillets (cod, hake, salmon, etc. could be substituted)

½ glass dry white wine

2 tablespoons cream

1 roasted sweet pepper, puréed

2 tablespoons sweet chilli sauce

1 fresh coriander sprig, finely chopped

100g/4oz orzo (rice-shaped pasta), cooked

Salt and pepper

Lime wedges and green salad, to serve

Serves 2

method

For the marmalade

· Place all the ingredients in a heavy-bottomed saucepan. Bring to the boil, then simmer and reduce for 30 minutes, stirring occasionally, until you get a sticky marmalade consistency.

For the fish

· Heat a little olive oil in a pan. Fry the fish until golden brown for approximately 3-4 minutes on each side. Finish briefly under a hot grill for 1 minute. Remove the fish from the pan and keep warm.

· Add the wine and deglaze the pan, add the cream, pepper purée, sweet chilli sauce and coriander. Reduce to thicken.

· Sprinkle the orzo into a pot of boiling, salted water. Cook for 5-7 minutes or until just cooked, according to the instructions on the package. Drain, rinse under hot water and then add to the sauce. Stir in well, then season to taste with salt and pepper.

To serve

· Place the orzo mix in the centre of each warmed plate. Arrange the fish on top and top with pepper marmalade. Garnish with lime wedges and serve with a little green salad.

Pappardalle pasta with Boilie cheese, spicy chorizo sausage and roast peppers

ingredients

For the sauce

Olive oil, for frying

100g/4oz chorizo sausage, (or salami) thinly sliced

2 red peppers, roasted, peeled, seeded and thinly sliced

450ml/15fl oz cream

For the pasta

2 tablespoons pesto

250g/9oz pappardalle pasta

Knob of butter

200g/7oz Boilie cow's milk cheese

Salt and pepper

Green salad and garlic bread, to serve

Serves 4

method

For the sauce

· Heat a little olive oil in a frying pan. Sauté the chorizo sausage and the red peppers. Add the cream and pesto to the pan and reduce to thicken. Season with salt and pepper.

For the pasta

· Cook the pasta in a large saucepan in boiling water with a knob of butter melted in the water. Do not overcook the pasta. When there is just a little 'chew' on the pasta, it is cooked enough – check the package for details.

· Drain the pasta and mix with the sauce from the pan. Drain the oil from the Boilie cheese, and add the cheese to the pasta mix. Stir gently.

To serve

· Serve the pasta in a large warmed bowl in the centre of the table, with side dishes of green salad and garlic bread. Set a warm plate at each place setting and allow your guests to help themselves.

Late summer berries
with Baileys Irish cream and crushed Amaretti biscuits

ingredients

100g/4oz Amaretti biscuits
225g/8oz strawberries
175g/6oz raspberries
175g/6oz blackberries
100g/4oz mascarpone cheese
1 dessertspoon caster sugar
100g/4oz cream
2 dessertspoons Baileys Irish cream

1 bar Cadbury's Flake and 4 fresh mint leaves, to serve

Serves 4

method

· Crush the Amaretti biscuits and divide into 4 long-stemmed glasses.
· Mix the berries together and add to the glasses.
· Whisk the mascarpone cheese, sugar, cream and Baileys together and spoon over the berries.
· Decorate with fresh mint and a crumbled bar of Cadbury's Flake.

The Coffee Corner

Dublin-born Stephen Morrissey, World Barista Champion 2008, provides his top tips on how to make a great coffee to finish off the perfect meal. Great coffee is achieved by adherence to the correct ratios, good technique and, of course, quality ingredients Brought to you by Avonmore.

Classic Cafetière

Cafetières are a staple in many homes today and are capable of brewing classic cups of coffee

Excellent Espresso

When espresso is good it is great. It should not require two sugars to be palatable

Creamy Cappuccino

When coffee meets milk it relies on an adherence to correct ratios, good technique and quality ingredients

Classic Cafetière

Cafetières (also known as French presses or plungers) are a staple in many homes across the country today and are capable of brewing classic cups of coffee.

method

- Make sure your cafetière is thoroughly clean. Any notion that leftover oils or bits of coffee are a good thing or a sign of a seasoned brew should be dismissed.

- Start with fresh whole coffee beans, within two weeks of roast date.

- To get the best flavour from your coffee, it is essential to get the correct ratio of coffee to water. Use a weighing scales to get the proportions correct: around 60g/2½oz of coffee per litre of water will give a well flavoured coffee. If you like a different strength brew, adjust around this quantity.

- Use a good coffee grinder for best results. A coarse grind is best for cafetière coffee. Anything finer will result in an over-extracted, bitter tasting cup, regardless of the coffee used. If you do not have a grinder, ask your supplier to grind it coarse for a cafetière and aim to use it as quickly as possible.

- Once the kettle boils, wait a few seconds for it to cool down a little before adding the water to the ground coffee - about ten seconds should be fine. Be sure to measure the quantity of water required.

- After 4 minutes, a crust should have formed on the surface of the brew. Break the surface of this crust. Some coffee will sink, leaving a light brown foam on top; spoon off the foam and any floating coffee.

- Take your filter, carefully place it on top and plunge to press any remaining grinds to the bottom. Pour a little bit down the sink as, occasionally, a few ground particles make it past the press.

- Enjoy! Taste it black first as great coffee is wholly satisfactory by itself though many coffees work well with milk. Sugar should not be necessary if you are buying good coffee.

Excellent Espresso

When espresso is good it is great. It should not require two sugars to be palatable. The distinguishing characteristic of espresso is 'crema'. It should be reddish brown in colour, not yellow or black.

An espresso machine is required.

method

· Start with fresh whole coffee beans.
· Grind the fresh coffee finely.
· Put the coffee in the espresso basket, level off with your fingers and use the tamper to press down, making sure it is even and level.
· Wipe the rim of the portafilter and spout clean and insert the espresso basket and start the machine.
· Ensure the espresso machine is creating the 'crema'. It should pour like honey at the start, yielding 25ml/1fl oz in roughly 25 seconds.
· If the coffee comes out too quickly and tastes sour, use a finer grind or more coffee in your basket.
· If the coffee pours slowly and tastes bitter, use less coffee or a coarser grind.
· Make sure you use preheated espresso cups (ideally, 85ml/3fl oz) and try to enjoy it within a minute of being brewed.

Creamy Cappuccino

When coffee meets milk, something lovely happens. It relies on an adherence to correct ratios, good technique and, of course, quality ingredients. Using a 225ml/8fl oz cup, a single espresso and steamed Avonmore milk will result in the perfect cup: sweet, balanced and wholly satisfying.

An espresso machine with a steam wand is required.

method

· Fill a clean jug half way with 170ml/6fl oz milk.

· If the machine is capable of it, steam the milk at the same time as the espresso is brewing. This way, both finish roughly at the same time allowing for immediate combining. If this is not possible, steam the milk first, as espresso will deteriorate faster after it has been brewed.

· Place the tip of the steam 'wand' into the jug of milk, not too deep but just below the surface of the milk and open up the steam.

· As the milk's volume starts to increase, slowly lower the jug so the wand is just below the surface. Exaggerated up and down movements that are often accompanied by spitty, gargling noise are not considered a sign of a good technique.

· Keep your hand on the side of the pitcher to gauge the temperature and, once it feels warm, raise the pitcher to push the steam wand further into the milk.

· From this point on, start tapping the side of the pitcher until it is too hot to touch. Once achieved, quickly turn off the steam and lower the pitcher away from the wand. Milk tastes at its best between 50°C and 60°C - warm enough to drink without fear of burning your mouth. The best cappuccino cannot be served boiling hot.

· The milk should achieve a glossy, chrome-like consistency. Should a few bubbles appear in the surface, knock the pitcher on the counter to get rid of them.

· Keep spinning the milk to maintain consistency.

· Once the espresso is ready, immediately pour the textured milk into the coffee.

Map

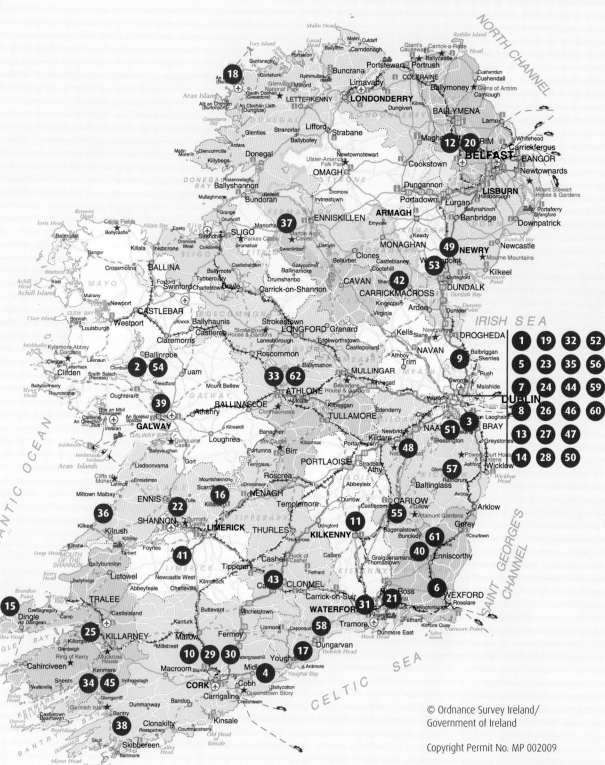

© Ordnance Survey Ireland/
Government of Ireland

Copyright Permit No. MP 002009

Map references

1. Ananda Restaurant
2. Ashford Castle
3. Avoca Cafés
4. Ballymaloe House and Cookery School
5. Bang Café
6. Beaches Restaurant
7. Bentley's Oyster Bar & Grill
8. Bistro One
9. Bon Appétit
10. Café Paradiso
11. Campagne
12. Cayenne
13. The Cellar Restaurant
14. Chapter One
15. The Chart House
16. Cherry Tree
17. The Cliff House Hotel
18. Danny Minnie's
19. Dax
20. Deanes Restaurant and Bar
21. Dunbrody Country House Hotel and Harvest Room Restaurant
22. Earl of Thomond
23. Eden
24. Fallon & Byrne
25. Gaby's Seafood Restaurant
26. Guinea Pig – The Fish Restaurant
27. Harvey Nichols First Floor Restaurant
28. Il Primo
29. Isaacs Restaurant
30. Jacques Restaurant
31. La Bohème Restaurant
32. L'Ecrivain
33. The Left Bank Bistro
34. The Lime Tree Restaurant
35. Locks Restaurant
36. The Lodge at Doonbeg Golf Club
37. MacNean House & Restaurant
38. Mary Ann's Bar and Restaurant
39. Matz at the g Hotel
40. Monart
41. The Mustard Seed at Echo Lodge
42. Nuremore Hotel and Country Club
43. The Old Convent
44. One Pico
45. Park Hotel Kenmare
46. Pearl Brasserie
47. Peploe's
48. Rathsallagh House
49. Restaurant 23
50. Restaurant Patrick Guilbaud
51. The Ritz-Carlton, Powerscourt
52. Roly's Bistro
53. Rosso Restaurant
54. Salt Restaurant at Lisloughrey Lodge
55. Sha-Roe Bistro
56. Shanahan's on the Green
57. The Strawberry Tree
58. The Tannery
59. Thornton's Restaurant
60. Town Bar & Grill
61. Via Veneto
62. Wineport Lodge

Index

Index

Index

Index

Index

Index

Index

Index

Index